India's Water Relations with Her Neighbours

India's Water Relations with Her Neighbours

Edited by

Rockin Th. Singh

Vij Books India Pvt Ltd
New Delhi 110002 (India)

Published   by

Vij Books India Pvt Ltd
(Publishers, Distributors & Importers)
2/19 (Second Floor), Ansari Road, Darya Ganj
New Delhi - 110002
Phones: 91-11-43596460, 91-11- 65449971
Fax: 91-11-47340674
web: www.vijbooks.com
e-mail   : vijbooks@rediffmail.com

Copyright © 2011, Publisher

ISBN: 978-93-80177-47-2

Contents

Preface

For India, water security implies effective responses to changing water conditions in terms of quality, quantity and uneven distribution. It can affect relationships at the inter-state level and equally contribute to tensions at the intra-provincial level if the government unheeded. The subcontinent has large river systems, and thus a number of bilateral treaties exist but are often hostage to the prevailing political animosity.

Resource nationalism will increasingly dominate the hydrological contours of South Asia and will largely define regional politics. The hydrological contours of India, both as an upper riparian and a lower riparian, will be at the epicenter of new riparian politics and diplomacy over transboundary rivers.

With continuously raising concerns over regulating and sharing of river waters, India's riparian relation with its neighbours will become progressively fragile with Pakistan, Bangladesh and Nepal. The friction in bilateral relations will increase if mutually acceptable bilateral or multilateral framework for cooperation to deal with integrated development of water resources is not effectively reworked.

For India, it is important to create global awareness about the water resources in Tibet and build regional pressure. As, China's aggressive south-to-north water diversion projects on the rivers that originate from the Tibet region, particularly on the Yarlung-Tsangpo, is opening up a new front of uncertainty in Sino-Indian relations as well as the overall hydrological dynamics in South Asia.

In spite of the UN Convention, riparian nations pitch their respective claims and counterclaims based on their interest and interpretation. This raises fundamental questions on whether formal arrangements on long lasting peaceful sharing of river waters can be achieved particularly in regions where the political climate is hostile to cooperative endeavours.

Water as an instrument and tool of bargain and trade-off will assume predominance because the political stakes are high. Though the importance of politics cannot be discounted in India's water relations with Nepal and Bangladesh, this book is however far more delving the scope to overcome and break political deadlocks through sensible water sharing arrangements and resource development.

- *Editor*

1

India and the Law of the Sea

Over the centuries the international law of the sea had come to be based on the basic principle of "freedom of the seas". Beyond the narrow coastal strip of territorial waters, the seas could be freely used by all nations for fishing and for navigation. Coastal states used to be content with exclusive rights in their narrow belt of territorial waters. The discovery of petroleum and natural gas in the shallow waters of the continental shelf led the United States to issue the Truman Proclamation in 1945, which claimed sovereign rights over the resources of the continental shelf adjacent to its coast.

Around the same time, coastal states found that the fishing areas near their coasts were being poached by larger and better equipped fishing ships of distant foreign states. Both these developments, combined with the emergence of newly independent states after the decolonisation of Asia and Africa, led to a spate of unilateral claims by the coastal states to extend national jurisdiction over large adjacent sea areas to protect their fishery resources. On attaining independence in 1947, India had been content to proclaim the traditional territorial sea of three miles.

In view of the above developments, India issued four presidential notifications to safeguard its interests:

(a) On 30 August 1955, India claimed full and exclusive sovereign rights over the seabed and subsoil of the continental shelf adjoining the coast but beyond territorial waters. Neither the depth nor the distance from the coastline was indicated.

(b) On 22 March 1956, India claimed Territorial Waters of six miles from appropriate baselines.

(c) On 29 November 1956, India claimed a Conservation Zone for fisheries up to a distance of one hundered miles from the outer limit of territorial waters.

(d) On 3 December 1956, India claimed a Contiguous Zone.

After the disintegration of the Roman Empire, the Rhodian tradition of the freedom of the high seas came to be debated. But it was not until the end of the Second World War in 1945 when the freedom of the high seas came to be seriously questioned. President Truman on September 28, 1945 made the twin declarations relating to fisheries and continental shelf extending the coastal jurisdiction to areas of the high seas adjoining the coasts of the United States. It immediately unleashed a series of divergent standpoints by different maritime nations on the territorial sea, fisheries, continental shelf and other issues of the law of the sea.

In an endeavour to end the resulting impasse, the United Nations through the International Law Commission convened a conference in 1958 which came to be known as the Geneva Conventions or United Nations Conventions on Law of the Sea (UNCLOS-I). The four conventions that were opened for signature of UNCLOS-I in 1958 effectively codified the international customary law on the sea existing till that point of time. However, it left a number of issues unsettled. States were selective in becoming party to the conventions and with advancing technology continued to exploit resources beyond the limits envisaged in the conventions.

It was only in 1980, with the Vienna Convention, the law of the sea had been evolved into a hard law from soft law. The UNCLOS-III had consolidated all past treaties, codified customary law and put in place new law for new issues. It was a global agreement as for the first time even land locked states were addressed in maritime affairs. By the end of nineteenth century 'Freedom of the High Seas' became established as a fundamental principle of international law and were divided into zones of maritime jurisdiction. Each of these zones had further been subjected to varying 'control and regulations' by specifying rights and responsibilities of all states.

The freedom of navigation by a flag state, through coastal state territorial waters continues to exist as part of international customary law but in a more controlled and regulated manner by the coastal state. Unthinkable environmental damage has turned to reality in certain parts of the world with oil tanker disasters like the Exxon Valdez and Torrey Canyon. Economically, exploiting and controlling the mineral wealth of the oceans has become a necessity for the sustenance of the world economies. Politically, a host of nations, particularly coastal nations have gained their independence. Besides, the global reach of organised transactional crime and its evasion of national controls challenge every nation's economic well being, social stability and political peace.

However, the effectiveness of control and regulation depends not only upon establishing jurisdiction in the coastal state legislation but actually exercising such jurisdiction in practice. There must be a recognition in India that we have interests and obligations in coastal and marine activities occurring within our maritime zones of jurisdiction. Managing the multiple activities in our maritime zones require a range of potential responses - operational, political, legal and non-governmental for which India must maintain or have access to capabilities for surveillance, monitoring and control.

This will enable India to effectively meet the responsibilities and challenges to marine resource management, environmental protection, marine safety, illegal activity and maritime sovereignty. The International

Court of Justice rulings in the 1950s implied a certain priority of the coastal states' preferential rights of fishing in waters adjacent to its coast while recognizing the concurrent historical rights or interests of foreign fishing states. This was largely due to the need to introduce some mechanism over the allowable catch and sharing of the resources with an overarching view to preserve the fish stocks. The notion of the EEZ (Exclusive Economic Zone) thus began to be conceived by the establishment of the exclusive fishing zone as a zone separate from the territorial sea.

The rapid pace of technological, environmental, economic and more importantly political changes altered the equation of relationship at sea. Technological advances brought in the need to monitor sea traffic. Two thirds of the world populace is expected to be living near the coastline by 2025. Several other developments were also taking place. The USA and the Soviet Union were unable to agree on the width of territorial waters - the Soviet Union wanted twelve miles whilst the USA wanted only three miles.

Technological developments in the industrialised West began to make it possible to extract oil and gas from the seabed. The newly independent nations of Asia and Africa began to feel that the International Law of the Sea would be exploited to their disadvantage. To sort out all these matters, the first United Nations Conference on the Law of the Sea (UNCLOS-1) was convened in 1958.

UNCLOS 1 – 1958

UNCLOS 1 was able to codify the traditional law. It adopted what came to be known as the Geneva Conventions on the Law of the Sea. The four Conventions were:-

(a) the freedom of the seas as long conceived.

(b) the sovereignty of coastal states in the territorial sea.

(c) the ancillary physical, customs, sanitary and

immigration rights of coastal states in a Contiguous Zone.

The acceptance by UNCLOS 1 of the Continental Shelf convention enabled the countries bordering the North Sea to divide the sea area for extracting oil and gas.

The UNCLOS 1 participants remained divided on several issues:

(a) The rights of coalitions of coastal states, land locked states and archipelagic states.

(b) Certain states contested the rights of passage through straits used for international navigation like the Straits of Gibraltar, Hormuz and Malacca.

(c) Land based mineral producers tried to carve out for themselves as much as they could of the newly found seabed mineral resources.

UNCLOS 1 completely failed to agree on:-

(a) The precise width of the Territorial Sea (three miles or twelve miles) and the extent of the Exclusive Fisheries Zone.

(b) The prior authorisation and/or notification of the passage of foreign warships through the territorial sea of a coastal state.

The Second Conference, UNCLOS 2, was therefore convened in 1960 to resolve these issues.

UNCLOS 2 - 1960

UNCLOS-2 attempted to extend the jurisdiction of coastal states over territorial waters to six miles, with an additional six miles as an Exclusive Fishing Zone. This failed to gain the required two thirds majority for its acceptance.

After UNCLOS 2 failed to achieve agreement on the width of the territorial sea, many countries unilaterally extended their offshore jurisdiction. The South American countries reaffirmed their earlier claim of their territorial waters extending two hundred miles from the coast. African states like Nigeria, Congo, Mauritus and Ghana also extended their territorial sea to distances much beyond 12 miles.

Passage of Warships through The Territorial Sea

At UNCLOS 1, India has proposed that the passage of foreign warships through the territorial sea of a coastal state should be subject to prior authoritisation and notification to the coastal state. As this requirement was not accepted and therefore not included in the 1958 conventions on the Territorial Sea and the Contiguous Zone, India declined to ratify all four Geneva Conventions. In subsequent years, India reviled from this position. As a growing maritime nation interested in the freedom of navigation both for itself and the international community, India sought only prior notification for the innocent passage of foreign warships through territorial waters.

Developments After 1965

India's Extension of territorial Waters

On 12 September, 1967, India extended its territorial waters to twelve miles. This was largely a reaction to Pakistan's extension of her territorial waters from three to twelve miles, rather than an act of maritime policy.

The Seabed Committee

During the 1960s political, technological, economic and naval developments began to change the situation. Advances in seabed exploitation technology made it possible to exploit the seabed much beyond a depth of two hundred metres, thereby rendering the 1958 Conventions outmoded. The deployment of submarine launched ballistic missiles and worldwide apprehensions of a competitive scramble to achieve predominant control over the seabed led the United Nations to discuss the need to evolve means for the peaceful use of the oceans.

In 1968, the UN General Assembly constituted a 42 member "Seabed Committee" on the peaceful use of the seabed. In December 1970, the General Assembly adopted the "Declaration of Principles" governing the Seabed, the ocean floor and the subsoil thereof, beyond the limits of national jurisdiction. The Declaration stated that these areas and their resources are the common heritage of mankind and shall be subject to an international regime as established by an international treaty.

Seabed Mining

India's interest in the mining of polymetalic nodules from the seabed derived from its long term strategy for metals like nickel, cobalt, copper and manganese. In the early 1970, the Indian Government had initiated a programme of scientific investigation and evaluation of the manganese nodule resources in the Indian Ocean.

Offshore Oil and Gas

By the early 1970's, India had discovered oil and gas in Bombay High and promising fields were being forecast in the Godavari, Krishna and Palk Bay basins, as also gas in the Andaman Offshore. With a view to establish and equitable international regime for the exploitation of seabed resources, the UN General Assembly convened the third conference, UNCLOS 3 in 1973.

UNCLOS 3 - 1973 TO 1982

It took UNCLOS 3 nine years of discussions to adopt the United Nations Convention on the Law of the Sea on 30 April 1982. Thereafter this convention took twelve years to formally come into force on 16 November 1984.

UNCLOS 3 aimed to define an agreed set of rules to govern the use of the seas which would strike a fair balance between:

(a) those who considered that a coastal state should have no right whatsoever over the living resources of the seas beyond a territorial sea of twelve miles and

(b) others who maintained that a coastal state should have full or limited sovereignty over the sea and its resources out to an Exclusive Economic Zone of two hundred nautical miles.

The acceptance of this concept of the Exclusive Economic Zone (EEZ) was a landmark contribution of UNCLOS 3.

At UNCLOS 3, India's stand at was that as a developing country centrally located in the Indian Ocean, with a coastline of over 64000 kilometers, its basic national interests were:-

(a) To obtain assurance of smooth and free navigation though traditionally used waters and straits used for international navigation.

(b) To achieve archipelagic status for the Andaman and Nicobar Island group and the Lakshadweep Island group which between them, comprised over 1280 islands and islets.

(c) To protect essential strategic and security interests in the waters around its coast.

(d) To secure the free mobility of naval war ships.

(e) To preserve the marine environment in the sea areas adjacent to its coast, because the channels of navigation passed near its long coastline.

(f) To regulate within its EEZ, the conduct of marine scientific research by foreign research agencies.

India advocated from the baselines, a territorial sea of twelve miles, an EEZ of two hundred miles and a continental shelf to the outer edge of the geological continental margin. India also made specific proposals on the requirement of prior notification for warships passing through the territorial sea, enlargement of safety zones around offshore oil rigs, designation of special areas for the protection of the resources located therein (as for example the coral lagoons in the Lakshadweep where tankers could run aground) and several other proposals.

The 1982 Convention on the Law of The Sea

The 1982 Convention on the Law of the Sea met most of India's interests. It adopted:

(a) Twelve miles as the uniform limit for the width of the territorial sea.

(b) a two hundred miles EEZ, within which the coastal state exercises sovereign rights and jurisdiction for certain specified economic activities.

(c) a Continental Shelf extending to the outer edge of the continental margin, to be delimited with reference to either three hundred and fifty miles from the baselines of territorial waters or one hundred miles from the 2500 - meter isobaths.

(d) regimes for the abatement and control of marine pollution, for marine scientific research, for the international seabed area and for unimpeded transit passage through straits used for international navigation.

(e) The 1982 Convention included India as one of the four states named as "pioneer investor' for seabed mining. On 17 August 1987, India became the first state to be so registered, after having fulfilled the criteria stipulated in the Convention.

There were several areas where India's stand was not accepted. The major ones were:

(a) Passage of Warships through the Territorial Sea.

There was vehement opposition from the USA and the Soviet Union to prior notification before warships transited through territorial waters, on the grounds that it would seriously jeopardise their strategic and security interests. There is therefore no provision in the 1982 UN Convention on the Law of the Sea requiring prior notification or authorisation for the passage of foreign warships through the territorial waters of a coastal state.

But by 1977, Pakistan, Bangladesh, Sri Lanka and Burma (Myanmar) had all unilaterally promulgated that prior authorisation and notification was required for the passage of foreign warships through their respective territorial seas. India's Maritime Zones Act 1976 also requires foreign warships to give prior notification for passing through India's territorial waters and enjoins all submarines and other underwater vehicles to navigate on the surface and show their flag while passing through these waters.

(b) Archipelagic Status for the Andaman and Nicobar Islands.

The Convention granted the status of an archipelago only to those groups of islands that were political entities by themselves as for example Indonesia, the Philippines and the Maldives. This was because of fear of interference with the freedom of navigation through archipelagic waters that might be created if the off-lying islands of continental coastal states were to be granted archipelagic status.

For example, the distance between the Andaman group and the Nicobar group of islands is 76 miles. If archipelagic status had been granted to these groups of islands, India would have had full regulatory control over the navigation of ships passing through the Ten Degree Channel, which would then have been part of India's archipelagic waters, and therefore subject to the restricted regimes of archipelagic sealanes passage.

(c)   Enlarged Safety Zones for Offshore Installations.

The UNCLOS 1 Continental Shelf Convention had provided for a safety zone of 500 meters around artificial islands, installations or structures on the continental shelf. India's view at UNCLOS 3 was that this zone was inadequate, considering the time that a huge supertanker takes to come to a stop. India therefore advocated Enlarged Safely Zones. The suggestion did not receive adequate support. A provision was however incorporated in the 1982 Convention that if authorised by generally accepted international standards or as recommended by the competent international organisation, then a coastal state may promulgate safely zones larger then 500 metres.

India's Gains After the 1982 UN Convention of the Law of the Sea.

Apart from the benefits of an agreed Law of the Sea, India gained in two significant areas:-

(a)   India's EEZ became the twelfth largest in the world. The extension of the EEZ to 350 miles or 100 miles beyond the 2500-metre isobath added 2 million square kilometers to India's jurisdiction.

(b)   Pursuant to the 'pioneer investor' status, the International Seabed Authority allotted to India a 150,000 square kilometer mine site in the central Indian Ocean for the seabed mining of polymetalic nodules. The richest area at this site has a density of 21 kilograms of nodules per square metre.

The Genesis of The Coast Guard

While UNCLOS 3 was still in the early phase of

discussing the EEZ and well before India had enacted the Maritime Zones Act of 1976, discussions had commenced in India on how the EEZ was going to be sageguarded. In 1974, Naval Headquarters had suggested to the Government to have an armed force on the lines of the US Coast Guard and stressed the importance of inter-ministerial coordination while selecting Coast Guard vessels, recruiting experienced personnel, setting up communication networks, using naval repair facilities, indigenisation etc. Such integrated Navy-Coast Guard development would avoid duplication and economise effort.

On 25 August 1976 India passed the Maritime Zones Act which claimed a 12 mile territorial sea, a 24 mile contiguous zone, a 200 mile EEZ and a continental shelf up to 200 miles or the outer edge of the continental margin, whichever is greater.

Soon after this Act, a committee was set up to consider the type of force that should be created to enforce compliance with its provisions. Three options emerged:

(a)   To entrust this responsibility to the marine wing of the Ministry of Finance, which already had a number Cental Board of Revenue (CBR) anti smuggling vessels? This option was not pursued as the functions were too onerous.

(b)   To set up a separate Coastal Command, as a part of the Navy, to oversee these functions. This option was seriously considered since it would avoid the expenditure of raising and maintaining a separate armed force. The Ministry of External Affairs however felt that patrolling of the EEZ and protection of national assets was a peace time role for which defence assets should not be used.

(c)   To set up a separate armed force of the Union, along the lines of the US Coast Guard. This option was finally chosen, as it avoided the Navy being distracted from its primary role of preparing for hostilities.

An interim Coast Guard was constituted on 1 February 1977, which operated under the aegis of the Navy until 18 August 1978. A permanent Coast Guard was constituted as an armed force of the Union on 19 August 1978. The Coast Guard Act 1978 requires the Coast Guard to:-

(a)   Ensure the safety and protection of offshore terminals, installations and other structures and devices.

(b)   Provide protection to fishermen, including assisting them when in distress at sea.

(c)   Protect the marine environment by preventing and controlling marine pollution.

(d)   Assist the customs in anti smuggling activities when patrolling the seas beyond Indian customs waters.

(e)   Enforce the Maritime Zones Act of 1976.

(f)   Take measures for the safety of life and property at sea.

(g)   Collect scientific data.

The Coast Guard thus became the principal agency for enforcing all national legislation in the Maritime Zones of India, working in close liaison with other Government authorities to avoid duplication of effort. During hostilities, India's Coast Guard would function under the overall operational command of the Navy as is done by other Coast Guards of the world.

Maritime Boundaries

India has maritime boundaries with five opposite states (Sri Lanka, the Maldives, Myanmar, Indonesia, and Thailand) and two adjacent States (Pakistan and Bangladesh).

Maritime boundary agreements were amicably concluded with:-

(a) Sri Lanka in 1974 and 1976.

(b) Indonesia in 1974.

(c) The Maldives in 1976.

(d) Thailand and Indonesia, on the trijunction point, in 1977.

(e) Myanmar in 1982.

Maritime boundary agreements with the adjacent states of Pakistan and Bangladesh have yet to be concluded. Meetings have been held with Bangladesh since 1976 and with Pakistan since 1986. More than two decades of negotiation culminated in 1982 with the approval of the Law of the Sea Treaty (LOST) by the Third United Nations Conference on the Law of the Sea (UNCLOS). The United States was not among the 117 nations (and two other delegations) that penned their approval of the treaty, which opened for signature amid great fanfare. American opposition was not without effect, however; the LOST, as the treaty is known, failed to gain the 60 ratifications necessary to go into effect.

Even the Soviet Union, which had proudly proclaimed its solidarity with the developing nations pushing the treaty's ratification, did not formally bind itself to the LOST. No one noticed the treaty's failure. Much of what the LOST covered was already customary international law. Navigation proceeded without hindrance. The treaty's most dramatic innovation, the seabed mining regime, proved unnecessary because seabed mining turned out to be a bust rather than the financial bonanza once predicted; land-based production remained far more accessible and affordable than ocean operations.

The international redistributionist campaign known as the "New International Economic Order," of which the LOST was a key component, collapsed amid the socialist wreckage commonly known as the Third World. It became evident that the sort of collectivist economics that wouldn't work domestically also would not work internationally. But enthusiasm for international agreements is always strong in Washington. The Clinton administration renegotiated the treaty and proclaimed that the problems involving the seabed mining provisions cited by President Ronald Reagan had been fixed. The United States signed the LOST in 1994, setting off a stampede of foreign ratifications.

The Republican Senate refused to vote on the LOST under President Bill Clinton, but Senate Foreign Relations Committee Chairman Richard Lugar (R-Ind.) won committee approval in 2004 with the support of President George W. Bush. At her confirmation before Lugar's committee, soon-to-be Secretary of State Condoleezza Rice stated that the President "would certainly like to see it pass as soon as possible." Continuing opposition has prevented the treaty from reaching the Senate floor, but even some critics of the treaty argue that ratification would be harmless since the LOST doesn't matter—if there's no seabed mining, the regulatory regime does not matter, no matter how awful it is.

So why not ratify the convention? The answer: a bad agreement is a bad agreement. If seabed mining ever becomes economically profitable, it could be crippled by the LOST's unnecessarily complicated rules. The precedential impact of the treaty is even more detrimental to U.S. interests. The LOST creates a collectivist, highly politicized system to govern much of mankind's unowned resources. The more than two decades of experience following negotiation of the treaty have demonstrated that a free and unfettered market is not only more efficient, but also more fair than political control. At a time when the spread of free economic systems has proved to be a boon for the world's poor, the LOST is a reactionary step back into the collectivist past.

Collectivism or Chaos

Former Maltese UN Ambassador Arvid Pardo, who coined the phrase "common heritage of mankind" for the seabed's resources, reversed his earlier opinion and now calls the system "fatally flawed," complaining that it could "prove to be an enduring economic burden on the international community." Still, some treaty proponents contend that no matter how unfavorable the LOST might be for international mining—most importantly, the mining of manganese (polymetallic) nodules, polymetallic massive sulfides, and cobalt-rich ferromanganese crusts—it is better than having no treaty at all.

Without some security of tenure to deep-sea mining sites, it is said that companies would not invest the millions of dollars necessary to begin operations. Certainly, firms would not take the potentially enormous risks of such a new venture if they might face conflicting site claims that the LOST addresses. However, most businessmen understand that it makes little difference whether or not, say, Zimbabwe recognizes its right to harvest manganese nodules in the Pacific because it is incapable of mining the seabed itself or interfering with the operations of others. Indeed, given the dynamics of seabed mining, it probably does not even matter if other industrialized nations, with firms capable of mining the ocean floor, recognize other countries' claims.

In all but the most unusual case, the seabed's irregular geography and surplus of nodules make "poaching" uneconomical; it would make more sense to develop a new site than to attempt to overrun someone else's. In any case, it would have been quite simple to build an alternative to the LOST. In 1980, Congress passed the Deep Seabed Hard Minerals Act to provide interim protection for American miners until Congress ratified an acceptable LOST. The Act could simply be amended to create a permanent process for recording seabed claims and resolving conflicts. Such legislation could then be coordinated with that of the other leading industrialized states.

In September 1982, the United Kingdom, France, Germany and the United States signed the Reciprocating States Agreement to provide for arbitration of competing claims. Such an informal system could have been upgraded to a formal treaty, authorizing each nation to oversee its own companies' activities and creating a mechanism to resolve any conflicts. No international bureaucracy would have been necessary. America's refusal to sign the treaty after its completion in 1982 generated substantial global anguish, but the world has since moved the United States' way. As mineral prices declined, so too, did the prospects of massive resource harvests from the seabed. Poorer states saw their expected LOST windfall disappear.

And as developing countries started experimenting with market economics, they backed away from the wide-ranging "New International Economic Order," which sought to promote income redistribution from the industrialized "North" to the impoverished "South." By the early 1990s, some Third World diplomats were privately admitting that the Reagan administration had been right to kill the LOST.

But bad ideas never seem to die. Washington should have pressed to separate seabed mining, for which the treaty was unnecessary, from other maritime issues, where the LOST offered some benefits, if it desired to return to the issue. Instead, the first Bush administration began consultations to "fix" the LOST in 1990, and these negotiations were accelerated under the Clinton administration. After winning changes in some of the treaty's most burdensome provisions governing seabed mining, the United States signed on 29 July 1994. United States Ambassador to the United Nations, Madeleine Albright, praised the LOST for providing "for the application of free-market principles to the development of the deep seabed" and establishing "a lean institution that is both flexible, and efficient."

"We have been successful in fixing all the major problems raised by the Reagan administration," explained chief State Department negotiator Wesley Scholz. "We have converted the seabed part of the agreement into a market-based regime." The current Bush administration is making essentially the same argument. The Department of State's legal adviser, William H. Taft IV, testified before the Senate that the changes in "the 1994 Agreement overcome each one of the objections of the United States to Part XI [covering the seabed] of the convention and meet our goal of guaranteed access by the U.S. industry to deep seabed minerals on the basis of reasonable terms and conditions."

John F. Turner, assistant secretary of state for oceans and international environmental and scientific affairs, contended, "the changes set forth in the 1994 Agreement meet our goal of guaranteed access by U.S. industry to deep seabed minerals on the basis of reasonable terms and conditions." In fact, the Clinton administration only succeeded in slightly improving an accord that was disastrous to begin with; the treaty has not been completely fixed. More than enough negative provisions remain, even though some good has been done by the revisions to the LOST prompted by the United States. In certain places, the negotiators substituted slightly less harmful ambiguity for what had been clearly negative provisions.

The result is an improvement, and a dramatic testament to the distance that market ideas have traveled since the LOST was opened for signature in 1982. Nevertheless, the original collectivist framework remains. Even the State Department acknowledges that the new "Agreement retains the institutional outlines of Part XI." The revised treaty would still create a Rube Goldberg system to govern seabed operations, with an International Seabed Authority (ISA), Enterprise, Council, Assembly and more, that is likely to become yet another multilateral boondoggle. The LOST retains revenue sharing with developing states and other organizations, international royalties, a council veto for land-based minerals producers, and the like.

The publicly run enterprise is an international version of the ubiquitous parastatals that have failed so miserably in almost every debt-ridden Third World nation. The financial redistribution clauses remain a special interest sop to poor states. Facing the usual incentives afflicting any organization that separates the few that fund it from the many that constitute a voting majority, the ISA is likely to end up bloated and politicized. Today, with low mineral prices that discourage development of a vibrant seabed mining industry, the ISA sometimes emphasizes the trivial. It generates many reports as well as wastes paper; protecting "the emblem, the official seal and the name" of the ISA, as well as "abbreviations of that name through the use of its initial letters," has become one of the ISA's missions.

Among the other crises the authority has confronted: In April 2002, the Jamaican government turned off the ISA's air-conditioning, necessitating "urgent consultations with the Ministry of Foreign Affairs and Foreign Trade." One year later, Jamaica used the same tactic in the ongoing battle over Authority payments for its facility. The LOST revisions restrict some of the ISA's discretionary power, but still submerge seabed mining in the bizarre political dynamics of international organizations. Private firms must continue to survey and provide, gratis, a site for the enterprise for each area they wish to mine. The treaty encourages public cartels yet includes anti-monopoly and anti-density provisions that still would apply disproportionately to American mining firms.

ISA fees have been lowered, but companies would continue to owe a $250,000 application fee and some, as yet undetermined, level of royalties and profit sharing. The "system of payments," intones the compromise text, shall be "fair both to the contractor and to the Authority," which has no practical effect. Fees "shall be within the range of those prevailing in respect of land-based mining of the same or similar minerals," even though seabed production is more expensive, riskier and occurs in territory beyond any nation's jurisdiction.

The revised LOST establishes a new "economic assistance fund" to aid land-based minerals producers.

Surplus funds would still be distributed, "taking into particular consideration the interests and needs of the developing States and peoples who have not attained full independence or other self-governing status," like the Palestinian Authority, a provision unchanged by the 1994 agreement. Theoretically, the United States could block inappropriate payments—at least so long as it was a member of the finance committee—but over time U.S. ISA representatives would feel enormous pressure from their peers to be flexible and reasonable.

In fact, redistribution has been an important objective for the ISA during its short life. For example, a proposal was made for an African institute of the oceans, as if that was the highest priority for countries suffering from civil war, economic collapse and social chaos. Voluntary trust funds have been established to aid developing countries, though few people or nations have rushed forward to contribute—the response was "rather slow," explained the ISA—forcing it to fill the fund coffers. The International Tribunal for the Law of the Sea is supposed to offer dispassionate adjudication of disputes. Yet membership is decided by quota; each "geographical group" is to have at least three representatives.

On the tribunal were some of the early conference participants who pushed the treaty's redistributionist agenda: Cameroon's Paul Engo, who chaired the committee responsible for drafting Part XI, and Tanzania's Joseph Warioba, whose term has since ended. Even some of the specific fixes look inadequate. Consider the voting system, which admittedly has been improved. According to the revised treaty, the United States would be guaranteed a seat on the council, though still not a veto. The council would consist of four chambers, any one of which could block action if a majority of its members voted no.

On matters of serious interest, the United States could probably, but not necessarily, win the necessary extra two votes in its chamber to form a majority. Moreover, this purely negative veto power does not guarantee that the ISA would act when required to approve rules for mining applications. The interest of the land-based mineral producers is antagonistic to the very idea of seabed mining, which is expected to reduce resource prices.

Yet they, as well as the "developing States Parties, representing special interests," such as "geographically disadvantaged" nations, each have their own chamber, and thus a de facto veto over the ISA's operations. Thus, the voting power of such groups essentially matches that of the United States.

Moreover, the qualification standards for miners are to be established by consensus, essentially unanimity, which could give land-based producers as much influence as the United States. The possession of a veto provides them with an opportunity to extract potentially expensive concessions from nations that support mining—new limits on production, for instance, or redistributionist payments—to let the ISA function by promulgating mining rules. Unfortunately, once the ISA asserts jurisdiction over seabed mining, potential producers would be hurt by a deadlock, which would prevent them from mining.

Indeed, production controls, one of the most controversial provisions in the original text, have been preserved in the new agreement. The revision does excise most of the LOST Article 151 and related provisions, which set a convoluted ceiling on seabed production. However, it leaves intact Article 150, which, among other things, states that the ISA is to ensure "the protection of developing countries from adverse effects on their economies or on their export earnings resulting from a reduction in the price of an affected mineral, or in the volume of exports of that mineral."

That wording implies that the ISA has the right to impose production limits. The United States might have to rely on its ability to round up allied votes to block such a proposal in the council in perpetuity. Funding remains a problem as well. The United States, naturally, would be expected to provide the largest share of the ISA's budget, which would be 25 percent of the total budget in the ISA's initial stages.

How much that would be exactly is impossible to predict; the budget is to be developed through "consensus" by the finance committee, on which the United States is temporarily guaranteed a seat ("until the Authority has sufficient funds other than assessed contributions to meet its administrative expenses").

The Clinton administration argued for the new agreement to "[reduce] the size and costs of the regime's institutions." This was to be accomplished by adopting a paragraph in the revised text pledging that "all organs and subsidiary bodies to be established under the Convention and this Agreement shall be cost-effective."

Similarly, states the new accord, the royalty "system should not be complicated and should not impose major administrative costs on the Authority or on a contractor." These sentiments might be genuine, but the revised agreement changed none of the underlying institutional incentives that bias virtually every international organization, most obviously the United Nations itself, towards extravagance.

Absent firm institutional limits, poorer voting majorities typically find it impossible to resist the temptation to spend the resources of the wealthier minority. In fact, concern over bloated budgets was a major factor in Moscow's initial decision in 1994 not to endorse the treaty.

Russian UN Ambassador H.E. Ostrovsky explained that a particular concern was the fact that "general guidelines such as necessity to promote cost-effectiveness can not be seriously regarded as a reliable disincentive." Before the treaty had even gone into force, Ambassador Ostrovsky pointed to "a trend [within the United Nation's seabed office] to establish high paying positions which are not yet required."

Technology Transfer

The provisions covering technology transfers to the enterprise and mining operations through developing states constitute some of the most odious redistributionist clauses left over from the original text.

The mandatory transfer requirement, which would have required turning over private, proprietary technology to competing mining operations, has been discarded, replaced by a duty of sponsoring states to facilitate the acquisition of mining technology "if the Enterprise or developing States are unable to obtain" equipment commercially.

However, the enterprise and developing nations would find themselves unable to purchase machinery only if they were unwilling to pay the market price or preserve trade secrets, or if a government restricted the sale of the technology because it had important dual-use capabilities.

The new clause might be interpreted to mean that industrialized states and private miners, whose "cooperation" is to be ensured by their respective governments, are therefore responsible for mandating and subsidizing the enterprise's acquisition of technology.

Presumably the United States and its allies could block such a proposal in the council, but, again, it is hard to predict the future legislative dynamics and potential log-rolling in an obscure UN body in upcoming years.

Moreover, the amended agreement leaves intact a separate, open-ended mandate for coerced collaboration. The authority, states Article 144, "shall take measures":

> 1. (b) To promote and encourage the transfer to developing States of ... technology and scientific knowledge....
>
> 2. To this end the Authority and States Parties shall co-operate in promoting the transfer of technology and scientific knowledge.... In particular they shall initiate and promote:

(a) Programmes for the transfer of technology to the Enterprise and to developing States ... under fair and reasonable terms and conditions;

(b) Measures directed towards the advancement of the technology of the Enterprise and the domestic technology of developing States, particularly by providing opportunities to personnel from the Enterprise and from developing States for training.

At best, this suggests that Western firms would be expected to help equip and train their competitors. At worst, it could end up authorizing some sort of mandatory system, one close to that explicitly enshrined in the original treaty text. Private companies would be forced to subsidize their competitors and would lose control of expensive technologies.

At issue is not just technology, useful for seabed mining. For instance, dual-use technologies with military applications might also fall under ISA requirements. Peter Leitner, a Defense Department advisor, points to "underwater mapping and bathymetry systems, reflection and refraction seismology, magnetic detection technology, optical imaging, remotely operated vehicles, submersible vehicles, deep salvage technology, active and passive military acoustic systems, classified bathymetric and geophysical data, and undersea robots and manipulators" as technology that developed countries might also be potentially required to provide to poorer ones.

The treaty has become a solution in search of a problem. A good international treaty would be useful, but it is not necessary. Until Washington ratifies the LOST, U.S. citizens retain the liberty to mine the seabed. This makes it all the more important that the United States rejects the accord. If the United States ever joins the ISA, a future renunciation of the LOST might not be considered enough to reestablish Americans' traditional freedoms on the high seas.

Admittedly, objections based on seabed mining might seem to be of little importance today since the promise of recovering ocean resources is far less bright than it was when UNCLOS was initially convened. But operations might still become economically feasible in coming years, especially as technological innovation makes the mining process less expensive.

Moreover, principle also is important. Even if no minerals are ever lifted commercially from the ocean's floor, the LOST remains unacceptable because of its coercive, collectivist philosophical underpinnings, most notably declaring all seabed resources to be mankind's "common heritage" under the control of a majority of the world's nation states.

The Failure of the New International Economic Order

The treaty negotiations were held in a different era, a time when communism reigned throughout much of the world, Third World states were proclaiming socialism to offer the true path to progress and prosperity, and multilateral organizations were promoting the "New International Economic Order," or NIEO, to engineer massive wealth redistribution from the industrialized to the underdeveloped states. Indeed, many of the provisions of the original LOST, particularly those provisions regarding seabed mining, were dictated by the so-called Group of 77, the developing states' de facto international lobby.

These nations saw the LOST as the leading edge of a campaign that included treaties covering Antarctica and outer space, expanded bilateral and multilateral aid programs, and activism by a veritable gallery of UN alphabet-soup agencies—CTC, ILO, UNCTAD, WHO and WIPO. Ambassador Pardo commented that American acceptance of the treaty, "however qualified, reluctant, or defective, would validate" international political control of private economic activities, or what he euphemistically termed "the global democratic approach to decision making." Luckily, economic reality has since hit many poorer nations. Even formerly kleptocratic one-party states like Mexico, one-time authoritarian collectivist regimes like Tanzania and formally communist states like Vietnam have moved in varying degrees towards the market economy.

Before Ronald Reagan left office, the NIEO had disappeared from international discourse, along with any mention of the LOST. Although American ratification of the LOST would not be enough to resurrect the NIEO, it would nevertheless enshrine into international law some very ugly precedents that are reminiscent of the collectivist spirit of the NIEO. One such precedent is that the nation-states of the world collectively own the world's unclaimed resources. Granting ownership and control to petty autocracies with no relationship to the resource nor any ability to contribute anything to their development makes neither moral nor practical sense.

Much better on both counts is the simple Lockean notion that mixing one's labor with resources—by developing complex machinery capable of scouring the ocean floor, for instance—grants one a property interest in them. The Lockean standard also would better suit the interests of developing peoples. The LOST may purport to promote international justice, fairness and cooperation, but, in fact, it advances none of these principles.

Rather, it raises to the status of international law self-indulgent claims of ownership to be secured through an oligarchy of international bureaucrats, diplomats and lawyers. And the treaty's specific provisions, which still, even if in an attenuated form, mandate global redistribution of resources, create a monopolistic public mining entity, restrict competition and require the transfer of technology, reflect the sort of statist panaceas that were discredited by the historical wave that swept away Soviet-style communism.

Countervailing Benefits

Throughout the treaty's development, some observers acknowledged the treaty's failings, but nevertheless contended that it had enough positive benefits to warrant signing. Typical is the argument by members of the Center for Law and Social Policy: "Although the draft is not perfect, we believe that the benefits to U.S. interests from the treaty far outweigh the disadvantages." There are gains in non-seabed areas, though they are limited. Many of the non-seabed provisions are marginally beneficial, while a number are somewhat harmful. Sections governing fishing and maritime research, for instance, make few changes in current law, and the treaty's authorization of 200-mile exclusive economic zones (EEZs) merely reflects what has become customary international law.

Provisions that work to the detriment of the United States include the boundary-setting process that strips some non-seabed resources away from the United States, the pollution provisions that restrict America's ability to control some emission sources, and the clauses that imply that the United States might eventually have to share oil revenues from development of the Outer Continental Shelf.

Perceived as far more important by many treaty supporters are the provisions covering rules of navigation. For instance, Rear Adm. William Schachte Jr., a Pentagon official who backed the LOST during the Reagan years, argued that the document was vital to guarantee American naval rights. Washington's refusal to sign the LOST left critics predicting chaos and combat on the high seas two decades ago, yet we have witnessed not one incident as a result of the failure to implement the LOST.

Nor is the treaty unambiguously favorable to transit rights. The document introduces some new limitations on navigation involving the EEZs, territorial seas and water surrounding archipelagic states. Even seemingly innocent restrictions might have a negative impact; Alfred Rubin of

Tufts University worries that the ban on "research or survey activities" could limit U.S. naval rights. At other times, the LOST's language is ambiguous regarding transit rights for submerged submarines, for instance, thus limiting the value of the treaty guarantee. Ambassador Pardo complains that the treaty "is often studiously unclear, and predictability suffers."

Gary Knight of Louisiana State University argues that "the difficulty of establishing our legal right to EEZ navigation and submerged straits passage would be no more difficult under an existing customary international law argument than under the convoluted text of the proposed UNCLOS." In short, there is only modest theoretical advantage arising from the navigation section for which to trade away the mining provisions. Even if the LOST offered a definite and positive interpretation, the legal protections for navigation would provide little practical gain over existing customary procedures.

Analysts Benjamin Friedman and Daniel Friedman contend that "by signing the Convention, the United States gives added weight and stability to customary rights, and pushes recalcitrant states to respect navigational freedoms." Bush administration representatives make the same argument: "The navigation and over-flight freedoms we require through customary international law are better served by being a party to the Convention that codifies those freedoms," testified Adm. Michael G. Mullen, vice chief of naval operations for the Joint Chiefs of Staff. While that may be true, the practical benefits of the LOST are far outweighed by negative factors. Adm. Schachte acknowledged in Senate testimony that "the Convention alone is not enough, even [with the United States] as a party Our operational forces must continue to exercise our rights under the Convention."

The LOST is unlikely to influence countries that have either the incentive or the ability to interfere with U.S. shipping. In practice, few do; nations usually have far more to gain economically from allowing unrestricted passage. However, where countries perceive their vital national interests to be at stake—Great Britain in the First World War and Iran during its war with Iraq in the 1980s, for instance—they rarely allow juridical niceties to stop them from interdicting or destroying international commerce. In a crisis, most maritime nations are ready to sacrifice abstract legal norms in pursuit of important policy goals.

Indeed, LOST membership has not prevented Brazil, China, India, Malaysia, North Korea, Paldstan and others from making ocean claims deemed excessive by some. In his testimony last October, Adm. Mullen warned that the benefits he believed to derive from treaty ratification did not "suggest that countries' attempts to restrict navigation will cease once the United States becomes a party to the Law of the Sea Convention." As for military transit, America should concentrate on maintaining good relations with the handful of countries that sit astride important sea lanes.

At a time when Washington is combating lawless terrorism, it should be evident that the only sure guarantee of free passage is the power of the U.S. Navy to ensure free passage. Of course, even with friendly nations, Washington would prefer not "to have to use muscle to exercise our rights," observed Carter-era LOST negotiator Elliot Richardson. Moreover, Mark T. Esper, deputy assistant secretary of defense for negotiations policy, told the Senate that sea and air lanes should "remain open as a matter of international legal right—not contingent upon approval by coastal and island nations along the route or in the area of operations."

But LOST or no LOST, those rights in practice will remain contingent on the acquiescence of maritime states. Consider the luckless USS Pueblo, the U.S. intelligence ship seized by North Korea in international waters in 1968. Pyongyang held the crew for 11 months and turned the ship into a propaganda attraction. International law did not prevent North Korea from illegally seizing the intelligence ship; approval of the LOST would have offered the Pueblo no additional protection.

The United States was similarly unaided by international law in its confrontation in 2001 with China over its EP-3 surveillance plane. Adm. Schachte contends that "if you look at the Persian Gulf situation, for example, we didn't have problems with Iran or Oman in using the Strait of Hormuz, because they recognized that the language of the treaty was clear."

Yet Iran, which bombed Kuwaiti oil tankers during its war with Iraq, is unlikely to be deterred by an international treaty, however unambiguous its provisions. If Iran, or any other maritime state, believed it to be in its vital interest to prevent the passage of U.S. ships, then its signature on the LOST would not likely prevent it from acting; rather, the country would be primarily concerned about America's willingness and ability to force passage. And in a world in which the USSR has disappeared and its Red Navy is rusting in port, China has yet to develop a strong blue water navy, and Third World conflicts are largely unconnected to the United States as they were during the Cold War, Washington is rarely going to have to fight for access to waterways.

Moreover, the administration's positive assessment of the treaty depends on Washington's ability to insulate military operations from the LOST in his October 2003 testimony, the State Department's William H. Taft IV noted the importance of conditioning acceptance "upon the understanding that each Party has the exclusive right to determine which of its activities are 'military activities' and that such determination is not subject to review."

Whether other countries will respect that claim is uncertain. Adm. Mullen acknowledged the possibility exists that a LOST tribunal could assert jurisdiction over American military operations, resulting in a ruling that adversely impacts "operational planning and activities, and our security."

Indeed, the impact of the LOST on President Bush's Proliferation Security Initiative (PSI) for interdicting illicit weapons transfers is uncertain. Treaty advocates contend that the LOST would provide an additional forum through which to advance the PSI. Assistant Secretary of State John Turner testified before the Senate that "joining the Convention would strengthen PSI efforts." At the very least, "it imposes no new restrictions," write Daniel Friedman and Benjamin Friedman. That is not so clear, however. Washington's ability to intercept weapons shipments currently legal under existing international law is problematic, and will remain so under the LOST.

After all, any anti-proliferation policy, such as the PSI, treats nations differently based upon a subjective assessment of the stability and intention of a particular government; the LOST incorporates no such distinctions. Controversy is inevitable due to the ambiguous nature of the LOST towards the seizure of WMD shipments. China and India already have insisted that the PSI be barred by the treaty. Accepting the LOST might end up adopting ambiguity, which would weaken Washington's position. Convention advocates further contend that even if the LOST is flawed, only participation in the treaty regime can prevent future damaging interpretations, amendments and tribunal decisions. Professor Bernard Oxman, a University of Miami Law School professor who also serves as a Judge Ad Hoc on the International Tribunal for the Law of the Sea, contends that "what we gain by becoming party is increased influence over" the interpretation of the convention's rules.

Senator Lugar worries that failing to ratify the treaty means the United States could "forfeit our seat at the table of institutions that will make decisions about the use of the oceans." David Sandalow of the Brookings Institution warns that staying out of the LOST risks existing navigation freedoms through "backsliding by nations that have put aside excessive maritime claims from years past." However, American friends and allies, both in Asia and

Europe, have an incentive to protect navigational freedom, including that of the United States. So long as Washington maintains good relations with them, although admittedly a more difficult undertaking because of strains in the aftermath of the war in Iraq, it should be able to defend U.S. interests indirectly through surrogates.

If the nations, which alongside the United States benefit from navigational freedom—countries such as Germany and Japan are as, if not more, dependent than the United States on international trade—are unwilling to aid the United States (i.e., defend navigational rights currently guaranteed by the treaty) while Washington is outside the LOST, they are unlikely to prove any more steadfast with Washington inside the LOST. In October 2003, Assistant Secretary Turner told the Senate Foreign Relations Committee that America had "had considerable success" in asserting "its oceans interests as a non-party to the Convention."

Critics of the United States' refusal to sign in 1982 predicted chaos on the oceans, but, as noted earlier, not once has an American ship been denied passage. No country has had either the incentive or the ability to interfere with U.S. shipping; if a nation was willing and able to do so, the LOST would have been of little help. Ironically, potential problems cited by U.S. shippers, such as the creation of a "particularly sensitive sea area" off of Europe, have involved alleged misinterpretations of the treaty, not America's lack of membership. Also, foreign shippers have attempted to use LOST to escape application of U.S. environmental controls. Joining the treaty would provide no panacea for eliminating ocean controversies.

Finally, the LOST may encourage the United Nations to venture into new, unexplored territory. The United Nation's Division for Ocean Affairs and the Law of the Sea boldly announced that the LOST "is not, however, a static instrument, but rather a dynamic and evolving body of law that must be vigorously safeguarded and its implementation aggressively advanced." If international jurists exhibit the same creativity as shown by activist judges domestically, the LOST might prove to be dangerously unpredictable and be detrimental to U.S. interests.

For instance, in 2001, Douglas Stevenson, representing the Seamen's Church Institute, a private aid group for mariners, complained about "trends that erode traditional seafarers' rights," such as medical care, as well as abandonment by insolvent and irresponsible ship-owners.

Stevenson explained that "when mariners' health, safety or welfare is in jeopardy," they "looked to the United Nations Convention on the Law of the Sea to protect them." There obviously are real and tragic abuses of seamen by irresponsible shipping companies, but what the international community should do as part of the LOST about such issues is not obvious. Washington might find out to its detriment that the treaty ultimately reaches far beyond what it expects to if it signs on.

If the stakes are that high, then it is even more important that the treaty be a good one, which it manifestly is not. Someday, seabed resources might be worth recovering, giving life to the provisions of the so-called Part XI. In the meantime, the LOST sets undesirable precedents, reflecting its birth when collectivist economics as represented by the New International Economic Order permeated international relations. Unfortunately, notwithstanding the 1994 revisions, the LOST remains captive to its collectivist and redistributionist origins. It is a bad agreement, one that cannot be fixed without abandoning its philosophical presupposition that the seabed is the common heritage of the world's politicians and their agents, the authority and enterprise. But the issue is more than abstract philosophical principle. Much depends on the practical operation of the ISA and ultimate interpretation of the LOST.

2

Towards a National Water Law

In the face of growing freshwater scarcity, most countries of the world are taking steps to conserve their water and foster its sustainable use. Water crises range from concerns of drinking water availability and/or quality, the degradation or contamination of freshwater, and the allocation of water to different users. To meet the challenge, many countries are undergoing systemic changes to the use of freshwater and the provision of water services, thereby leading to greater commercialization of the resource as well as a restructuring of the legal, regulatory, technical and institutional frameworks for water. India does not have an exclusive and comprehensive water law. Water-related legal provisions are dispersed across various irrigation Acts, central and state laws, constitutional provisions and court decisions.

Laws relating to water in India have diverse origins, including ancient local customs and the British Common Law. The in-depth chapters in this compendium pertain to issues on water – water-resource policy, management, conservation, conflict-resolution etc. – and proceed to a discussion of the legal questions that arise. Water laws in India have been changed drastically in the last two decades. The legal framework for the management of water resources, the role/rights of the government and users, and the institutional frameworks are some of the important areas where considerable reforms have been happened or are happening. Ongoing reforms tend to incorporate a number of norms into the legal framework, such as participatory management, viewing water as an economic good and redefining the role of government from 'service provider' to 'independent regulator'.

These norms are not unique features of water law reforms in India. Ongoing reforms, in this respect, seem to have relation with the policies of international financial institutions, such as the World Bank. The nature and extent of these norms could be varied for different competing uses, such as domestic, agriculture, industrial and commercial. The reforms, as above stated, are largely applicable to surface water resources. The reforms in the legal regime of ground water have been initiated and to some extent implemented in an entirely different background. Previously, ground water was considered as part of land rights and therefore was in a 'private domain'.

The reforms brought about significant change in this legal position by a shift from 'private domain' 'government control'. The ground water legal reforms provide a legal and institutional framework to regulate ground water use. Ongoing reforms of the ground water legal regime seem to work in a different plane. Ongoing reforms in water laws have invited mixed responses. The evaluation of the water law reforms are mainly based upon the norms of equity, human rights, caste and gender.

Another base for evaluation could be the 'environmental concerns', that is, the protection and preservation of the resource in the larger interest of present and future generations. Reforms of water law in the broader context of water sector reforms include a number of new laws. In the context of drinking water, which is arguably one of the most fundamental aspects of water law because of the direct link with the human right to water, neither Parliament nor Legislative Assemblies have been involved in ongoing reforms.

Rather, the significant reforms that have been progressively put in place over the course of this decade have been introduced through series of government proposals that have not been put to the test of parliamentary scrutiny.

Since the new policies propose a system which is likely to restrict access to drinking water for the poorest that should be the primary beneficiaries of any new scheme, this raises significant questions concerning the realisation of the human right to water. This chapter examines proposed drinking water reforms and their broader impacts.

Constitutional provisions

According to the state list, under the Seventh Schedule of the Constitution, states have jurisdiction over water resources within their borders. The powers of the states are subject to:

(a)   The Union list under the Seventh Schedule of the Constitution that allows the central government to regulate and develop inter-state rivers and river valleys when declared by Parliament as a matter of public interest.

(b)   The central government's regulatory role in inter-state water projects, under Article 252.

(c)   The Environment (Protection) Act, 1996, and notifications issued under it by the Union Ministry of Environment and Forests (MoEF), which require states to get central clearance for major water projects.

(d)   The central government's role in resolving inter-state water disputes as per the provisions under Article 262. Under this Article, Parliament enacted the Inter-State Water Disputes Act of 1956, under which a number of tribunals have been set up to resolve water disputes among the states.

The central government can also acquire legislative powers on water when two or more states desiring uniform water legislation request the Union government, with the approval of their respective Assemblies, to provide such legislation. Subject to the above limitations, and limitations enforced by central administrative, policy and financial decisions, legislative powers over water rest with the states. Water-related legislations in Maharashtra are listed below:

Maharashtra's water-related laws:

(a) Maharashtra Fisheries Act, 1960

(b) Water (Prevention and Control of Pollution) Act, 1974

(c) Maharashtra Irrigation Act, 1976

(d) Maharashtra Kharland Improvement Act, 1979

(e) Maharashtra Groundwater (Regulation for Drinking Water Purposes) Act, 1993

(f) Krishna Valley Development Corporation Act, 1996

(g) Vidarbha Irrigation Development Corporation Act, 1996

(h) Tapi Irrigation Development Corporation Act, 1997

(i) Konkan Irrigation Development Corporation Act, 1997

(j) Godavari Marathwada Irrigation Development Act, 1998

(k) Maharashtra Project-Affected Persons Rehabilitation Act, 2001

(l) Maharashtra Water Resources Regulatory Authority Act, 2005

(m) Maharashtra Management of Irrigation Systems by Farmers Act, 2005

Water Ownership

India does not have any specific law defining ownership and rights over water sources. The rights are derived from several legislations and customary beliefs.

Rights over Surface Water

Rights over water in rivers and lakes are defined by land and state irrigation Acts. Formulated first in colonial times, these Acts explicitly state that the government has absolute right over this water. For instance, the Northern India Canal and Drainage Act, 1873, states that the government has the right to "use and control for public purposes the water of all rivers and streams flowing in natural channels, and of all lakes". Irrigation Acts or their rules specify who can use canal water, and for what purpose. Only use rights — not ownership rights — are granted.

Typically, use rights are granted only to people who have land in command areas. However, in Maharashtra, lift irrigation schemes have been permitted to take water to lands outside the command area. Further, a new law allows 'bulk' users such as water users' associations to sell the water allotted to them. But such sale will be regulated by the authority that grants the bulk allotment in the first instance.

Rights over Groundwater

Several court judgments in post-Independent India have affirmed that all natural resources — resources that are by nature meant for public use and enjoyment — are held by the State in public trust. For instance in M C Mehta v Kamal Nath (1997), the Supreme Court declared that "the State is the trustee of all natural resources"; as a trustee, the State has "a legal duty to protect the natural resources," and "these resources meant for public use cannot be converted into private ownership".

However, the legal position on whether groundwater is a resource meant for public use is fuzzy, and India has no law that explicitly defines groundwater ownership (Orissa did amend its irrigation Act to assert State right over groundwater, but this has been challenged in court). Some grounds for determining groundwater rights are provided by the Indian Easement Act of 1882. An 'easement' is a right that the owner or occupier of certain land possesses, for beneficial enjoyment of that land. Examples of easements are right of way, right to light and air, and right to standing or flowing water not on one's land.

Section 7 (g) of the Indian Easement Act states that every landowner has the right to "collect and dispose" of all water under the land within his own limits, and all water on its surface that does not pass in a defined channel. Hence, by this Act, the owner of a piece of land does not, strictly speaking, "own" the groundwater under the land or surface water on the land; he only has the right to collect and use the water.

However, it is customarily accepted across India that a well on a piece of land belongs to the owner of that land, and others have no right to extract water from the well or restrict the landowner's rights to use the water. This belief and practice is indirectly supported by various laws such as land Acts and irrigation Acts that list all things on which the government has a right. These Acts do not mention groundwater. Interpretations of the Transfer of Property Act of 1882 and the Land Acquisition Act of 1894 also support the position that a landowner has proprietary rights to groundwater; it is connected to the 'dominant heritage' (land) and cannot be transferred apart from the land.

But the right to property in India is not absolute. It is not a fundamental right and government has the power to restrict it in the interests of the larger public good. Thus, the government enjoys the right to take over anybody's land to construct dams, build roads, etc. While the government has to follow due process and pay due compensation (failure to do so can be challenged), its right to acquire the property itself is unchallengeable. Further, the government is duty-bound by the directive principles of the Constitution to work towards social, political and economic justice and equity, and protection of the environment.

For instance, Article 39 (b) lays down that: 'The State shall, in particular, direct its policy towards securing that the ownership and control of the material resources of the community are so distributed as best to subserve the common good.' Article 51-A (g) says it is the fundamental duty of every citizen 'to protect and improve the natural environment including forests, lakes, rivers...'

Hence, the government has the right as well as the duty to regulate use of groundwater in the interests of justice, equity and environmental protection. This duty was emphasised by a Supreme Court order that directed the Centre to constitute a groundwater authority. Accordingly, the Central Ground Water Authority was set up in 1986.

Right to Water

The Constitution guarantees every citizen fundamental rights to equality, life and personal liberty. Article 15 (2) of the Constitution further states that no citizen shall be subjected to any restriction with regard to "the use of wells, tanks, bathing ghats". Various courts have upheld that the right to clean and safe water is an aspect of the right to life. For instance, in Narmada Bachao Andolan v Union of India (2000), the Supreme Court said that "water is the basic need for the survival of human beings and is part of right to life and human rights as enshrined in Article 21 of the Constitution of India".

But judgments do not constitute law or policy; at best, they provide directions for the formulation of laws and policies. As yet, no laws or policies have been formulated asserting that water is a fundamental and inviolable right enjoyed by every citizen of the country. The 'right to water' can therefore be obtained in India only on a case-by-case basis, by going to court.

Responsibility for providing Water

Groundwater plays a major role in meeting irrigation, industrial and drinking water needs. Groundwater in India largely remains as a part of private property right. This facilitates uncontrolled extraction of groundwater for various purposes. The subsidized power supply for agricultural purposes also catalyses the large scale extraction of groundwater. The purity and consistency in availability of groundwater coupled with the insufficiency of surface water promote the uncontrolled extraction of groundwater.

Hence the growing needs, the 'favourable' legal framework, availability of technology etc. seems to have caused the deterioration of quantity and quality of groundwater across the country. One of the major reasons for this continuing deterioration can be attributed to the existing law and policy framework. India, even after, independence, followed the colonial laws and principles. So is the case with the groundwater legal regime.

As a result, groundwater largely remained as a part of land right. The right over groundwater was considered as, more or less, a real property right. This legal framework made groundwater a resource that could be enjoyed by the propertied class in an uncontrollable manner. The technological development and policies of the government such as electricity pricing, lending policy etc. also facilitated the indiscriminate extraction of groundwater. A shift in this legal regime started recently. One of the major features of the evolving legal regime is the shift from uncontrolled private regime to government control. This shift could be traced from the model bill prepared by the Ministry of Water Resources in 1970. Subsequently, several states have enacted separate groundwater laws.

This process is not yet completed because some states are in the process of enacting separate laws while some other states do not feel it necessary to enact such laws. Apart from the statutory framework, there are policy documents, principles and doctrines forming part of the groundwater legal regime in India. In this background of multiplicity of laws, policies and institutions, this chapter attempts to analyse the groundwater legal regime in India. There is no legislation in India that says governments have to provide water to citizens. But, as noted earlier, courts have ruled that the right to water is part of the constitutional guarantee of right to life.

It has also been implicitly accepted since Independence that central and state governments have a primary responsibility for providing water for drinking, and, subsequently, for other purposes. Provisions for supplying drinking water have been made in all the Five-Year Plans, and the responsibility was made explicit in the Twenty-Point Programme drafted in 1975 and modified in 1982 and 1986.

Accordingly, a host of programmes have been framed and implemented at the central and state levels, such as the Accelerated Rural Water Supply Programme and the Rajiv Gandhi National Drinking Water Mission. A gamut of laws has also been drafted, including:

(a) Laws establishing water boards for urban water supply.

(b) Laws enacted for water supply in metropolitan cities.

(c) Laws for water supply in the state as a whole.

(d) Laws on regulation of groundwater extraction and use.

(e) Laws on protection of water sources.

(f) Laws for supply of water to specific industrial areas.

Elaborate institutional mechanisms have been set up to provide water. The mechanism in Maharashtra is briefly discussed below.

Supply of Water

Maharashtra's surface water resources are managed by the irrigation department, which allocates water for different uses: irrigation, drinking water and sanitation, and industry. When non-irrigation usage (for example, domestic use) of a particular surface resource exceeds 15% of the water available, the allocation is done by a committee headed by the chief minister.

The following institutions are involved in the supply of water:

(a) Maharashtra Jeevan Pradhikaran formulates and executes schemes in rural and urban areas.

(b) Groundwater Directorate Survey and Development Agency implements schemes based on groundwater resources in rural and semi-urban areas.

(c)   Maharashtra Industrial Development Corporation supplies water to its industrial estates and a few industrial townships.

(d)   Zilla Parishads (ZPs) are responsible for rural water supply schemes.

(e)   Urban local bodies such as municipal corporations are responsible for the provision of drinking water in cities.

Responsibilities of PRIs

Under the 73rd and 74th constitutional amendments, states may transfer powers and responsibilities to Panchayati Raj Institutions (PRIs) with regard to minor irrigation, watershed development (panchayats) and water supply for domestic, industrial and commercial purposes (municipalities). Devolution of power to panchayats has generally not occurred. Devolution of drinking water-related powers and responsibilities to ZPs has, however, taken place.

In Maharashtra, the Maharashtra Village Panchayat Act, 1938, inter alia lists the duty of gram panchayats to maintain minor irrigation works with a cultivable command area of less than 100 hectares, which are not entrusted to ZPs. ZPs have been entrusted with the task of maintaining irrigation projects with command areas of less than 250 hectares, under the Maharashtra Zilla Parishads and Panchayat Samitis Act, 1961.

ZPs are also responsible for rural water supply schemes. Under Section 79 A of the 1961 Zilla Parishads Act, every ZP has to set up a water conservation and drinking water supply committee. The committee must include one or two people with "special knowledge or experience in the subject of water conservation and drinking water supply". These associate members of the committee do not enjoy voting rights. The committee can exercise powers related to the subject as allotted to it under the provisions of the Act.

The chief executive officer of the ZP has the power to:

(a) Order the owner of any water supply source, such as a well or tank, to keep it clean and in good repair (Section 192).

(b) Set apart public springs, tanks, wells and parts of public water courses for drinking purposes, for bathing or for washing clothes and animals (Section 194).

(c) Prohibit the use of water from any source to which the public has access (Section 194).

Regulation of Groundwater Use

Groundwater is the main source of water across India, for all purposes. Around 80-90% of rural drinking water needs are met by groundwater, and groundwater serves around half of India's net irrigated area. Groundwater extraction has risen exponentially since the 1950s due to various reasons such as the introduction of Green Revolution technologies, increased cultivation of cash crops, and electricity subsidies for irrigation pumpsets. Extraction exceeds natural recharge in many parts of the country.

In response to an emerging crisis that threatens the life and livelihoods of millions, the Centre, in 1970, framed a Model Groundwater (Control and Regulation) Bill for adoption by the states. Revised in 1972, 1996 and 2005, the Bill provides the framework to regulate use of groundwater in India. Some states like Karnataka, Maharashtra and Tamil Nadu have passed legislation based on this model Bill.

The revised version of the central Bill proposes:

(a) Compulsory registration of borewell-owners.

(b) Compulsory permission for sinking a new borewell.

(c) Creation of a groundwater regulatory body.

(d)   Restrictions on the depth of borewells.

(e)   Establishment of protection zones around sources of drinking water.

The Bill mandates:

(a)   Periodical reassessments of groundwater potential on a scientific basis, considering quality of water available and economic viability.

(b)   Regulation of exploitation of groundwater sources so that extraction does not exceed recharge.

(c)   Development of groundwater projects to augment supplies.

(d)   Integrated and coordinated development of surface water and groundwater so that they are used conjunctively.

(e)   Prevention of over-exploitation of groundwater near the coast to stop the ingress of seawater.

These mandates, which have yet to become law in most parts of the country, sound good on paper. But there is one basic flaw: implementation is entirely in the hands of government authorities; the people who use groundwater have no role in decision-making or implementation. This runs contrary to customary belief regarding ownership of groundwater (discussed above) and the experience of groundwater regulation anywhere in India and the rest of the world. All the evidence so far clearly shows that groundwater use cannot be controlled solely by government; it can be controlled only with the close involvement of all primary stakeholders — those who use groundwater excessively as well as those who suffer because of over-use.

In Israel, for instance, control over use of water has worked effectively because it is almost a matter of faith among the people of that country — anyone who abuses water resources is considered 'anti-national'. Likewise, experiences from India such as the water conservation movement initiated in Saurashtra by Pandurang Shastri

Athavale following the 1985-87 drought, the movement initiated in Alwar district in Rajasthan by Rajendra Singh, and several models developed in Maharashtra (for example, Ralegan Siddhi) show that regulation by people themselves can and does work. If regulation by people has to cover the entire state, the government obviously has a role to play. That role is providing an enabling legal and policy framework.

Water Policy

Following a severe drought across the country in 1987, the Centre framed a National Water Policy (NWP) that laid down certain principles, listed below. Specifically, the NWP recommended the promotion of:

(a) Conjunctive use of water from surface and sub-surface sources.

(b) Supplemental irrigation.

(c) Water-conserving crop patterns.

(d) Water-conserving irrigation and production technologies.

Other important recommendations included:

(a) Raising canal water charges.

(b) Promoting user participation in canal management.

Though the policy recognized the need to limit individual and collective water withdrawals, it did not identify the institutional mechanisms needed to define and enforce such limits. The 1987 NWP was modified in 2002. Major policy additions included recognition of the role of private sector participation and the need to shift from development of new projects to performance improvements in existing ones. Several states, including Maharashtra, came out with their own water policy statements along the lines of the NWP.

National Water Policy: key principles:

(a) Water is a precious national resource and its development should be governed by national perspectives.

(b)   Available sources of both surface and groundwater should be made utilisable to the maximum extent.

(c)   Appropriate organisations should be established for planned development and management of river basins.

(d)   Water should be made available in areas where there is a shortage by transfer from other areas including transfers from one river basin to another, after taking into account the requirements of the basins.

(e)   In the allocation of water, ordinarily, first priority should be for drinking purposes, with irrigation, hydro-power, industrial and other uses following in that order.

(f)   Groundwater potential should be periodically re-assessed and its exploitation regulated with reference to recharge possibilities and considerations of social equity.

(g)   Maintenance, modernisation and safety of structures should be ensured through proper organisational arrangements.

(h)   There should be close integration of water use and land use policies; distribution of water should be with due regard to equity and social justice.

(i)   Water rates should be such that they foster motivation for economy in use, and should cover maintenance and operational charges and a part of the fixed costs.

(j)   Farmers should be progressively involved in the management of irrigation systems.

(k)   The needs of drought-prone areas should be given priority in the planning of projects for the development of water resources.

Contrast with Israel

It is useful to compare India's water law framework with the framework in Israel, a country that has recorded impressive progress on all fronts, despite experiencing severe water shortage. The first principle of Israel's water law of 1959 is that water sources are the property of the public; there is no private ownership of water resources. The absence of private water ownership is further clarified in Section 4 of the country's water law, which states: "A person's right in any land does not confer upon him a right in a water resource situated therein..."

The second principle of the water law is that "every person is entitled to receive and use water, subject to the provisions of this law". The right to water is not an absolute. It is always for one of the purposes recognised by the water law: domestic use, agriculture, industry, handicraft, commerce, services, and public services. Each and every water use requires a licence. That is, licences are required to extract water, supply or consume water, sub-surface recharging, and water treatment. All licenses are issued for one year only.

The licence lists conditions that relate to quantity, quality, increasing the efficiency of water use, preventing pollution, etc. A licence may be revoked if these conditions are not met, or if use of the water endangers the water source. Until 1995, domestic users in municipalities were subject to quota allocations. Since that year, domestic water use is regulated through a strict differential pricing mechanism. Each consumer has an individual water meter, and water is charged separately through municipal levies.

Water rates applicable increase in proportion to the amount of water consumed. Water rates for domestic use are higher than rates for industrial and agricultural use, on two grounds:

    (i)   water for agriculture and industry is designated for production

(ii)   water for agriculture is supplied on a less reliable basis and is of poorer quality.

Industrial users are subject to quotas based on water use tables for various industrial purposes. An industrial user whose waste water disposal system does not meet the required criteria will not receive a water consumption license.

Most regions in the country are declared "rationing regions", meaning regions where water consumption is limited to fixed rations. Usage norms are established for different crops; multiplication of norms by the scale of crop cultivation determines the water quota for a farm. Water tariffs and several other matters can be enforced only after consultations with a water council, which includes representatives of government, consumers, suppliers and producers. Disputes between the government and individuals pertaining to the water law are adjudicated before a special judicial forum, the water tribunal, composed of one professional judge and two public representatives.

Water allocations are based on water needs in various parts of the country. Normally, water is not allotted to regions where particular growth is considered uneconomical. Efforts to introduce privatization in the water sector in India have increased in the last one decade. It could be seen as a part of the new economic policy introduced in 1991 in the country. There are several examples showing the rapidly growing privatisation of water services and resources in India. Privatization in the water sector involves all elements such as hydropower, industrial, irrigation and drinking water supply.

Privatization as a policy has been introduced as a 'panacea' to address many ills of the public sector such as insufficient finance, bad management etc. However, experiences from developing countries reveal a different picture showing that 'promises' for which the privatisation has been introduced were hardly met. Moreover, implications of privatisation on equity and human rights were severe. Despite of the worst experiences from across the world, the privatisation policy in the water sector is being promoted and implemented in India. The privatisation agenda could be seen as an important part of the ongoing water sector reform in India.

By promoting norms such as full cost recovery, creation of tradable water tights, elimination of subsidy, removal of public stand posts, creation of independent regulators etc., ongoing reforms tend to transform water sector into a fully commercial and market based operation. At the same time, civil society resistance against water privatisation has been remarkable. The public resistance against the proposed water privatisation in Delhi and the Sheonath project could be considered as examples of the growing civil society resistance against water privatisation and the privatisation policy in general.

The public resistance in India needs to be viewed as part of resistance movement at the global level. Apart from criticising the policy of water privatisation, the resistance movement remarkably presents some alternatives also. Hence, it is critical to understand the motives, driving forces and implications of water privatisation and the ongoing water reform in India. It is equally relevant to record the civil society resistance and some of the public alternatives.

Some Case Study

The history of relations over shared water resources is replete with incidents of conflict. Examples range from intrastate violence along the Cauvery River in India, to California farmers blowing up a Los Angeles water pipeline, to much of the violent history in the Americas between indigenous peoples and European settlers. The desert state of Arizona in the United States even commissioned a navy (made up of one ferryboat) and sent its state militia to stop a dam and diversion on the Colorado River in 1934.

At the international level, water has likewise led to hostilities between Arabs and Israelis, Indians and Bangladeshis, Americans and Mexicans, and among all ten

Nile basin co-riparian nations. While direct manifestations of water conflict are well documented, water disputes can also have broader political and geographic implications. For example, during 30 years of Israeli occupation in the Gaza Strip, the quality of surface and groundwater supplies steadily deteriorated and water-related disease rose. In 1987, the intifada, or Palestinian uprising, broke out in the Gaza Strip and quickly spread to the West Bank.

While it would be simplistic to claim direct causality, water was undoubtedly an irritant exacerbating an already tenuous situation. Issues of water security have played a role in regional instabilities in other parts of the globe as well. India's decision in the 1 960s to build the barrage at Farakka on the Ganges River to control siltation at Calcutta's seaport some 100 km to the south had a number of adverse impacts on Bangladesh, including degraded surface and groundwater supplies, impeded navigation, declining fisheries and public health risks.

In Southern Africa, water security concerns have been suggested as one possible motive behind South Africa's 1998 deployment of troops to Lesotho, the upstream riparian to the regionally important Orange River, in response to political turmoil in the mountain kingdom. These examples illustrate the geographic complexities of water disputes and the possibility for water issues to extend across political boundaries and to become entwined with other political issues.

Despite the history of water-related discord, however, conflict and cooperation over water has rarely been assessed methodically to determine if quantifiable relationships exist between water-related events at varying geographic scales (e.g. domestic and international) and between water and non-water relations. While a recent empirical study assessing the factors contributing to international water conflict and cooperation found an overall correlation between general bilateral relations among nations and bilateral relations regarding water resources, the study did not clarify the direction of linkage nor whether the nature of the linkage is consistent across countries and regions.

Furthermore, it did not explain if international issues drive domestic relations over water or v ice versa. The overall purpose of the present work is to establish a conceptual framework for evaluating the spatial relationships between water events — that is, for determining the extent to which domestic and international conditions influence the state of national and international water conflict and cooperation as well as the direction, or existence, of causal flow. The interrelationships between water and broader political events are also examined by investigating the direction of linkage between international relations in general and water relations specifically.

Three regions have been selected for the application of the framework — the Middle East, South Asia and Southern Africa — to assess not only the efficacy of the proposed framework but also the consistency of the results across geographically distinct regions. Within each region, one representative country (termed the 'primary country') is selected to assess both domestic water conditions and water and non-water relations with co-riparian states (terme d 'secondary countries').

The chapter begins by briefly discussing the political and resource settings of each primary country both domestically and within broader regional contexts. A proposed statistical framework for analyzing each region is then described, followed by an application of the framework to the three case study regions. Finally, the fidelity of the quantitative analysis is examined by comparing the statistical results with the initial qualitative descriptions.

Case Study Descriptions

The three geographic regions selected for this study are the Middle East, South Asia and Southern Africa. These regions were chosen as it was hypothesized that their divergent climatic, historic and political settings might provide insights into the range of variation in internal/external water relation dynamics. Within each of the three regions, one nation was selected as the primary country of analysis — Israel, India and South Africa, respectively. Like the larger regions, the three primary countries differ in many respects: politically, socio-economically and physically.

Furthermore, the historic relations of the primary countries with their neighbouring, co-riparian states ('secondary countries') contrast sharply with one another. The resource and general political settings of each of the three primary countries are briefly described below. These descriptions will serve as a qualitative assessment against which quantitative findings will later be compared.

Israel

Even before the establishment of Israel, Zionists viewed access to water resources as a necessary component for the long-term viability of a Jewish state. At the 1919 Paris Peace Conference, for example, the World Zionist Organization insisted that the future Jewish state control not only the water resources within the British Mandate of Palestine, but also the sources of their flow. Since Israel's founding in 1948, water has remained inextricably linked with national security, and water use has been viewed as a means for both agricultural and economic output as well as national survival.

Access to adequate water supplies to support a growing population and an agriculture largely dependent upon irrigation has been a constant concern for Israel's leaders since the nation's establishment. Located in one of the driest areas on Earth, Israel is reliant upon the Jordan River and its tributaries as well as delicate groundwater reserves to meet ever-increasing water-resource demands.

Since 1949, for example, Israel's population and irrigated area have both increased approximately sixfold, severely straining the nation's water supplies. Uneven spatial and temporal water distribution further complicates an already precarious resource situation. The country's primary water sources are located in northern Israel, a substantial distance from the nation's agricultural, industrial and population centres, and the Mediterranean climate separates winter rainy season supplies from peak summer irrigation demands.

Viewing agriculture, and the supporting water resources, as necessary for the nation's economic and political vitality, the Israeli government has maintained central control over water supplies and management. From the country's establishment, the Israeli government has committed substantial resources to increase the efficiency of the country's scarce water supplies through research and development; water allocation, monitoring and pricing structures; and financial incentives.

Israel's first national project, in the 1950s, for example, was the draining of the Huleh swamps just north of the Sea of Galilee, expanding agricultural land and increasing runoff to the Sea of Galilee, Israel's only major surface reservoir. Its second national project, in the 1960s, was to build the National Water Carrier to bring approximately 500 mcm [year.sup.-1] from the Sea of Galilee to the coastal plains, which contain the bulk of Israel's population, agriculture and industry.

Israel's water supplies, however, depend not only on conditions within its borders. The Jordan River is shared with four other political units — Lebanon, Syria, Jordan and the Palestinian Authority — and the hydrologic interdependency of these countries and territory has become increasingly apparent as utilization rates within the Jordan basin increase. Currently water demand regularly meets or exceeds the naturally replenished supplies of 1800 mcm, the differences being made up by groundwater over pumping and wastewater reclamation.

With rising demand and significant water supply constraints, disputes between Israel and its co-riparian neighbours over water have not been an uncommon occurrence. These disputes have included not only numerous verbal exchanges but also two incidents of armed conflict between Israel and Syria in the early 1950s and mid-1960s over proposed water development projects.

Regional water-supply issues have also been linked to broader relations in the region. For most of its history, Israel has been at a state of war with its Arab neighbours.

While territorial issues lie at the heart of Arab-Israeli conflict, notable connections to water exist. The Arab League's plans to divert the headwaters of the Jordan River away from Israel in the early 1960s, for example, has been cited as one contributing factor to the tensions leading up to the 1967 War. Furthermore, as the territory occupied by Israel since the 1967 War supplies a substantial percentage of the country's total water supplies, water is undoubtedly an integral part of the continued territorial conflicts in the region.

This linkage between water and non-water events can also be seen in more recent movements towards peace in the region. In the 1990s, Israel signed two bilateral peace agreements, both of which included substantial provisions concerning shared water: the 1994 Treaty of Peace between Israel and Jordan and the 1995 Israeli-Palestinian Interim Agreement on the West Bank and the Gaza Strip. In the 1994 agreement, Israel and Jordan outlined the allocation of shared surface and groundwater supplies and agreed to cooperate in the areas of supplementing water supplies and improving the quality of shared water sources. The 1995 interim agreement between Israel and the Palestinian Authority, while postponing full elaboration on water-sharing units until permanent status negotiations are held, did incorporate joint water-sharing principles and provided for the establishment of cooperative water-sharing mechanisms.

India

India demonstrates a substantially different water resource dynamic than Israel. As the world's largest democracy and second most populous country, India's vast physical and demographic size includes a great diversity of human and climatic conditions. Consequently, water resource issues in one area of the country can vary dramatically from another. Additionally, the country's federal system, combined with disparate relations with its neighbouring states, further regionalizes not only resource issues themselves but also the corresponding policy responses. A review of India's two primary international basins — the Ganges—Brahmaputra—Meghna and the Indus — serves to illustrate the incongruent water and broader political relationships across the Indian landscape.

The Ganges—Brahmaputra—Meghna (GBM) is India's largest river system. The basin, which in total covers an area of 1.7, occupies over 30% of India's territory, with 15 Indian States and one union territory falling either fully or partially within its hydrologic bounds. While India is the largest areal contributor to the GBM, the basin's resources are of great importance to downstream Bangladesh, which lies almost entirely within the GBM's topographic limits and, to a lesser extent, to parts of China, Nepal, Bhutan and Myanmar.

Climatically, the GBM basin extends through the Indian subcontinent's main monsoonal region and, as a result, receives some of the highest rainfall levels in the world. The vast majority of the rains, however, occur during a four-month period from July to October. A result of the basin's temporally uneven hydrologic regime is oscillating episodes of severe flooding and drought. Such adverse climatic conditions, coupled with weak institutions and inadequate regional cooperation, have contributed to the basin's desperate economic situation. For just India alone, the GBM region accounts for some of the country's poorest and most densely populated states. More telling, the basin as a whole, which covers approximately 1% of the Earth's total land surface, is home to 10% of the world's population and contains the largest concentration of poor on Earth.

The Indus basin, in contrast, is characterized by a very different set of physical and social characteristics. While its headwaters commence less than 200 km from the Ganges in the Tibetan Plateau of China, the Indus proceeds through the much drier climatic region of northern India and eastern Pakistan before draining into the Arabian Sea. The Indus basin covers about two-thirds the area of the GBM basin and has Pakistan as its primary riparian. Indian Territory, including six Indian States and one union territory, contributes about one-quarter of the total basin area.

Historically, the Indus basin was home to one of the world's earliest civilizations and supported a highly stratified and powerful irrigation society. In the modern era, the Indus has continued to play an important role in the regional economy. The British, Pakistanis and Indians have all constructed irrigation systems within the Indus and, as a result, the basin now has some of the most extensive irrigation networks in the world, accounting for nearly 6% of total irrigated land globally.

Beyond the physical and developmental differences between the GBM and Indus basins, India's political structure also promotes inter-basin variability. With a federal system, responsibility for India's water resources is shared between the national government and the individual Indian states. When water resources are shared by two or more states, as is the case with the GBM and Indus basins in India, the national government retains overall management authority.

However, while still under the control of the central government, inter-state river boards, such as the Bhakra Beas Management Board on the Indus basin and the Upper Yamuna River Board on the Ganges, allow for more local level involvement in the management of shared waters among India's individual states. Furthermore, India's state governments are encouraged to cooperatively resolve inter-state water disputes with central government intervention only as needed through a tribunal process.

India's divergent international relations with its riparian neighbours on the Indus and GBM seem also to have influenced disparate regional dynamics. Since the partition of India in 1947, India's relations with Pakistan have been especially tense, with the two countries involving themselves in full-scale war on two occasions and continued hostilities over conflicting territorial claims in Kashmir. From 1947 to 1971, Pakistan was a riparian to both the GBM and Indus basins. However, in 1971, when Bangladesh achieved independence, a new dynamic began to evolve in the Indian subcontinent. While Indo-Pakistani relations remained tense, India's assistance to Bangladesh during its war for independence created a new Indian ally in the region.

The history of water relations in the two basins is somewhat different than the history of political relations. In fact, India and Pakistan have demonstrated a remarkable ability to separate water issues from larger conflicts between the two countries. While India and Pakistan approached the 'brink of wart' in 1948 over the division of the Indus basin, since the 1960 conclusion of the Indus Water Treaty, India and Pakistan's water relations have remained remarkably stable, despite continued general tensions between the two states.

While India's general relations with its immediate neighbours on the Ganges — Nepal and Bangladesh — have been generally positive, cooperative water relations have only recently emerged. The Indian Farakka Barrage, first announced in 1951 and later constructed just a few kilometres upstream from the Bangladesh border to flush the port of Calcutta, resulted in a decades long disputes between India and Bangladesh (and East Pakistan prior to 1971), ultimately becoming 'on e of the most dominant and important elements in the Indo-Bangladesh relationship'.

It was not until 1996, nearly 30 years after the completion of the Barrage, that the two countries were able to conclude a long-term water-sharing agreement on the Ganges. Similarly, after several decades of unfruitful water negotiations between India and Nepal over the Ganges waters, the 1996 bilateral Mahakali Treaty constituted an important breakthrough in Indo-Nepal water relations.

South Africa

South Africa illustrates yet another set of resource and political relations. Like the other two case study countries, water resources are extremely valuable to South Africa, an overall 'water stressed' country with water availability fluctuating between 1000 and 1700 per person annually. In addition, as a major consumer of the region's water resources and co-riparian to five international basins, South Africa's international water relations are important to the country's water management.

Distinct from the previous two country studies, however, South Africa's pervasive apartheid history uniquely shaped the country's domestic and regional relationships for much of South Africa's post-World War II history.

South Africa's hydrologic regime varies significantly from its dry western regions to the more rainfall abundant areas in the south and east. On average, however, the country receives less than half of the world's average mean annual precipitation of 860 mm. Additionally, even in areas with relatively high precipitation, water demand is outstripping local supply. The country is thus faced not only with periodic droughts but also with the challenge of linking incongruent water supply and water demand centres. To respond to this challenge, South Africa has relied upon large storage and transfer schemes to control the natural hydrologic variations.

During the country's apartheid years, beginning just after World War II and continuing until South Africa's 1994 all-race elections, the natural inequities of the country's water resource supplies were further exacerbated by the government's discriminatory political system, the legacies of which the new South African government is now trying to redress.

During the apartheid era, significant portions of South Africa's population had virtually no access to the political system and were systematically excluded from full participation in the economy. Moreover, the country's discriminatory practices meant that black townships and nominally autonomous homelands were essentially detached from the central government's water supply mechanisms and did not receive the same level of water and sanitation services available to the white population. As a result, by 1994, the year in which apartheid ended, an estimated 30% of the country's inhabitants lacked access to adequate potable water supplies and more than half were without basic sanitation services.

South Africa's apartheid regime also had significant consequences for the country's regional relationships. As its neighbours gained independence and/or majority rule during the course of the apartheid period, South Africa was increasingly surrounded by 'front-line' states hostile to its structure. The polarization of the region became institutionalized through the creation of two regional institutions from which South Africa was excluded until the abolition of apartheid: the Southern African Development Coordination Conference (SADCC) created in 1980 and the Southern African Development Community (SADC) created 12 years later.

With the dismantling of the apartheid system in 1994, the majority of South Africa's population was enfranchised and allowed fuller entry into its political and economic systems. On the domestic front, the new, democratically elected South African government has instituted significant policy reforms in an effort to rectify the previous regime's discriminatory practices. The reforms initiated since 1994 have included fundamental changes to the country's water management ethic. South Africa's new constitution, adopted in 1996, for example, declares a universal right to water.

Similarly, the 1998 National Water Act designates the national government as trustee of the nation's water resources, responsible for ensuring that 'water is protected, used, developed, conserved, managed and controlled in a sustainable and equitable manner, for the benefit of all persons ...' [emphasis added] (Article 3 (1)). Internationally, the country's former regional enemies were converted almost overnight into allies, and less than six months following its historic 1994 national elections, South Africa acceded to the Treaty of the Southern African Development Community. With this move, South Africa was integrated into a regional body whose stated goals include not only economic growth and integration but also 'sustainable utilization of natural resources and effective protection of the environment'.

In comparison with its general political relationships, South Africa's international water relations appear to have improved at a substantially earlier stage. As noted above, South Africa is riparian to five international rivers: the Orange/Senque and Limpopo, Incomati, Maputo and Umbeluzi, which, in sum, occupy approximately 65% of South Africa's land territory. Reliant on much of these shared water sources to support the country's agricultural, industrial and domestic water needs, South Africa began concluding bilateral and multilateral water agreements with some of its riparian neighbours prior to the end of apartheid.

Despite the country's general political isolation, South Africa concluded an agreement with Mozambique and Swaziland in 1983, and three years later signed the notable Treaty on the Lesotho Highlands Water Project, which outlined a multi-stage plan to transfer water from Lesotho to South Africa's industrial heartland in Gauteng Province. Three additional treaties were signed with Namibia and Swaziland in 1992 during a period of clear reform in South Africa but still two years prior to its welcoming into SADC.

Since 1994, South Africa has continued to support international water cooperation efforts. South Africa has concluded at least one new bilateral water treaty with additional agreements in progress and is a signatory to SADC's two regional water protocols. South Africa's commitment to coordinated shared water resource management is also supported by its ratification of the 1997 UN Convention on the Non-Navigational Uses of International Watercourses.

Comparing the Qualitative Assessments

The general review of the water resource and political settings of the three case study countries illustrates a variety of regional dynamics. In the case of Israel, water scarcity issues not only play a central role in the country's domestic policies but have also created international hydrological links, which have both provoked co-riparian disputes and enhanced broader regional peace initiatives. In contrast, water issues in India display a more regionalized character that is manifested not only in the nature of water and non-water relationships but also in the connectivity between the two domains. Finally, South Africa's unique post-World War II history produced shifting, and at times incongruent, water resource and political relationships both domestically and with its neighbouring states.

Analytical framework Description

It is these complex and diverse geographic water resource relations that this study seeks to methodically examine. The proposed analytical framework described in this section explores, through a three-stage process, the relationships between national and international water cooperation and conflict and the related role of non-water related events. More specifically, the study seeks to address four explicit questions:

1   What, if any, relationships exist between water and non-water relations at the international scale for each of the three primary countries?

2   What, if any, relationships exist between international and domestic water cooperation and conflict for each of the three primary countries?

3   If relationships are found to exist, can the direction of causation be established?

4   If relationships are found to exist, is it possible to generalize across geographic regions?

To answer these questions, the following sections describe in detail the analytical framework developed for this study and its application to the three case study regions.

Stage one — data collection

The principal analytical tool utilized in this study is event data. A dataset was developed of conflictive and cooperative interactions ('events') between nation-states. The dataset draws information from two international conflict and cooperation databases — the Conflict and Peace Data Bank (COPDAB) and Global Event Data System (GEDS) Project, the combined coverage of which span the years 1948-1994. COPDAB and GEDS — together with news sources (primarily the English language Foreign Broadcast Information Service) and the academic literature — were also utilized to develop a specific international water relations dataset for the years 1948-1999.

For the years noted, this dataset includes, to the extent possible, every reported interaction between two or more nations, whether conflictive or cooperative, that involves water as a scarce and/or consumable resource or as a quantity to be managed — i.e. where water is the driver of the event. To date 1831 water related events — 507 conflictive, 1228 cooperative and 96 neutral or non-significant — have been compiled. Non-water related events between co-riparian states from COPDAB and GEDS total over 300 000. For the present study, similar sources and methodologies were used to collect and code domestic water events pertaining to the three case study countries for the years 1989-2000.

This dataset currently includes over 400 internal water-related events between and among governmental and non-governmental actors. For all events, both international and domestic, the intensity of each interaction was given a value ranging from -7, the most conflictive, to +7, the most cooperative, with 0 denoting neutral exchanges. The event descriptions were modified slightly to categorize domestic events.

Stage two — data analysis

After collecting and coding international water and non-water related interactions, domestic water events, and supporting hydrologic, socio-economic and political information, a framework for assessing the possible linkages between international and domestic conflict and cooperation over freshwater resources was constructed. The established framework systematically evaluates the event data beginning from the international scale and works towards specific water events at the domestic level. The framework begins with an investigation of general relationships between nations on issues other than water, followed by examinations of water-specific relationships between nations and finally on internal water events.

The fundamental quantitative tool used to carry out the statistical analyses of the data is the Friendship/Hostility (FH) index. For general, non-water relationships, the Friendship/Hostility value is calculated by averaging the scale values, described above, assigning all events between two nations or other actors during a given timeframe.

By selecting only water-related events, a similar calculation yields a Water Friendship/Hostility index (WFH). Water Friendship/Hostility can be determined at either the international (International WFH) or domestic scale (Internal WFH). For both FH and WFH, higher numbers represent more cooperative relationships, and lower numbers suggest greater conflict levels. Water-related events were additionally coded by the international basin in which they occurred, allowing WFH to be calculated by basin as well as by country.

International Analysis

Building from the event data collected for each of the three regions, the international analysis involves three sequential questions. The process begins with an analysis of FH levels (excluding water-related events) between the country of interest (the primary country) and each of its neighbours (the secondary countries). The question to be answered is whether FH between the primary country and each of its neighbours is correlated (e.g. if relations between South Africa and Namibia are correlated with relations between South Africa and Botswana).

Correlation, either positive or negative, would suggest that the relations of a primary country with its neighbours may be influenced by an overarching regional issue rather than some set of bilateral issues. If, in contrast, no correlation exists, specific bilateral issues may be of significance. The second question concerns the relationship between FH (again excluding water relations) and WFH.

In this case, a correlation, either between a primary country and one of its neighbours, or between the primary country and its neighbours in aggregate, would suggest a connection between water and non-water relations. In general it is assumed that non-water relations drive water relations, but it is conceivable that water issues can play a non-trivial role in a country's overall relations with a neighbour or group of neighbours. If no relationship is found between water and non-water events, regional water relations are likely distinct from other foreign policy matters, suggesting further analysis of water affairs should be undertaken if a fuller understanding of the primary factors driving water relations is to be gained.

The final question in the international scale analysis involves a comparison of WFH between the primary country and each of its neighbouring riparian states. If WFH levels of the primary country and each of its neighbours are correlated (e.g., if water relations between South Africa and Namibia are correlated with water relations between South Africa and Botswana), this suggests that the primary country's national water policies, rather than basin-specific or other local issues, may be driving its water relations with its neighbours as a group.

However, the findings from the FH-WFH relationship analysis described in the preceding paragraph would need to be reviewed to see if in fact water is the likely driving force in the relationships, or if water relations simply move with overall bilateral relations. If bilateral relationships over water are not correlated, more localized (e.g. basin level) issues may drive the primary country's water relations with each of its neighbours individually. Given this finding, further analysis at the basin scale would be warranted.

The next step in the analytical framework is to review internal water relations and compare the domestic event data results with those from the international analyses. The domestic analysis can either be concentrated at the national level or at the basin level. If the relationships derived in the international analysis above indicate that regional rather than bilateral issues dominate the primary country's relations with its neighbours, national-level water issues may be of more interest, If, for example, the primary country's FH and WFH relations with each of its neighbours are correlated in aggregate, then this might suggest that the primary country's national water policies and related events influence its external water relations (or vice versa). In this case, the primary country's average external WFH level at the nation-state level could be compared with the average internal WFH level (encompassing all basins and localities). Conversely, if the primary country's water relations with each of its neighbou rs are divergent, a comparison of the primary country's internal and external water relations within specific international basins may be more appropriate.

Stage three — contextual evaluation

The sequential questions set out in Stage Two above systematize an approach to analyzing potential linkages between international and domestic water events. This approach, however, does not substitute for an in-depth knowledge of a country or region's past and present political and environmental settings. Thus, to measure the fidelity of the analytical results, the final stage of the research framework involves a qualitative review in which the case study descriptions presented above are compared with the statistical findings.

Utilizing the research framework described above, the following sections detail the event data findings from each of the three case study regions. The relations between each of the primary countries and their neighbours are assessed along with the domestic water relations within each primary country. To test the fidelity of the analytical framework, the final section compares the qualitative findings from the statistical analysis with the quantitative descriptions outlined in the first part of the paper.

The first step in the statistical analysis was the examination of each primary country's Friendship/ Hostility (FH) level with its neighbouring countries over the period 1948-2000. Using correlation coefficients as a means of analysis, the relationship of annual FH levels between sets of primary-secondary country pairs was ascertained (e.g. the average annual FH level between South Africa and Namibia was correlated with the average annual FH level between South Africa and Botswana).

The test revealed on average mild correlation between Israel and South Africa and their respective neighbours, suggesting that the two nations' international relations are affectedly some set of overarching regional issues. The same analysis for India revealed no correlation, suggesting that India's relations with its neighbours is more a function of bilateral rather than regional issues.

The average annual FH and Water Friendship/Hostility (WFH) levels for the primary countries were then compared with their respective secondary countries in aggregate and bilaterally. Israel's overall FH and WFH levels were found to be correlated, though the relationships were weaker when correlations were considered bilaterally rather than in aggregate. In the case of India, no correlation either in the aggregate or bilaterally was found. Too few chronologically overlapping FH and WFH data points were available to make substantive statements concerning relationships for South Africa.

The final stage of the international analysis involved an examination of WFH levels between each of the primary countries and their respective neighbours. Analogous to the first step above, the relationship of annual WFH between sets of primary-secondary country pairs was ascertained (e.g. the average annual WFH level between South Africa and Namibia was correlated with the average annual WFH level between South Africa and Botswana).

On average, aggregate bilateral WFH levels were found to be mildly correlated between Israel and South Africa and their respective neighbours, while no correlation was found between India and its neighbours. These results suggest that for Israel and South Africa, overarching regional issues may influence international relations over water just as they were found to influence overall international relations. For India, the findings suggest that relations over water, like the country's non-water relations, are related to bilateral, rather than regional, issues.

As described above, the national level analysis involved a comparison of each primary country's internal WFH and external WFH levels for the years for which the two data sets overlapped. In the case of Israel, internal and external water relations were correlated. A mild correlation was found between the two datasets for India and no correlation for South Africa. For Israel, and to a lesser extent India, the results suggest a relationship between national water policies and external water relations.

For both India and South Africa, a comparison of internal and external WFH levels at the international basin level may have offered insights into more localized water dynamics. However, insufficient internal basin-specific data precluded an analysis at this scale.

In addition to the analyses just described, we examined a large set of variables hypothesized to be correlated with overall FH and WFH levels, such as precipitation patterns by basin, trends in Gross National Product (GNP), population and change in government structure.

No correlation was found between any of these variables and FH or WFH levels in the three-country sample. These findings are consistent with the results of the Wolf et al.'s (forthcoming) study, which found through cross-sectional time series analysis of all the world's international basins a mild, at best, correlation between these variables and WFH. In summary the framework as applied to the three case study countries found that for Israel overarching regional issues drive the overall friendship/hostility level.

Friendship/Hostility in turn appears to be connected in some manner to Israel's external water relations. Israel's external water affairs are also likely associated in some manner with the country's national water policies. Whether water issues, either internal or external, drive the country's overall relations cannot be clearly determined from this analysis. As with Israel, the results for South Africa suggest that overarching regional issues drive international relations in general and over water. However, because of a lack of data it is not possible to make a connection between non-water and water related events for South Africa.

For India, the results suggested that bilateral relations drive India's foreign affairs both overall and as related to water, but that water and non-water relations appear to move independently of one another. This conclusion is slightly obscured by the fact that internal and external water relations were mildly correlated, suggesting some connection between India's national water policies and water relations with its neighbours in general.

Placing the quantitative findings in context

While data constraints limited a full analysis of all the potential spatial and political relationships, the application of the framework to the three case study countries and surrounding regions did offer insights into possible linkages between water and non-water events and between international and domestic water relations. To ascertain the effectiveness of the analytical framework and associated event data, the results of the quantitative analysis must be placed within their regional contexts. Drawing from the case study descriptions presented above, the following section compares the quantitative results with the general qualitative understanding of the three selected primary countries.

Israel

For the Israel case study, a substantial degree of conformity can be found between the quantitative results and conventional understanding of the country specifically and the Middle East region in general. The correlation between Israel's Friendship Hostility (FH) and International Water Friendship Hostility (WFH), for example, is supported by the explicit linkages that exist between regional water issues and broader political conflict and cooperation in the Middle East.

Furthermore, until the peace agreements of the 1990s, Israel's Arab neighbours have generally been in alliance against the Jewish state, a finding consistent with the mild correlation between Israel's FH and WFH with each of its neighbours. Finally, the relationship found between Israel's internal and external water events conforms with the fact that water resources within the country are controlled at the national scale and that the internationally shared Jordan River also serves as the primary water source for Israeli citizens as well as fo r many of Israel's neighbours.

India

In the case of India, the regionalized character of water and non-water relations is at least in part evident in the results of the statistical analysis. For example, that fact that no correlation was found in any of the statistical analyses of FH and International WFH between India and its neighbours in the aggregate is consistent with the general picture of India's diverse geographic conditions, post-independence international history, and government structure.

The lack of a relationship between water and non-water related events is also consistent with India's relationship with Pakistan on the Indus, exemplified in the resiliency of the bilateral water treaty despite continued hostilities in other realms between the two countries. Furthermore, when Pakistan was riparian to both the Ganges and the Indus prior to 1971, India and Pakistan demonstrated an ability to differentiate between basin-distinct issues, when, for example, bilateral negotiations continued on the Indus despite Pakistan's disagreements over the Farakka Barrage on the Ganges.

A correlation between water and non-water events would have been expected, however, between India and Bangladesh, given the elevation of the Farakka Barrage issue to the realm of high politics from the 1970s up until the 1996 treaty between the two countries. Additionally, the mild correlation found between external and internal water events appears dis-synchronous with the South Asia regional setting. Given the decentralized nature of India's water regime and the dissimilarities between India's bilateral relations with Pakistan and with Bangladesh and Nepal, no relationship between India's domestic and aggregate international water affairs would have been expected.

South Africa

The South African case study likewise demonstrates a general correspondence between the statistical results and the qualitative description of the country and the Southern African region. South Africa's shifting political conditions in its post-World War II history, for example, supports the correlation found in the country's bilateral Friendship—Hostility levels. While the bilateral FH relations were found to be only mildly correlated, a closer analysis of the data indicates collective oscillations in regional relationships consistent with the dominancy of the apartheid government and its recent downfall.

For the years in which event data were available, demonstrates generally positive overall relations between South Africa and its colonized neighbours from 1963 to

1971, a decline in relations in the succeeding ten years as South Africa's neighbouring states gained independence, and an improvement in relations in the early 1990s as South Africa moved closer to abolishing apartheid.

The mild correlation of bilateral international WFH levels is also supported by the region's resource relationships. Unlike FH, however, generally positive relations are apparent from the mid-1980s onward, a finding consistent with South Africa's conclusion of water treaties while still in the midst of general apartheid-based political isolation. While insufficient overlap between FH and international WFH data precluded a comparison of these two data sets, a strong relationship would not have been expected as South Africa's water relations improved significantly in advance of its general regional relationships in the later apartheid years.

Since 1994, however, a correlation between FH and international WFH would be likely. Finally, the lack of correlation between international and domestic WFH also corresponds with South Africa's recent history. The two data sets were compared over the years 1989-2000, which encompasses both apartheid and post-apartheid years. As described above, the discriminatory practices of the apartheid years extended to the provision of water sanitation services to the majority, black population.

It was not until the dramatic political changes of 1994 that the South African central government assumed the responsibility for the country's water resources, both national and international, for the benefit of South Africa's entire population. With additional data, further analysis of the domestic and international water events might indeed reveal correlation between domestic and international water events in the recent post-apartheid years.

This chapter presented a methodology for systematically examining the geographic complexities of water conflict and cooperation. The framework developed for the study — which involved data collection, statistical analysis and contextual evaluation techniques — sought to answer four specific questions related to the existence and nature of water relationships. The framework was applied to three regional case studies focused on Israel, India and South Africa, and while certain limitations were present, the framework provided valuable insights into the study of water conflict and cooperation.

The findings from the quantitative analysis, supported by qualitative description, indicated that water-related events at the national level are related to both water and non-water events at the international scale. The nature of these relationships and the extent to which they are present, however, appear to vary considerably by country and region. This result highlights not only the intricacies of hydro-political dynamics and their variation across geographic space, but also the need to consider the often distinct historical and political conditions within a region or basin if water relations are to be well understood. As Gilbert White stated almost half a century ago: '[i]f there is any conclusion that springs from a comparative study of river systems, it is that no two are the same'.

3

Large Dams Trans-Boundary Waters Conflict

India and Bangladesh Water Down Differences

Sharing of water of trans-boundary Rivers has been a major cause of dispute between India and Bangladesh. In its bid to improve its bilateral relationship with Bangladesh before the upcoming SAARC summit India has been keen to remove the apprehensions of its eastern neighbour on this ground. Dhaka on its part wanted to show that it has recovered from the recent countrywide bomb blasts carried out by the Islamists. As a result both sides agreed to hold their first ministerial-level water talks in two years in Dhaka to mend differences between the two countries over a whole range of water issues.

Though no major breakthrough was achieved in sharing of Teesta water India appears to have succeeded in dispelling the Bangladeshi concern regarding the multibillion-dollar Indian River Linking Project (RLP). India and Bangladesh share 54 common rivers' waters and in 1996 inked the landmark Ganges River Water sharing Treaty. Because of the large number of trans-boundary Rivers disputes are also bound to happen. To sort them out, both sides have formed an Indo-Bangla Joint Rivers Commission (JRC).

The mandate of JRC calls for at least two meetings a year. But the latest meeting took place two years after the 35th JRC meeting was held in New Delhi in September 2003. At the two-day meeting, Water Resources Minister Priya Ranjan Dasmunshi headed the 13-member Indian delegation while his counterpart Hafizuddin Ahmed represented the Bangladeshi side. Indian minister approached the talks with a friendly attitude. Dasmunshi, who had meetings with chief ministers of West Bengal, Tripura and Assam prior to attending the JRC meet, had expressed confidence in Kolkata that the Dhaka meeting will be successful. He reportedly said, "Bangladesh is our friendly neighbour. Not only do we have diplomatic relations, but there are cultural and social ties as well. There may be occasional differences of views in a democracy but those can be solved through discussions."

But the complexity of the issues involved became obvious as soon as the talks began. In the first session itself there were debates over setting of agenda as Bangladesh tried to introduce India's river linking project (RLP) as a separate issue. Finally it was agreed to have RLP under the miscellaneous category. The other important issues included water-sharing of seven trans-boundary rivers including Teesta, bank erosions of common rivers, sharing of Ganges water as per the 1996 treaty, construction of Tipaimukh Hydrological Dam on river Barak and more advance flood forecast data exchange. Though both countries share 54 rivers, they have so far agreed only on sharing water of the Ganges River. Bangladesh, a flood and drought prone country claims that its miseries are due to the improper sharing of water.

Issue of Farakka Dam

At the JRC meeting Bangladesh alleged that it was not getting its due share of Ganges water as per the 1996 treaty. Bangladesh claimed that it received lower amounts of water from the Ganges in 10 out of 15 slots during the lean period in January-May this year. But India rejected Bangladesh's complaints that it was not getting its share of the river's water as provided for in the agreement. India's contention was that in fact Bangladesh had drawn more than its agreed share of water on nine occasions. Only in March they had received less than their share. However, Dasmunsi explained that this was due to delayed monsoon and hydrological reformation of the river itself in certain period. Still, India agreed to review the "operational implementation" of the treaty.

River Linking Project Issue

In 2003 India showed its intention to go for a multi-billion plan to divert surplus water from rivers in its flood-prone northeast to dry western and southern parts of the country, but set no deadline. Bangladesh, which gets about 70 percent of its river water from the Ganges and Brahmaputra rivers in the dry season, has asked India to shelve plans to siphon more water from their shared rivers. Bangladesh says the plan violates a 1996 water-sharing treaty and will hit its environment, agriculture and forests as well as water transport system. A formal protest was lodged by Dhaka about two years ago at the JRC meeting held in New Delhi.

Dispelling Bangladesh 's concern over this river linking project (RLP), Dasmunsh stated in Dhaka that his country will not interlink the Himalayan rivers, including the Ganges and Brahmaputra . He acknowledged completion of feasibility reports on several planned links under the Himalayan Component of the RLP. He, however, clearly asserted, "Completion of feasibility reports by the National Water Development Agency of India does not necessarily mean the links will be established at the cost of our neighbours." He also assured Bangladesh that India would not do anything in this regard without taking it into confidence.

Terming Bangladesh's concern over the RLP "uncalled for apprehension", the Indian water minister said Indian states of Bihar and West Bengal will start a hue and cry even before Bangladesh if India ever ventures for water-diversion from the Ganges. He said water will not be diverted from the Ganges and Brahmaputra, the two rivers having immense bearings on Bangladesh, as India is concentrating on the Peninsular Component of the RLP in southern India only rather than implementing the Himalayan Component.

No Agreement over Teesta and Six Other Rivers

During the talks there was little progress on sharing of Teesta and six other common rivers—Dharla, Dudhkumar, Monu, Khowai, Gumti and Muhuri. While Bangladesh favours a 40-40 or a 38-40 percent share of the Teesta water by the two countries and retaining the rest 20 percent for the river itself, India prefers keeping only 10 percent for the river. Moreover, India wants other factors to be taken into account before distributing water of these rivers. In the case of Teesta, 85 percent of agricultural land served by the river was in India and the remaining 15 per cent in Bangladesh.

On the Teesta water-sharing, Dasmunsi said, "We have to reach a point where two countries can make a sacrificed-share of Teesta. You know, some rivers are flowing with longer catchment area in India and shorter in Bangladesh. So, we need sacrificed-sharing here." Though no breakthrough was made over the sharing of Teesta water both sides expressed optimism that they would reach a mutually beneficial arrangement very soon after conducting a study on the water flow of the river. The issue meanwhile has been referred to the joint experts committee who would report back to the Commission.

India is very much willing to look into Bangladesh's request for water-sharing treaties with respect to six more rivers besides Teesta. But at the same time it wants Dhaka to agree to dredge its side of the river Ichhamati. Dasmunsi urged Bangladesh to go for immediate joint dredging programme to save the region from unwanted flooding. Massive deposits of silt in the river Ichhamati is a major cause of floods along the river.

Tipaimukh Hydrological Dam (THD)

Dhaka also objected to the construction of Tipaimukh Hydropower Dam (THD) on the Barak River that feeds the Kushiara and Surma rivers in greater Sylhet. Bangladesh claims that diversion of the Barak waters through interventions like the THD would "drastically change the hydrological regime of Meghna." India dispelled Bangladesh's concern over THD, saying Tipaimukh is a power generating venture, not an irrigation scheme, and it will not affect Barak's flow to Kushiara and Surma that eventually contribute to the Meghna.

India, however, agreed to provide Bangladesh with detailed plan of the THD beforehand. It also agreed to accommodate concerns of Bangladesh, if any. Indian side also pointed out that the project would help the north-eastern region of Bangladesh in managing floods. India turned down a proposal of Dhaka to include Nepal to discuss the issue of constructing a reservoir in Nepal to solve water sharing issues of the Ganges. It maintained that a third country should not be involved in a bilateral framework. India also rejected the idea to raise the issue at the SAARC meet saying that the regional body was a forum for handling economic issues.

The JRC meet, also decided that from now on India will provide its lower-riparian neighbour with flood forecasting data keeping more lead-time. India will now provide Bangladesh with information for the Ganges at Farakka point keeping 67-hour lead-time, extending it by 26 hours from the existing lead-time, and for the Brahmaputra at Guwahati point 66 hours ahead, extending it by 24 hours. As Bangladesh feels more comfortable with further extension of lead-time, Dasmunsi assured Hafiz Uddin of discussing the scopes for more extension of lead-time at the next JRC meeting to be held six months later. The issue of land erosion by some trans-boundary rivers has been a major cause of conflict between the border guards of the two countries.

To deal with this issue both Bangladesh and India agreed on a joint inspection by their water ministers of the bordering areas affected by erosion of trans-boundary Rivers. After examining the ground realities, both the countries will start revetment work from January 2006 on respective sides to prevent erosion. Though no major breakthrough was achieved at the latest round of Indo-Bangla JRC meet, it managed to end on an optimistic note. India succeeded in convincing Bangladesh that the Himalayan streams would be excluded from its river-linking project.

Speaking at the joint press conference with Indian Water Resources Minister Priya Ranjan Dasmunsi upon conclusion of the two-day JRC meet in Dhaka, Bangladesh Water Resources Minister Hafiz Uddin Ahmed said that he was satisfied with the talks and hoped that this would lead to an acceptable solution to the existing problems in the common river water sector shared by Bangladesh and India. Besides this optimism the talks also produced some tangible results as India agreed to cooperate with Bangladesh on advanced flood forecasting.

Tipaimukh Dam

The world is rife with conflicts over waters, especially over use and management of transboundary waters. Rivers with transboundary nature, Brahmaputra, Mekong, Barak etc are becoming subjects of controversy over the right to manage the waters. Some countries exercise power through military or economic means to weaker countries to justify control of transboundary waters. Conflicts emerge when countries upstream of a water resource use the water available to them to wield more power and when certain countries downstream use other forms of power such as military to get more water.

Stronger countries use "exploitation potential", both technical capacity and infrastructure to exploit water resources. Two expressions of concerns, one Bangladesh's opposition to Tipaimukh Multipurpose Hydroelectric Project over Barak River in Manipur in India's North East and the other, India's objections to Chinese Government's plan to dam and divert waters of Yarlung Tsangpo (Brahmaputra) River in Tibetan Plateau, elucidates potentials of conflicts over the use of transboundary waters and the need to explore feasible means to avoid conflicts. The critiques of Tipaimukh dam to be built in Manipur is moving beyond imposed frontiers, the traditional expression of concerns once confined limitedly in Manipur and parts of Bangladesh now resonates from afar.

Never had Tipaimukh Dam been focus of international diplomacy, media attention, intelligentsia critics, environmentalist and those with high tentacles as in 2009. The Prime Ministers of India and Bangladesh discussed the contentious issue at the recently concluded Non Aligned Movement (NAM) summit, July 2009 in Egypt. The issue has now moved from the confines of Manipur Assembly discussion to the British and Bangladesh parliamentary debates to the deliberations of several United Nations human rights forums. The Tipaimukh Multipurpose Hydroelectric Project is to be constructed 500 Meters downstream from the confluence of Barak and Tuivai Rivers in Manipur over Barak River with firm generation capacity of 401.25 MW.

The main objective of the project is to generate 1500 MW hydropower and flood control on 2039 Sq. km. The North Eastern Electric Power Corporation (NEEPCO) was earlier slated to undertake the project with the Manipur Govt at 5% equity till it was replaced recently by National Hydroelectric Power Corporation (NHPC). The Government (Govt) of India had a tough time pursuing the Tipaimukh project in Manipur since 1970's due to vigorous peoples' opposition to the project and also in clearing out the armed insurgents who dominates the Tipaimukh dam site area.

Manipur is afflicted with armed conflict as national liberation movement groups battle Indian armed forces operating under the Armed Forces (Special Powers) Act, 1958 for full secession of Manipur since 1949, the year Manipur was merged to India without peoples consent. The Tipaimukh project is also opposed by several national liberation groups terming it as India's yet another sinister effort for hegemony and exploitation of the natural resources of Manipur.

Concerns and Responses

The Tipaimukh dam issue currently continues to dominate the domain of political, media, intellectual and civil society's discourse in Bangladesh with a unilateral demand for revocation of India's decision for the project. Massive rallies, protest meetings, strikes and other forms of protest against the dam continues to gain momentum in Bangladesh. The Tipaimukh Dam concern is not a recent phenomenon as the first international Conference on Tipaimukh Dam, held way back in December 2005 had resolved against the project. The peoples' concerns in Bangladesh are based on their bitter experience of severe water shortage and multifaceted impacts after commissioning of Farakka Barrage over the Ganges River by India.

Concerns raised include staggering environmental degradation, economic crisis and hydrological drought. The damming of Barak River, seriously limiting free flowing Surma and Kushyara rivers will disrupt agriculture, irrigation, drinking water supply, navigation etc and reduce recharge of ground water during lean season, affecting all dug wells and shallow tube wells. Bangladesh gets 7 to 8 percent of its total water from the Barak River. The Surma-Kushyara with its maze of numerous tributaries and distributaries support agriculture, irrigation navigation, drinking water supply, fisheries, wildlife in the entire Sylhet division and in peripheral areas of Dhaka division and industries like fertilizer, electricity, gas.

The dam would also leave millions jobless with the drying up of the two rivers. Millions of people are dependent on hundreds of water bodies, fed by the Barak, in the Sylhet region for fishing, agriculture and allied activities. The Barak-Surma-Kushyara is an international river with Bangladesh as a lower riparian country having rights over any decision over River. "Construction of a dam at Tipaimukh would be a death-trap for Bangladesh, it rather involves the very existence of the lives of the 15 Crore people of the country," Bangladesh National Party (BNP) vice president Hafizuddin Ahmed asserted.

In Manipur, where the dam is to be built, the concerns are diverse and premised on three aspect, first the direct physical aspect of displacement, loss of biodiversity, loss of economic activities of indigenous peoples, social and environmental impacts etc, the second being the procedural lapses, absence of holistic impact assessment and limitations of developmental and environmental regulations, weak enforcement mechanisms and lack of people oriented accountability norms and thirdly, unclear benefits of the project to the people of Manipur and nuances based on traumatic experiences from similar projects in Manipur such as NHPC's 105 MW Loktak Multipurpose Hydroelectric Project (NHPC) which remains irresponsible and unaccountable for its devastation of Loktak wetlands ecosystem, submergence of vast tract of agricultural land, loss of species and failure to rehabilitate several thousands of affected peoples of Manipur even after nearly three decades of project commissioning in 1984.

The NHPC further insisted on reaping more profits by filing Loktak project as Clean Development Mechanisms project for carbon credits under Kyoto Protocols of the United Nations Framework Conventions on Climate

Change. A large number of Zeliangrong and Hmar tribes will be displaced permanently and deprived of livelihood. Official figures states 1,461 Hmar families will be directly displaced due to the project. The dam will submerge 311 sq. km covering 90 villages with 1,310 families, including 27,242 hectares of forest and cultivable land and posing serious threat to the rich biodiversity, flora and fauna of the region. Social impact due to demographic changes due to migration of workers from outside Manipur has not been addressed.

The site selected for Tipaimukh project is one of the most active in the entire world, recording at least two major earthquakes of 8+ in the Richter scale during the past 50 years. The dam is envisaged for construction in one of the most geologically unstable area and the dam axis falls on a 'fault line' potentially epicenters for major earthquakes. The Memorandum of Understanding between the Govt. of Manipur and the NEEPCO was signed on 9 January 2003 even as the affected peoples both in the upstream and downstream of Barak River called for a wide consultation on Tipaimukh Dam based on provision of project information.

Against peoples' wishes, the power Minister of India, Sushil Kumar Shinde laid the foundation stone for Tipaimukh Dam on 15 December 2006. Of late, the Ministry of Environment and Forests (MoEF) of the Govt of India accords environmental clearance on 24 October 2008 despite peoples' objection to Tipaimukh Dam during the projects' five public hearings held from the year 2004 to 2008.

The environmental clearance of MoEF is despite the fact that the downstream impact assessment of the project in Assam and Bangladesh is still pending. Notwithstanding serious lack of information, Detailed Project Report (DPR) and Environmental Impact assessment and management plans of the dam, the Govt. of India floated international tenders inviting bids for construction of the project. Largely the Govt. of India rely on militarization of dam site area and suppression of voices for fair decision making process and sustainable development to pursue construction of the dam.

The Indian Govt's response to Bangladesh concerns has long been marked by a state of denial. Indeed, the Indian High Commissioner Pinak Ranjan Chakrabarty's statement of absence of an international law that could prevent India from constructing the Tipaimukh Dam and that Bangladesh's concerns are based on ignorance on 21 June 2009 at Dhaka provoked an intense resentment in Bangladesh even calling for his expulsion. Experts counter reacted his statement as totally erroneous in view of the status of the 1996 Indo-Bangladesh Ganges Water Treaty and the applicability of the 1997 UN Convention on the Law of Non-Navigational Uses of International Watercourses.

Bangladesh experts though agreeing that it is not yet binding as an "international treaty" law, opined there is every reason to argue that the Convention, being adopted by a vote of 103 - 3 in the UN General Assembly, is applicable as "evidence of international customary law" to Tipaimukh dam or any such project on shared rivers. The 1997 Convention put heavy emphasis on comprehensive cooperation for equitable utilization of any trans-boundary watercourse, no-harm to all the co-basin states, and adequate protection of the watercourse itself. Sensing a political crisis in South Asia over Tipaimukh Dam, the U.S. Ambassador to Bangladesh, James F Moriarty urge the people and the government of Bangladesh to discuss with India to settle the Tipaimukh dam issue," while speaking at a discussion on 'Engaging South Asia: Obama's South Asia Policy,' held in Dhaka.

Dams over Transboundary Waters in South Asia and Challenges

As Bangladesh engaged India to drop construction of Tipaimukh dam, India too is busy raising concerns with Chinese Govt's efforts to dam and generate 40,000

Megawatt power from Yarlung Tsangpo (Brahmaputra) in Tibet and to divert 200 billion cubic meters of waters to the Yellow River for easing water shortages in cities of Shaanxi, Beijing and Tianjin in Northern China. The dam and diversion plan is at the Tsangpo River's big U-turn at 7,782-meter-high Namcha Barwa, the world's deepest canyon before entering India. Shu Yinbiao, vice president of State Grid Corp. of China opined, "An initial study shows the river can accommodate hydropower stations with a total capacity of 70 gigawatts, or about 10 percent of the nation's overall generating capacity".

The diversion of the waters is part of a China's larger hydro-engineering project, the South-North water diversion scheme. The 2,906-km long Brahmaputra is one of Asia's largest rivers that traverse its first stretch of 1,625 km in China's Tibet region, the next 918 km in India and the remaining 363 km in Bangladesh before converging into the Bay of Bengal. The Tsangpo is now perhaps the only Transboundary Rivers yet to be dammed in China after dams are constructed over Mekong, Salween, Irrawady, Sutlej, Indus etc.

The water diversion project at the Great Bend will spell disaster for the Tibetan plateau and the lower riparian countries, India's North East and Bangladesh. India is also facing a security dilemma over the Chinese control over the principal watershed of South and Southeast Asia in Tibet. India fears Chinese reported plans to use nuclear technology in the project will lead to environmental concerns in the Eastern Himalayas. Indian experts say the mega scheme could be disastrous for the 185 million people of India's North East and Bangladesh.

In Assam, 80 per cent of the population is involved in agriculture, depending on Brahmaputra for irrigation and the region's regular earthquakes, that can hit 8.0 on the Richter scale, can destroy the proposed Chinese dam and cause devastating floods downstream. India's proposed Tipaimukh dam and China's proposed dam over Yarlung Tsangpo bears much similarity in terms of scale of destruction, threats and challenges both in upstream and downstream portion of the rivers. In the latter scheme, both India and Bangladesh shares common challenges when China proceeded with diversion of Brahmaputra waters in its territory primarily due to shortage of water.

Bangladesh exists because of its waters coming from the Mighty Rivers Ganges, Teesta, Brahmaputra, and Barak etc. India's Farakka Dam over River Ganges burdens Bangladesh with an irreparable crisis of unfathomable magnitude. India pursued a perfidious double game. While objecting China's plan to dam Yarlung Tsangpo, India aggressively pursued mega dams construction spree in India's North East, including gigantic dams over the same river Yarlung Tsangpo, called Siang (the Brahmaputra) in Arunachal Pradesh, notwithstanding concerns in India's North East and Bangladesh.

The Siang Upper HE Project is a massive 11000 MW project to be built over Siang River in East Siang district of Arunachal Pradesh. The Middle and Lower Siang Hydel project with 750 mw and 1700 mw power generating capacity are other mega dams planned over the same river. The 2000 MW Lower Subansiri Hydroelectric project is another mega dam over River Subansiri, a main tributary of Brahmaputra River. Other dams over the tributaries of Brahmaputra includes the Ranganadi I and II (450 and 150 mw respectively), Kameng (600 mw), 3000 MW Dibang HE project etc. the construction of series of dams over Siang River and its tributaries will exacerbate the water crisis and related problems in Assam and Bangladesh.

India's plan to construct more than 169 dams in India's North East and connotation of the region as India's Power house has been met with stiff opposition from the region. The Assam Govt strongly opposed proposed construction of mega dams on the Siang River and several other rivers in Arunachal Pradesh. "I am aware of Assam's concerns over the dams and I feel there is no need to construct mega dams", Governor of Assam, Shiv Charan Mathur said while addressing his first press conference. The Assam Govt set up a commission to study the environmental impact of mega dams in Arunachal Pradesh and other neighboring states on Brahmaputra valley region.

"Large-scale diversion of water would adversely hit the state's economy and could even lead to environmental problems and affecting the surface water table" according to Chief Minister of Assam, Tarun Gogoi. Anti dam movement is increasing In Arunachal Pradesh where most of the dams are being planned. India uses all means, mis-information, flouting of norms, manipulations, militarization, brute use of force and nepotism etc to push through dam projects. India is proactive in addressing concerns with the Chinese Govt. on the proposed dam over Tsangpo River, relaying its concern to Beijing in 2006.

However, the Govt. of Bangladesh needs be more proactive to the whole scheme to dam the Brahmaputra River and its tributaries in China and India, which will worsen water crisis in Bangladesh and Assam. Bangladesh faces a big challenge to confront the "exploitation potential" of both China and India over the use of transboundary waters. There is indeed, a primary urgency for Bangladesh and the people of India's North East to explore all means to ensure China and India to adopt a multilateral, multiparty decision over transboundary water use with due and full respect of rights and participation of indigenous peoples depending on waters.

All States indeed, should refrain from unilateral and contradictory decisions over transboundary waters disregarding downstream concerns and rights of indigenous peoples. Towards multilateral and human rights based approach to manage transboundary waters. Diplomatic engagement between India and Bangladesh over proposed Tipaimukh Dam, latest being the Prime Ministers meet at NAM summit in Egypt and past experience of efforts to resolve water dispute between the two countries, such as the Indo-Bangla Ganges Water sharing treaty, 1996 and setting up of Teesta River Commission, 1997 etc, indicates possibility of the two countries converging towards establishing dialogues for resolution of differences.

Intervention of the United States envoy to Bangladesh favoring a dialogue to settle the row further reinforces this possibility. Indeed, Bangladesh Prime Minister called for political unity with the opposition BNP to be able to "bargain better with India" over Tipaimukh Dam issue. However, the Statement of Mr. Razzak, proposed head of Bangladesh parliamentary team to visit Tipaimukh dam site, that the Tipaimukh dam is beneficial for Bangladesh, is premature given that Bangladesh Govt. is still yet to take an official position on the dam and despite absence of comprehensive and multilateral impact assessment.

The statement seriously negates and undermined the rationale and objectives of the visit to Tipaimukh dam site. In transboundary waters such as Mekong River, Yarlung Tsangpo, Barak River etc, question looms large as to whether a single country or States solely decide over the use of the waters in exclusion of indigenous people who lives and depends on the waters over millennia and whose cultures, identity and traditions evolved with such relationships? The big question still remains, will the people of Manipur accept any compromise bargaining, if any and exclusively crafted between India and Bangladesh.

Any bilateral Agreement between India and Bangladesh without the people of Manipur will be unacceptable. The people of Manipur have inalienable rights over the transboundary waters. International law has also evolved that Indigenous peoples have right to self determination over their land resources, need for recognizing their rights over their land and resources and having clear rights to define their develop priorities on how to use, manage their land and resources in accordance with the UN Declaration on the rights of Indigenous peoples, 2007 and recommendations of the sessions of UN Permanent Forum on Indigenous Issues at UN HQs, May 2009.

Such approach can prevent all sufferings of indigenous peoples affected by Bangladesh's Kaptai Dam in Chittagong Hills Tract, India's Loktak Hydroelectric Project in Manipur or India's Dumbur dam in Tripura etc. The resolution of Tipaimukh dam seriously needs a multilateral, inclusive and human rights based approach to development and sensitivity to the concerns & established rights of all affected peoples. Bangladesh Govt's announcement of sending an all-party parliamentary committee to visit Tipaimukh dam site in end July 2009 to review the dam's impact will be a right step if the visit forms the basis for an inclusive process to conduct detailed impact assessment of the dam in upstream and downstream of the Barak River based on recommendations of World Commission on Dams, 2000 and other applicable Int'l law on transboundary waters, such as the UN Convention on the Law of Non Navigational Uses of International Watercourses of 1997.

The visit can be a good grounding for a multilateral approach in addressing Tipaimukh Dam issues. Bangladesh and the indigenous peoples of India's North East needs be fully sensitive to the multitude of mega dam projects planned both by India and China in transboundary waters and tributaries and should strategize for a multi dimensional and multi party approach in the use and management of transboundary waters with due respect of rights of people in lower riparian areas and indigenous peoples dependent on such waters. India should refrain from constructing Tipaimukh dam to avoid multidimensional conflicts and complications as the project is potentially rife for causing conflicts between states, between state and indigenous peoples and between indigenous peoples all over control and management of resources and definition of developmental priorities.

4

The Narmada Judgement

The Narmada Dam Project is a large hydraulic engineering project involving the construction of a series of large irrigation and hydroelectric multi purpose dams on the Narmada River in India. The project was first conceived of in the 1940s by the country's first prime minister, Jawaharlal Nehru. The project only took form in 1979 as part of a development scheme to increase irrigation and produce hydroelectricity. Of the thirty large dams planned on river Narmada, Sardar Sarovar Project (SSP) is the largest structure to be built. It has a proposed final height of 136.5 m (448 ft). The project will irrigate more than 18,000 km (6,900 sq mi), most of it in drought prone areas of Kutch and Saurashtra.

Critics maintain that its negative environmental impacts outweigh its benefits. It has created discord between its government planners and the citizens group Narmada Bachao Andolan. The Experts' Committee of the Ministry of Environment and Forests (MoEF) made a clear finding of the egregious failure of the government machinery on virtually all aspects of the planning and implementation of environmental safeguards of the project and recommended that no further reservoir filling be done until failures of compliance on the various environmental parameters have been fully remedied. The controversy over the giant Dams and large Dams on the Narmada river, altogether 30 large and 135 medium Dams, displacing a few million people, not even fully and fairly counted, and destroying thousands of hectares of agricultural land and forest, affecting the whole riverine ecosystem is decades old.

Yet, the same is again reaching its peak in the case of the Sardar Sarovar Interstate Project. The Dam, with the wall completed upto 122 mts, as per the demand by the Government and politicians of Gujarat and Madhya Pradesh is to be pushed ahead by raising piers and erecting gates 17 mts high even when 2,00,000 and more people; adivasis, farmers, fish workers, artisans, traders live in the village communities and township densely populated with pakka houses, markets, best of agriculture and horticulture since generations.

The demand that the Centre must fund the Project with thousands of crores or declare it to be a 'national' project, contrary to the stand of its own sanctioning and monitoring authorities, is also indicative of Gujarat's politics, stinking of irrationality and immaturity, showing neither prudence nor progressive outlook. The Finance Ministry has declared 3000+ crores in the latest budget, but this cannot and should not be done, without looking back and looking forward to the reality of the Project – its claims and achievements.

The absolutely illegal push given to the Dam in the past (1987 – 2006) violating conditions on rehabilitation and environmental mitigatory measures is tried again, when on both grounds and on the issue of costs and benefits too, the Project stands fully exposed. It is obvious that the Report by the Group of three Ministers including Former Union Minister of Water Resources, Shri Saifuddin Soz, Former Union Minister for Social Justice and Empowerment Ms. Meira Kumar and Union Minister of State for Earth Sciences, Shri Prithviraj Chavan after their visit to the Narmada valley in 2006 was most truthful and depicts the situation of "Rehabilitation on Paper" and "Massive corruption", which is the reality further confirmed, even today.

There are thousands of families , including adivasis who have lost their lands and habitats since 1994, who are yet to be given their land entitlements in Madhya Pradesh (with the largest submergence and 'oustees') as also in Maharashtra and Gujarat where the Governments are not able to allot land to the eligible, since private land is not being purchased at the market value, any more. Not even one resettlement site for its own adivasis wishing to resettle in Madhya Pradesh, as per legal provision is located and established by the state of MP, while the corporates are given land as per their whims and interests, at whatever costs, financial to social and environmental.

Corruption worth a few hundred crores in rehabilitation exposed by the affected farmers of Narmada Bachao Andolan has resulted in the High Court appointing a Judicial commission of Inquiry in Madhya Pradesh and its investigation is on. There is no political will to investigate and punish the guilty and hence the GoMP has challenged the Orders in the Supreme Court where hearing is yet to take place. It is unfortunate that the Narmada Control Authority, which is a central body also is not taking a clear position favouring the High Court' Judgement on the judicial commission on corruption and irregularities leading to derailment of the Rehabilitation Policy.

Drowning the lands and living communities with full life on, without an alternative source of livelihood (land for farmers, fisheries for fish workers) is absolutely in violation of the Narmada Water Disputes Tribunal Award (NWDTA), which is a decree; four judgements of the Supreme Court; constitutional and human rights, and justice. Is the UPA Government, with its Ministry of Social Justice and Empowerment incharge of rehabilitation and the Narmada Control Authority (NCA) with the statutory mandate, ready to permit these gross violations is a question.

Serious Environmental Non-compliance

The Project, along with its feeder Project, Indira Sagar Project (ISP) cannot proceed further in the present situation, due to serious environmental non-compliance, concluded by an Expert Committee chaired by the Former Director-

General, Forest survey of India and presently, Chairman of the Expert Appraisal Committee of River Valley Projects, Dr. Devender Pandey.

The Committee which has been appointed by the Ministry of Environment and Forests, which leads the Environmental Sub – Group of NCA, has brought out in its Second Interim Report that even after 20 years since the two giant Dams were cleared by the MoEF, there is an unprecedented apathy exhibited from the fact that the command area development plans necessary to prevent severe destruction of land with water-logging and salinization and ensure benefits are not even ready and final, nor approved by the Central Authority i.e. MoEF.

The unfounded hope of securing fulfilment with respect to the impacts on health, archaeology, seismic risks etc which are the most serious in preventing the Project from becoming more destructive, than developmental, has thus been diminished.

With a large percentage of SSP's and ISP's command area development not in place, catchment area (a few lakh hectares in each Dam) not yet treated and huge forest loss not proved to be compensated, the Committee's Report concludes that no construction on Dam and canal and no irrigation should be permitted.

Costs outweigh Benefits

Have the much drum-beaten benefits of the Dam come true, satiating the thirst of Kutch-Saurashtra in Gujarat or 'lightening' progress in Madhya Pradesh and Maharashtra with a share in power, but not a drop of water, in spite of bearing the largest share in submergence and finance?

No! Only 30% of the canal network of SP is built over 30 years and 66,000 kms long canals (70%) remain to be constructed, not due to NBA's opposition, but because Gujarat's own farmers are unwilling to part with 30000 hectares of land and also due to lack of finance, (estimates vary from 8000 crores to 20,000 crores) and absence of command area development plans. Inspite the pondage attained by submerging adivasis lands, forests, communities, not more than 7-10% of the available water is being utilized by Gujarat.

Moreover, with much of water supplied to the cities especially Gandhinagar, the Kutchis have moved the apex court, demanding their due share. Maharashtra is demanding for 1800 crores of compensation from Gujarat for loss in power allocation, but Madhya Pradesh is still keeping mum! Investment clearance for the SSP was for Rs. 6406 crores in 1988 Today, the project cost is Rs. 45,000 crores as per the Report of the Working Group on Water Resources of the Planning Commission and it will escalate upto Rs 70000 crores by 2012!

The Centre, in the past, under the Accelerated Irrigation Benefits Programme has allotted the largest amount of Rs. 5000 crores to this Dam and yet the CAG Reports have made a critical inditement of its misutilization. The Planning Commission should have by now or MUST, at least today, review the Project fully since not only the approved investment limit, but also the environmental conditions in the same are flouted by the states, with no monitoring.

The experience certainly explains the colossal gap of 1,20000 crores needed for completion of large Dams since the II Five Year Plan and huge discrepancy of 17 million hectares between the planned and attained irrigation potential. Not one hectare additional irrigation is achieved in the country is what the data of the Ministry of Water Resources for the years, 1990-2005 itself shows! Which way Sardar Sarovar and Narmada?

The most ancient of the world's civilization can't face any more destruction and death which is not a penalty but a political vendetta. For unexpectedly low and unsustainable benefits, if the Projects this and others, are pushed with illegal and unjustifiable expediency, not one state government, but the nation will be accused of connivance towards destruction.

Expected benefits of the Sardar Sarovar Dam

The expected benefits of the dam as listed in the Judgement of Supreme Court of India in 2000 were:

"The argument in favour of the Sardar Sarovar Project is that the benefits are so large that they substantially outweigh the costs of the immediate human and environmental disruption. Without the dam, the long term costs for people would be much greater and lack of an income source for future generations would put increasing pressure on the environment. If the waters of the Narmada river continue to flow to the sea unused there appears to be no alternative to escalating human deprivation, particularly in the dry areas of Gujarat.

The project has the potential to feed as many as 20 million people, provide domestic and industrial water for about 30 million, employ about 1 million, and provide valuable peak electric power in an area with high unmet power demand (farm pumps often get only a few hours power per day). In addition, recent research shows substantial economic multiplier effects (investment and employment triggered by development) from irrigation development.

Set against the futures of about 70,000 project affected people, even without the multiplier effect, the ratio of beneficiaries to affected persons is well over 100:1." The dam will irrigate 17,920 km (6,920 sq mi) of land spread over 12 districts, 62 talukas and 3393 villages (75% of which is drought-prone areas) in Gujarat and 730 km (280 sq mi) in the arid areas of Barmer and Jalore districts of Rajasthan. The dam will also provide flood protection to riverine reaches measuring 30,000 ha (74,000 acres) covering 210 villages and Bharuch city and a population of 400,000 in Gujarat.

Height issues:

(a)   In February 1999, the Supreme Court of India gave the go ahead for the dam's height to be raised to

88 m (289 ft) from the initial 80 m (260 ft).

(b) In October 2000 again, in a 2 to 1 majority judgement in the Supreme Court, the government was allowed to construct the dam up to 90 m (300 ft).

(c) In May 2002, the Narmada Control Authority approved increasing the heiaght of the dam to 95 m (312 ft).

(d) In March 2004, the Authority allowed a 15 m (49 ft) height increase to 110 m (360 ft).

(e) In March 2006, the Narmada Control Authority gave clearance for the height of the dam to increased from 110.64 m (363.0 ft) to 121.92 m (400.0 ft). This came after 2003 when the Supreme Court of India refused to stay the height of the dam again.

Controversy

Protest

The Narmada dam is India's most controversial dam project and its environmental impact and net costs and benefits are widely debated. The World Bank was a initially a funder of the SSP, but withdrew in 1990. The Narmada Dam has been the centre of controversy and protest since the late 1980s. One such protest takes center stage in the Spanner films documentary Drowned Out (2002), which follows one tribal family who decide to stay at home and drown rather than make way for the Narmada Dam. An earlier documentary film is called A Narmada Diary (1995) by Anand Patwardhan and Simantini Dhuru.

The efforts of NBA to seek social and environmental justice for those most directly affected by the Sardar Sarover Dam construction feature prominently in this award winning film (Filmfare Award for Best Documentary-1996). The figurehead of much of the protest is Medha Patkar, the leader of the "Narmada Bachao Andolan," the "Save

Narmada Movement." The movement was cemented in 1989, and was awarded the Right Livelihood Award in 1991.

Support for the protests also came from Indian author Arundhati Roy, who wrote the extended essay "The Greater Common Good" in protest of the Narmada Dam Project; the essay was reprinted in her book The Cost of Living. In that essay, Roy states:

Big Dams are to a Nation's 'Development' what Nuclear Bombs are to its Military Arsenal. They're both weapons of mass destruction. They're both weapons Governments use to control their own people. Both Twentieth Century emblems that mark a point in time when human intelligence has outstripped its own instinct for survival. They're both malignant indications of civilisation turning upon itself. They represent the severing of the link, not just the link - the understanding - between human beings and the planet they live on. They scramble the intelligence that connects eggs to hens, milk to cows, food to forests, water to rivers, air to life and the earth to human existence.

The Supreme Court Decision

Despite popular protest, the Supreme Court gave clearance for the height to be increased to 121.92 m (400 ft), but in the same judgment Mr. Justice Bharucha gave directions to Madhya Pradesh and Maharashtra (the Grievance Redressal Authorities of Gujarat) that before further construction begins, they should certify (after inspection) that all those displaced by the raise in height of 5 metres have already been satisfactorily rehabilitated, and also that suitable vacant land for rehabilitating them is already in the possession of the respective States. This process shall be repeated for every successive 5-metre increase in height.

Report of the Ministry of Environment and Forests (MoEF)

The Second Interim Report of the Experts' Committee set up by the Ministry of Environment and Forests (MoEF) of the Government of India to assess the planning and implementation of environmental safeguards with respect to the Sardar Sarovar (SSP) and Indira Sagar projects (ISP) on the Narmada River. It is a clear finding of the egregious failure of the government machinery on virtually all the aspects studied. The report covers the status of compliances on catchment area treatment (CAT), flora and fauna and carrying capacity upstream, command area development (CAD), compensatory afforestation and human health aspects in project impact areas.

The report is a severe indictment of the governments of Gujarat, Madhya Pradesh and Maharashtra and of the bodies set up by these governments to implement the projects for the 'integrated development' of the Narmada Valley. The report is peppered with phrases like 'gross violation', 'negligence', 'highly unsatisfactory,' 'inadequate,' 'serious lapse' and 'non compliance'. It states in strong and unequivocal terms that, with respect to virtually all of the aspects under consideration, compliance is either highly inadequate or absent altogether. A partial exception is compensatory afforestation. Construction, on the other hand, has been proceeding apace: the ISP is complete and the SSP nearing completion.

The report recommends that no further reservoir-filling be done at either SSP or ISP; that no further work be done on canal construction; and that even irrigation from the existing network be stopped forthwith until failures of compliance on the various environmental parameters have been fully remedied. The report of the World Commission on Dams is a step forward in the decades long struggle of the peoples' organizations questioning the social and environmental impacts and their justifiability on the basis of water and power delivery services as also economic benefits.

It is, however, ironical that at the same time, people in the Narmada Valley, who have been at the forefront of the worldwide struggle, challenging not just the dams in the

Narmada Valley but centralised, inequitous ecologically-destructive consumerist-oriented water and natural resource management as a development paradigm, Save Narmada Movement (Narmada Bachao Andolan - NBA) is compelled to fight unjustifiable, majority judgement by the Supreme Court of India allowing construction of Sardar Sarovar dam at the cost of people, especially the indigenous populations. The Report exposes the pro large dam bias in the judgment with a lopsided praise for the dams and beneficial and unsubstantiated premise that rehabilitation has brought higher standard of living for the project-affected, the oustees.

The WCD Report has clearly vindicated the issues that peoples' movements raised and struggled over, during the past half a century. By a majority judgement (by Chief Justice A.S. Anand and Justice B.N. Kirpal), the Court permitted the elevation of the dam from the present 88 metres to 90 metres. Further, the Court stipulated that construction beyond 90 metres could be made in stag es after obtaining clearances from the environmental and rehabilitation authorities. The maximum height of the dam allowed is 138 metres.

"The environmental subgroup in the Union Ministry of Environment and Forests (MoEF) will consider all aspects before giving clearance for the construction at each stage beyond 90 metres," the majority judgement stated. The Narmada authority was asked to draw up a plan, within four weeks, on relief and rehabilitation work. Dissenting from the majority judgement, Justice S.P. Bharucha said that the project required reconsideration as it had not obtained proper environmental clearance in the late-1980s when it was cleared by the Centre. He wanted immediate sto ppage of construction activities at the dam site.

The reactions from the two parties to the case were along expected lines. Crackers were burst and sweets distributed at the Gujarat State Secretariat. Chief Minister Keshubhai Patel declared a half-day special holiday for offices and sc hools in the State Capital, Gandhinagar. "The people of Gujarat have been waiting for this day for 40 years," he exulted. "Now, no power in the world will be able to stop us from going ahead with the project in full swing."

On the other side, Narmada Bachao Andolan (NBA) leader Medha Patkar went on a five-day protest fast at Bhopal from October 25 against the "anti-people judgement". There were demonstrations by NBA activists and supporters at Badwani, New Delhi, W ashington and San Francisco. "When there is no land, no master plan for rehabilitation even after 20 years, on what basis did the Court order a plan for rehabilitation and land acquisition in the next four weeks," the protestors asked.

The Narmada controversy has always evoked strong feelings. There was never a scope for compromise either among the proponents or the opponents of the dam. Several alternatives suggested at different stages of the controversy were brushed aside. There was enough symbolism from either side. The activists and tribals said, "doobenge par hatenge nahin" (we will drown but not move). The efficacy and the ethics behind the stance were questioned even by some of the supporters of the movemen t outside the valley.

On the other hand, last summer, the Gujarat Government transported 'water from the Narmada' to drought-hit regions by railways. Though the positions of the main proponents and opponents did not change, the reaction of the urban middle class (whose opinion, fortunately or unfortunately, has a bearing on much of the decisions taken in the country) to the controversy has changed over the years. The Supreme Court judgement was reported in the media and people spoke about it for a day or two before forgetting all about it. One of the most critical environmental judgements in recent decades has thus passed into obscurity rather soon.

This was hardly the case a decade ago. In December 1990, when tribals and activists from the valley marching towards the dam site were stopped at the Gujarat border by the police, the nation followed the developments with interest for days. The m arch had brought the Narmada issue to the national and international consciousness. Many people in cities and towns were disturbed by the plight of the tribals whose villages, culture and livelihood were facing the threat of submersion. In the recent past, the Narmada issue gradually faded from urban middle-class consciousness, except during two developments.

The more recent of the two was the drought that hit parts of the country, including Gujarat, this summer after a gap of 12 years. Dam proponents argued that the project, with its network of irrigation channels, was the only way to battle water sc arcity in the drought-prone regions of Kutch and Saurashtra. The anti-dam activists and other environmentalists argued that only micro-level water-harvesting structures could prevent water scarcity in times of drought. Instead of debating the pros and cons of the Sardar Sarovar project, the debate drifted to the issue of the dam size.

Earlier, during the monsoon of 1999, Booker-Prize winning author Arundhati Roy led a rally from urban centres to the villages of Domkhedi and Jalsindhi. Activists and villagers braved the rising waters of the river due to the additional construction on the dam. Arundhati's 'yatra' succeeded in drawing the attention of the urban middle classes to the plight of the people in the valley. Though her essay (published simultaneously in two magazines) did not add any data later than the Morse Committee report of 1993, it put the entire picture into perspective.

The writer had got a cause, the readers were moved by her prose, but her acidic remarks also raised the hackles of the Supreme Court judges. The third part was certainly unnecessary as it was the NBA which had petitioned the Court for justice in the case. In Arundhati's essay and in much of the arguments of the NBA, there is a strong dichotomy between 'us' and 'them' (the rich and the powerful), and 'we' and 'they'. This did appeal to the urban middle class in 1990 which was still under a socialist hangover. But the consumerist push of the post-1991, 'liberalised' economy has turned this class into a rather amorphous entity — the dichotomy between 'we' and 'they' has disappeared. Environmental movements such as the NBA are now being perceived more as a nuisance, thwarting the dream of 'development'.

This is the reason that the urban middle class cheered the Supreme Court when it teased and harangued the Karnataka and Tamil Nadu Governments on the Veerappan issue; or when the Special Courts sentenced Narasimha Rao and Jayalalitha t o prison terms... like the crowd cheering Rajnikanth decimating the bad guys single-handedly. The same class was quiet when two out of three judges crushed the prayer for justice that had come from the Narmada valley. The fault is not one-sided though. With its strait-jacketed, uncompromising position, NBA had also closed all doors for dialogue, not only with the dam proponents but also the larger body of people whose support can make or mar the environmental cause. More dangerous than losing the case in the Supreme Court would be the fading away of the movement from the national consciousness.

5

Water and Security in South Asia

The Indus Waters Treaty

The distribution of environmental resources as a potential contributor to conflict has been the subject of considerable research, and these linkages have dominated the post-Cold War interest in environmental security. Within this genre much attention has been given to water resources, owing to their vital importance for human survival. The distribution of environmental resources may contribute to conflict, but recent scholarship has begun to focus on the potential of environmental threats in stimulating conflict resolution. Uniting around a common aversion to environmental threats, as well as confidence-building through environmental cooperation, potentially hold great appeal for policymakers who aim to engage in proactive problem-solving rather than in precise problem identification.

What is most significant for government decisionmakers to consider is that even if a conflict is not environmental in nature, the remedy may well be achieved through environmental means. Environmental cooperation may offer pathways to confidence-building or peacebuilding, whether or not the conflict has environmental roots. This chapter explores the potentiality of such instrumental cooperation in the case of South Asia where regional conflict between two nuclear neighbors, India and Pakistan, is predicated in a history of religious rivalries and post-colonial demarcation. Despite inveterate antagonism, the two countries have managed to cooperate over water resources of the Indus River. How was this riparian cooperation enabled? And can it be reconfigured to provide for lasting peace in the region?

The Indian subcontinent quite literally owes its name to the waters of one river—the Indus. Regional politics are closely tied to the river's history and how different societies have used its waters for livelihood and for consolidating power. Hindu nationalists frequently recount that the very essence of their faith, dating back to the writings of the Rigveda in the second millennium B.C.E., is linked to the flow of the Indus. The name itself is a Latinized version of Sindhu, which means river in ancient Sanskrit, and from which the word "Hindu" and its concomitant ethno-religious identity emerged.

The partition of the subcontinent by the British in 1947 gave all but the very upper headwaters of the Indus to the newly formed Muslim majority country of Pakistan. More significantly, the major tributaries of the Indus that provided irrigation water for the fertile and densely populated region of Punjab on both sides of the border were divided. This was a classic conflict situation between upstream and downstream riparians, exacerbated by a lack of trust and intense territorial animosity between the two sides.

This led to a series of disputes related to the Indus and its tributaries. Both countries tried to settle the matter bilaterally several times after partition but no lasting agreement was reached until the World Bank got involved as a mediating entity. The resulting agreement, known as the Indus Waters Treaty, took nine years to negotiate and was signed in 1960.

It is a particularly remarkable treaty since both sides have otherwise had tremendous hostility for one another and have defied efforts at cooperation. It is therefore instructive to consider the development and history of the treaty in greater detail as a potential model for regional environmental cooperation. The treaty is often cited as a success story of international riparian engagement, as it has withstood major wars between the two signatories (in 1965 and 1971), several skirmishes over water distribution and derivative territorial concerns. The agreement is also heralded as a triumph for the World Bank, which played an instrumental role in its negotiation during the height of the Cold War.

The World Bank's role in this region was particularly unusual because India was a vanguard of the Non-Aligned Movement and wanted to disavow any pressure from international institutions or Western nations. The initiator and technical adviser of the agreement was David Lilienthal, the former head of the United States' Tennessee Valley Authority, who suggested that an engineering perspective could contribute to resolving this political stalemate. After a visit to India and Pakistan in 1951, he advised the two countries to divide the Indus Basin geographically. India would have unrestricted use of the three eastern rivers (the Ravi, Sutlej and Bias), while Pakistan would completely control the three western rivers (the Jhelum, Chenab and Indus).

The World Bank played a significant role by providing mediation, support staff, funding and proposals for pushing negotiations forward. Under the leadership of President David Black, the World Bank was able to persuade the international community to contribute nearly $900 million for impoundment construction. Nine years after Lilienthal's initial visit, both countries were finally convinced to sign the agreement. The Indus Waters Treaty obligated Pakistan to build a canal system, which, by utilizing previously less-developed rivers, decreased Pakistan's dependence on the Indus tributaries the treaty gave to India.

The treaty also charged India and Pakistan with exchanging information and establishing joint monitoring mechanisms of river flow to ensure enforcement. The key provisions of the agreement are as follows:

(a) An agreement that Pakistan would receive

unrestricted use of the western rivers, which India would allow to flow unimpeded, with minor exceptions;

(b)   Provisions for three dams, eight link canals, three barrages and 2,500 tube wells to be built in Pakistan;

(c)   A ten-year transition period, from 1 April 1960 to 31 March 1970, during which time water would continue to be supplied to Pakistan according to a detailed schedule;

(d)   A schedule for India to provide its fixed financial contribution of $62 million in ten annual installments during the transition period; and,

(e)   Additional provisions for data exchange and future cooperation.

As is often the case with riparian agreements, the treaty also established the Permanent Indus Commission, made up of one commissioner of Indus Waters from each country. In the technocratic spirit of the agreement, these representatives are often engineers rather than politicians. The two commissioners meet annually in order to:

(a)   Establish and promote cooperative arrangements for implementation of the treaty;

(b)   Promote cooperation between India and Pakistan in the development of the waters of the Indus system;

(c)   Examine and resolve by agreement any question that may arise between the two countries concerning interpretation or implementation of the treaty; and,

(d)   Submit an annual report to the two governments.

Both countries have upheld the Indus Basin Commission's information-sharing responsibilities; data on new projects, the water level in rivers and the water discharge of rivers are routinely conveyed to the other parties. If conflicts rise to the level of a dispute, the Indus River Commission will agree to mediation or arbitration, and the World Bank will appoint a neutral expert who is acceptable to both countries to resolve the dispute.

Remarkably, although India and Pakistan constructed and carried out this agreement amidst skirmishes, threats and full-scale war, and even during armed conflict, neither country sabotaged the other's water projects. One of the water negotiators for Pakistan has commented that the role of international institutions is vital in making this enterprise function:

Both the parties are under the obligation of the Indus Waters Treaty, which asked the signatories not to disrupt the functioning of the commission. Any hurdle in the working of the commission is challengeable under the treaty, the guarantor of which is the World Bank.

No projects allowed under the treaty's provision of "future cooperation" have been submitted since 1960, nor have any water quality issues. There have, however, been several other disputes that have arisen over the years. The first issues arose from Indian non-delivery of some waters during 1965 to 1966 that became questions of procedure and of the legality of commission decisions. Negotiators resolved that each commissioner acted as a government representative and had the authority to make legally binding decisions.

Another dispute involving the design and construction of the Salal Dam on the Chenab River in Jammu, India was resolved by way of bilateral negotiations. As noted in a recent World Bank study of Pakistan's water policy, India and Pakistan advocate conflicting principles of management: "equitable utilization" and "no appreciable harm," respectively. Both sides continue to foster misgivings about the treaty but accept it as the best option in a time of conflict. From the Indian perspective, the 75 percent allocation of water to Pakistan represented a fundamental violation of equitable utilization.

From the Pakistani perspective, the allocation of only 75 percent of the water when it possessed 90 percent of the irrigated land was a violation of the principle of no appreciable harm. As a mark of how leadership can achieve reconciliation despite high tensions, former Pakistani President Ayub Khan is quoted in the aforementioned study as saying, we have been able to get the best that was possible ... very often the best is the enemy of the good and in this case we have accepted the good after careful and realistic appreciation of our entire overall situation.... The basis of this agreement is realism and pragmatism.

As part of a study of the Tarbela and Mangla dams (the two Pakistani impoundments constructed as a result of the treaty), the World Commission on Dams concluded that:

The Indus Waters Treaty represents the only ongoing agreement between India and Pakistan that has not been disrupted by wars or periods of high tension. Cooperation that builds on this treaty could not only present opportunities for better water management between those two countries, but also serve as a model for water-sharing arrangements between India, Bangladesh and Nepal.

Prospects for Instrumental Peace

Although the Indus Waters Treaty has been able to overcome some minor issues (such as the Salal Dam dispute, which was resolved in 1978 through a new treaty), it has not been able to facilitate the resolution of larger conflicts, like Kashmir. The prospects for using the agreement over riparian issues as a means of conflict resolution more broadly can be traced back to a statement by U.S. Assistant Secretary of State George McGhee, who pointed out in 1951 that, a settlement of the canal waters question would signify those basic reversals of policy by the Governments of both India and Pakistan without which there can be no political rapprochement. Thus, the canal waters question is not only a functional problem, but also a political one linked to the Kashmir dispute.

As reported in the World Bank archives on this case, the British Prime Minister Anthony Eden felt that if this linkage were not possible, the resolution of the waters dispute could at least reduce tension over Kashmir. Interestingly enough, at one time it was argued by Pakistani politicians that the urgency of territorial claims on Kashmir for Pakistan also had a hydrological component. In 1957, the Pakistani prime minister, Hussain Suhrwardy, stated publicly that, "There are as you know six rivers (in the Indus Basin).

Most of them rise in Kashmir. One of the reasons why, therefore, that Kashmir is so important for us is this water, these waters which irrigate our lands." However, since then, the Pakistani government has de-linked the Kashmir dispute from the reconciliation over water allocation. Commenting for this research on the potential of using the treaty as a conduit for resolving the Kashmir conflict, the Pakistani government's senior spokesmen on foreign policy, Mohammed Sadiq, stated the following:

The Indus Waters Treaty has been an important document for the water issue between the two countries. It has also helped in a framework for the resolution of water disputes in the region. Pakistan is fully committed to the treaty in letter and spirit. As far as the Kashmir dispute, this is not a water issue. It relates to the inalienable rights of Kashmiri people to self-determination.

As early as 1951, the Indian government has argued adamantly that: "The Canal Waters dispute between India and Pakistan has nothing to do with the Kashmir issue; it started with and is confined to the irrigation systems of East and West Punjab." Yet this decision to de-link the two has been made consciously by politicians, despite the ecological reality that Kashmir does indeed lay strategically within the headwaters of the river systems. In fact the Indus flows right through the valley corridor that connects Indian and Pakistani-held Kashmir.

One can thus consider the cooperative role of water in this case at two levels. First, as suggested in the aforementioned statement by George McGhee, the resolution of the water dispute was a necessary but perhaps not a sufficient condition for conflict resolution over Kashmir. Second, since that condition for water cooperation has been met, the communication and opportunities for trust-building provided by the treaty continue to act as a potential means of further cooperation at the level of political psychology. Therefore, the Indus Waters Treaty has become the strongest link of cooperation between the two sides and, in times of crisis, it is often referenced as the ultimate cord of engagement that might be cut.

The latter proposition was put to the test in December 2001 following the Kashmiri militants' attack on the Indian Parliament two months prior, when India threatened to unilaterally abrogate the Indus Waters Treaty. However, six months later, the Permanent Indus Commission, which was established as part of the treaty, still met for the thirty-seventh time in New Delhi and the agreement weathered the story yet again. On a technical level, the Indus Waters Treaty was tested again when both India and Pakistan considered new dam projects to meet rising energy, demands. India is undertaking the Baglihar Hydropower Project (BHP) on the Chenab River in India, 160 kilometers north of Jammu, under severe opposition from Pakistan.

Apart from objecting to the project design of the BHP, Pakistan has expressed opposition to the Tulbul navigation project, the Sawalkote Hydroelectric Project and the Kishanganga Hydroelectric Project, all located in Jammu and Kashmir. The Baglihar dispute was taken to the World Bank, which appointed a neutral technical expert, Swiss engineer Raymond Lafitte, in August 2005 to make a binding decision on the case. Lafitte gave his ruling on the dispute in early 2007 and the matter was amicably settled, with both sides claiming victory. So far, the Indus Waters Treaty has served its purpose in de-escalating tensions over riparian water and has provided a direct avenue for regular, if technical, dialogue between the countries.

It has not led to greater peacebuilding between the two countries as some of the original motivators of the treaty may have hoped. However, these most recent dam projects in Kashmir raise some potential prospects for using the agreement more instrumentally in resolving the Kashmir dispute.

Increasingly, Kashmiri politicians are arguing that since the status of the territory is uncertain and so many of the disputes are in Kashmiri territory, they should be part of the Indus Basin negotiations as well. Whether such integrative solutions to the conflict would be found through cooperation on water remains to be seen, and is largely a question of leadership.

Even when all the ingredients of rational state behavior are in place, the ultimate action is dependent on individual leaders. The Indus Waters Treaty may also be relegated to a broad range of confidence-building measures that countries may develop during times of crisis.

As Shaista Tabassum has argued, the treaty did initially help to build some measure of conciliation between the two countries and was also framed as a "conflict avoidance measure." Soon after the treaty was signed, both countries did agree to negotiate actively on Kashmir and six rounds of talks were held from 1962 to 1964.

However, the talks failed because of territorial intransigence on both sides and the escalation of domestic political pressures. It may also be argued that the de-linkage of the substantive issues related to the Indus Waters Treaty and the development of Kashmir as a region might have provided an opening for dialogue which was not availed.

India's dominance as a hegemonic power in the region also gave it much more negotiating power that was not effectively countered by international pressure. For efficacy in such asymmetric circumstances, it is also important to consider the regional dynamics of cooperation over water.

Regional South Asian Strategies

South Asia has a remarkable history of cooperation over water-related issues in both maritime and riparian areas. India is South Asia's major littoral state, and shares maritime borders with several other South Asian states; in contrast, none of the other states have maritime borders with each other. India has settled its maritime boundaries with several of its neighbors, signing twelve bilateral agreements, including nine agreements with the Maldives, two each with Sri Lanka, Indonesia and Thailand, and one with Myanmar, as well as three trilateral agreements with Sri Lanka and the Maldives, Indonesia and Thailand, and Myanmar and Thailand.

Pakistan has also signed two bilateral agreements to settle its maritime disputes—one with Oman and the other with Iran. However, maritime disputes continue between India, Pakistan and Bangladesh. In the case of Bangladesh and India, the problem is not the maritime boundary, which can be defined fairly easily, but rather competing sovereignty claims over the island of Talpati. Bangladesh has a concave coast, and maritime boundaries in such geographical structures require integrative solutions and are extremely difficult to draw.

Nevertheless, if a comprehensive settlement is reached in such cases, environmental factors can play a pivotal role since they help link various issues such as economic development and security. For example, a joint conservation monitoring arrangement can allow both sides access to areas that would otherwise be off-limits and give both sides an opportunity to cooperate in reducing environmental degradation. In particular, states that are ecologically vulnerable to extreme climatic events, such as Bangladesh, are recognizing that poor environmental planning in coastal areas can have devastating economic impacts.

The old environment/economy tradeoff is becoming less relevant as environmental pressures begin to have direct economic impacts. Pakistan's maritime dispute with India over the Sir Creek region could conceivably provide an opportunity to forge such a link between economic development and environmental cooperation. In addition to maritime dispute settlements, several important river-sharing treaties have also been concluded in South Asia. India has agreements with Nepal, Bangladesh and Pakistan over riparian issues that are likely to be expanded in the future.

Nepal, a small landlocked neighbor of India, is the upper riparian on the Mahakali River, which flows from Nepal into India. After protracted negotiations, the two states agreed on a treaty for the river in 1996. The importance of water negotiations was highlighted by the fact that the Nepalese parliament passed the treaty with the required two-thirds majority, despite a serious political crisis in Nepal at the time. According to commentator Krishna Rajan:

> *The treaty attracted attention in a number of countries as an important indication of the ability of India and Nepal as multiparty democracies to reach an agreement on cooperation on water resources on the basis of equality, transparency and equitable sharing of costs and benefits.... it does offer a model for India and Nepal on how to reach important understandings despite the uncertainties of democratic politics and coalition governments.*

Also in 1996, India and Bangladesh signed a treaty on India's construction of the Farakkha Barrage, a dam that diverts the flow of the Ganges River into the Hooghly River during the dry season to flush silt from the port of Calcutta. The negotiations were spread over two decades and, after overcoming a number of controversies, finally concluded in the form of a thirty-year Farakkha Barrage Treaty. Regional organizations are often an important mechanism in promoting multilateral peacebuilding efforts.

South Asia, as an example, has the potential to engage in such a process through the South Asian Association for Regional Cooperation (SAARC), which was established in 1985. While bilateral dispute resolution is excluded from

SAARC's mandate, there are numerous aspects of bilateral disputes, which can have multilateral, or even global, implications. For example, the Siachen dispute between India and Pakistan has prevented scientists from studying glacial recession, hydrological impacts and climate change that can potentially influence the entire region. Arguments can thus be made that many of the so-called bilateral disputes that involve ecological factors have a salient global purpose.

Despite discouraging signs that both quantitative and qualitative environmental issues (scarcity and pollution, respectively) have historically been relatively low on the priority list of decisionmakers in the region, it is important to note the establishment of SAARC was preceded by the formation of a regional environmental organization. At the initiative of the United Nations Development Program, the South Asian countries—including Afghanistan and Iran—came together in 1980 and established the South Asian Cooperative Environmental Program (SACEP). The stated goal of SACEP at the time of establishment was:

to promote regional co-operation in South Asia in the field of environment—both natural and human—in the context of sustainable development and on issues of economic and social development which also impinge on the environment and vice versa; to support conservation and management of natural resources of the region and to work closely with all national, regional and international institutions, governmental and nongovernmental, as well as experts and groups engaged in such co-operation and conservation efforts.

In its early years, SACEP was able to establish a "Regional Seas" program that had the potential to bring forth the territorial contentions for potential resolution. The interactions at a regional level through SACEP may well have helped to establish SAARC, which has a broader mandate in its charter of regional cooperation, covering a wide range of activities from energy to tourism to environmental protection, as well.

While such instances of regional cooperation are promising, the South Asian case on its own does not provide us with enough structural coherence to develop an effective strategy, for moving forward with potential paths to making water an instrumental means of peacebuilding. Understanding the limitations of the current frames of policy analysis within international relations and considering alternative mechanisms for peacebuilding are important if we are to move beyond the self-fulfilling prophecy that tends to de-link environmental factors from peacebuilding.

Functionality of Water In Peacebuilding

Political geographer Kathryn Furlong has noted that dominant theories in international relations and international organizations tend to have five key flaws:

1) a mis-theorization of hegemonic influences at work;

2) undue pessimism regarding the propensity for multilateral cooperation;

3) an assumption that conflict and cooperation exist along a progressive continuum;

4) a tenet that conflict is restricted to state competition; and

5) a depoliticization of ecological conditions.

The Indus Waters Treaty exemplifies these challenges, which need to be addressed by scholars and practitioners alike. Theories of international relations that emphasize interdependence through mediating institutions such as the World Bank or the United Nations are most likely to offer some cooperative mechanisms in such asymmetric cases. The key to analyzing environmental cooperation as a potential pathway to peacemaking is to dispense with notions of linear causality and instead consider conflict de-escalation processes as nonlinear (not having a simple cause and effect relationship), often constituting a complex series of feedback loops. Positive exchanges and trust-building gestures are a consequence of realizing common environmental threats.

Often, a focus on common environmental harms (or aversions) is psychologically more successful in leading to cooperative outcomes than a focus on common benefits, which may lead to competitive behavior over the distribution of the gains. Specific research in game theory and operations research on the potential for cooperation over water is empirically showing that there are clear behavioral responses that suggest that such cooperation is possible. We also appear to have history on our side in this regard. An important historical study on water conflicts conducted by Oregon State University has noted that "the rate of cooperation overwhelms the incidence of acute conflict." In the last fifty years, only thirty-seven disputes involved violence, and thirty of those occurred between Israel and one of its neighbors.

Outside of the Middle East, researchers found only five violent events, while 157 treaties were negotiated and signed. The total number of water-related events between nations also favors cooperation: the 1,228 cooperative events are more than twice the number of 507 conflict-related events. Of these events, 62 percent are verbal, and more than two-thirds of these were not official statements. Realist scholars argue that cooperation on environmental issues among adversaries merely constitutes "low politics" and does not translate into larger resolutions over high-level national security concerns.

In this view, environmental conservation would be at best a means of diplomatic maneuvering between mid-level bureaucrats, and at worst a tool for influential elites to pursue their own narrow interests. Such critics give examples of cooperation on water resources between adversarial states such as India and Pakistan or Jordan and Israel without this cooperation translating into broader reconciliation or peace. Thus, it is presumed by some scholars looking at large historical data sets that environmental issues are not important enough in world politics to play an instrumental role in conflict resolution.

Meanwhile, recent research conducted by the International Peace Research Institute in Norway has tried to extricate some of the various geographical aspects of cooperation and conflict potential of riparian states using regression analyses. The basic conclusion of this study is that a shared river basin tends to accentuate conflict, but a shared river boundary as a border does not. However, such studies cannot provide the granularity of analysis required to understand how cooperative mechanisms might still operate in cases such as the Indus, where the principal cause of the overarching conflict is not water.

One of the earliest contributions to the study of environmental peacebuilding was Peter Haas' work in the context of the Mediterranean Action Plan. Haas focused on ways in which knowledge exchange promotes environmental cooperation through the formation of what he termed "epistemic communities," networks of professional experts who arrive at shared views on scientific policy questions. These networks often take the form of civil society groups—sometimes facilitated by development donors—that exchange information on environmental issues. There is also a growing commitment from donors to "bioregionalism," the notion that ecological management must be defined by natural delineations such as watersheds and biomes rather than by national or other borders.

Numerous joint environmental commissions between jurisdictions and countries have taken root all over the world, at times with implicit or explicit confidence- or peacebuilding goals. This evolution has also played out at various international forums in which bioregionalism and common environmental sensitivities have sometimes transcended traditional notions of state sovereignty.

An important role for such organizations is to improve an understanding of interconnections between distributive competitive issues of environmental scarcity with the mutual loss of deteriorated quality of the resource in the absence of cooperation.

Through such a process it may be possible to move functionally towards using water as a means of peacebuilding in South Asia and beyond. The Indus Basin agreement has often been heralded as a success story of riparian cooperation between warring states. The role of the World Bank as the mediating institution in resolving this dispute between India and Pakistan is often cited as a positive intervention that led to a win-win outcome for all sides in the dispute. Yet the cooperation between the two states on this technical matter has not catalyzed the resolution of the overarching conflict over the Kashmir region, giving some credence to realist assumptions about environmental factors being "low politics."

A closer examination of the cooperative arrangements reveals that the cooperation may still have played an important role in deescalating tensions during times of crisis. Consequently, it is possible to link such arrangements to larger narratives of conflict over territory that may be deemed "high politics." A more positive framing of the case might reveal that water resources in this context are so important that adversaries must show some semblance of cooperation over them, even when that does not spill over into broader peace. Furthermore, the use of environmental issues in building peace must be considered over longer time horizons and repeated interactions, premised empirically on the following conditions:

    (a) Development of a joint information base on a common environmental threat;

    (b) Recognition that cooperation is essential to alleviate that threat;

    (c) A cognitive connection and trust-building from initial environmental cooperation;

    (d) Continued interactions over time due to environmental necessity;

    (e) Clarification of misunderstandings and de-escalation of related conflicts; and,

(f) Increased cooperation and resultant peace-building.

These pathways are also considered the most empirically observed mechanisms, following a collective review by policy analysts for the United Nations Environment Program. The likelihood of environmental resources being used instrumentally in conflict resolution has increased in recent years.

Certain environmental resources are now better understood as fundamental to basic economic, environmental and social processes, including sustaining human life. There is a growing realization that environmental issues require integrated solutions across national borders since natural ecosystems do not recognize political boundaries. At the same time, politicians need to acknowledge that natural resources, particularly those as essential as water, can provide an important tool for resolving territorial disputes as well as providing a conduit for confidence-building measures between adversaries.

Cooperation over water and the environment is also a potential way of avoiding conflict if we can frame the matter appropriately While South Asia has exemplified some parts of this framing routine, there is far more which can be accomplished if leaders are more willing to explore inherent ecological linkages between technical collaboration on water and lasting territorial security.

The Ganges-Brahmaputra Delta

The management of water resources has played a vital role in the economic development of many countries in the South, but in a global context where large dams and water control projects face growing critical scrutiny and political opposition, the development of water resources shared by more than one state poses particular problems. Such development is increasingly understood to have vital geopolitical ramifications, nowhere more so than in the Ganges- Brahmaputra-Meghna system of the Bengal delta, shared between India and Bangladesh. This chapter explores the opportunities for enhancing effective use of the Ganges--Brahmaputra—Meghna waters through the development of a barrage complex at Farakka—Paksi—Mawa which would enhance the availability for both Bangladesh and India of currently surplus surface water flow in the Jamuna (Brahmaputra).

Set against the background of earlier disputes between India and Bangladesh over a wide range of alternative water development proposals since 1971, some of which were ultimately addressed in the Indo-Bangladesh Ganges Waters Treaty of December 1996, the chapter explores the arguments for a new barrage complex in southwestern Bangladesh. It analyzes the scale and nature of water demand in the trans-border region, and argues that an integrated development plan revolving around the construction of barrages in the Ganges delta within Bangladesh could bring major benefits to both Bangladesh and India. The Brahmaputra, the largest river in the Ganges—Brahmaputra—Meghna (GBM) river system, is one of the world's least utilized major rivers.

Although there are potential sites for major dams and barrages, none has yet been constructed. This chapter reviews some previous proposals for development and the reasons why they have not advanced. It focuses in particular on the issue of sharing the waters of the GBM between India and Bangladesh in the lower reaches of the system. In the past, negotiations over the sharing and joint development of the Ganges and Brahmaputra rivers have been protracted and unproductive, but the signing of the Ganges Water Treaty between India and Bangladesh in December 1996 suggests that both countries see a future in regional cooperation with respect to water development and management.

This chapter puts forward a new proposal for a barrage complex, integrating the existing Farakka barrage in India with new barrages on the Ganges and on the Padma in Bangladesh, and analyzes the changes in India and Bangladesh's geopolitical relationships which could make such a development feasible. As the scheme would depend for its success on making Brahmaputra water available to the water-short areas of both south-west Bangladesh and West Bengal, the geopolitical factors are just as important to the acceptance of the project as the technical features, which have been examined elsewhere by one of the authors. This chapter analyzes the relationship between technical and political feasibility for a project that has the potential significantly to augment the total water resources availability throughout the Bengal delta.

The River System

The term Ganges—Brahmaputra—Meghna region is used by India and Bangladesh to describe the three rivers which join within Bangladesh and flow together into the Bay of Bengal. Under the terms of the UN Convention on Non-Navigable Uses of International Watercourses (Article 1(a)), they form a single watercourse. It is a measure of the difficulty of finding common ground that India and Bangladesh have not been able to agree that this is the case, primarily because of the implications regarding water transfers from the Brahmaputra to the Ganges under the Helsinki accords.

However, it is also a measure of the need and determination to discuss the issues of sharing that the two sides have agreed on a term acceptable to both. The Ganges delta is defined as the area, limited in the west by the Hugh and the east by the Lower Meghna, with its apex at the Bhagirathi off-take in India — an area of 60 500km. The Brahmaputra adds, at a minimum, the area of alluvions between the Dhaleswari and the Ganges south of the Madhupur terrace, while the Meghna adds only its own channel bed (500km) from the confluence of the Kushiara and the Surma to the confluence with the Ganges. The total area of the GBM delta, can therefore be considered as 63 000km.

The three main rivers and the network of distributaries channels linking them mark the delta, Under natural conditions today, none of these distributaries carries significant flows during the dry season. The link between the Ganges and the Bhagirathi is maintained by the Farakka Barrage and its associated Feeder Canal, and between the Ganges and the Gorai by annual post-monsoon dredging. All three rivers have strongly seasonal flow characteristics. Their flows rise initially in response to snow melt, followed by monsoon rains in the Himalaya and, more importantly, on the piedmont plains.

The catchment area of the GBM system which has formed the Bengal delta now lies in five countries: Bangladesh, Bhutan, India, Nepal and China. Consequently, the control and development of the rivers in the delta itself has been subject to a range of geopolitical constraints which form as important a part of the development context as the more narrowly defined hydrological properties of the rivers themselves.

The geopolitics of development on Successive Rivers

While the development of large rivers for irrigation and power has been a major feature of the last century in river basins around the world, rivers that flow through a succession of different political territories, successive rivers, pose distinctive challenges on top of the increasingly widely recognized environmental questions which surround them. These include the rights of historic users in different parts of the catchment in relation to future potential users, and the implications throughout the river system of developing potential in one part of it.

In the contemporary state system, these interests and rights are mediated through the state and international system itself, and a growing body of international law plays an increasingly prominent role in defining rights of access and development to successive river waters. South Asia, which in the Indus, the Ganges and the Brahmaputra has three of the world's largest rivers, flowing through some of the world's most densely populated and poorest regions, is a geopolitical region whose internal post Independence political characteristics have interacted with its highly contrasted physical and economic environments to produce widely differing scenarios for large-scale water development.

In the Indus Waters Agreement, signed by India and Pakistan in 1960, it has what many still regard as one of the most successful international water development and sharing agreements in the world. Yet in contrast, apparently insuperable political obstacles have often beset the development of the eastern rivers, notably the Ganges and the Brahmaputra. In analyzing the reasons for this contrast, this chapter seeks to lay the basis for an alternative approach to cooperative development, especially between India and Bangladesh, most attempts at which to date have been vitiated by a spirit of competitive resource extraction rather than of cooperative development.

The Indus Waters Treaty

The political context against which the Indus Waters Treaty was signed could scarcely have seemed less propitious when it was under negotiation in the late 1950s. Yet despite the 15-month war in which India and Pakistan had been locked over Kashmir in 1947-8 and the deep distrust which has mired their relationship ever since, the agreement to share in the development of the Indus and its major tributaries has been strictly adhered to throughout the period of over four decades since its ratification. Why? The history of the Indus Waters treaty has been superbly discussed by Michel (1967).

The key geopolitical features underlying its success are:

    (a)   the interlocking characteristics of the geography of the catchment area;

    (b)   the nature and extent of pre-independence irrigation

development on the eastern tributaries of the Indus;

(c)   the Cold War significance of the northwestern part of the Indian subcontinent in the Western powers' containment strategy with respect to the Soviet Union; and

(d)   the enormous scale of advantage perceived by both India and Pakistan in the further development of the waters of the Indus system, none of which could be achieved without cooperation and full agreement between them.

In all fundamental respects, this context was quite different from that which has surrounded river development schemes in the GBM system. The geographical contrasts were vital in themselves. The Indus and its five major tributaries, fed by snowmelt from the high Himalaya and monsoon rainfall from the lower ranges, flowed from the Indian Himalaya into the semi-arid and arid plains of the western Punjab and Sind. Sparsely populated until the opening up of the great canal colonies from the 1840s onwards, by Independence the Punjab plains had become totally dependent on irrigation from the easternmost tributaries of the Indus.

Most of these plains were in Pakistan, which under Partition became the lower riparian state, and over 90% of Pakistan's agriculture dependent on the surface water irrigation derived from these rivers. After 1947, by the accident of the designation of India and Pakistan's Partition-inspired boundaries, all the headwaters of these rivers lay in India. India wished to lay claim to a substantial proportion of the water for its own development, and thus a resolution of the Indus waters crisis was essential to the economic and political security of West Pakistan. That this could be achieved was feasible because the western tributaries — the Jhelum and Chenab — and the Indus itself, were largely undeveloped.

Their damming and subsequent development would allow for the diversion of the eastern tributaries of the Indus

— the Sutlej, Beas and Ravi — to India. Hence, through the building of some of the world's largest dams, a project made financially possible by the World Bank, a treaty on sharing the Indus was made politically and economically attractive by the context of overwhelming mutual benefit, guaranteeing security of existing water supply and extensive development to Pakistan while also allowing the massive Rajasthan canal scheme and several other more minor works to take place in India. These benefits were sufficiently great to override the hostility which has dogged all other relationships between India and Pakistan since Independence.

By the end of the 1960s, the World Bank had drawn together six governments to provide the equivalent of $6700 million (in year 2000 US$) to finance projects in the Indus Basin that would provide a utilizable flow of 50 Maf (1954m) from the 70 Maf which was 'now wasting to the sea. The project would go on to cost $9510 million for dams and link canals, excluding the costs of distribution works. Even 35 years later, the World Bank was still proud of its contribution to the Indus Basin Project.

The Ganges-Brahmaputra-Meghna Basin

The geographical and the political situation in the GBM delta during the Pakistan period could scarcely have been more different from that obtaining in the Indus basin. Although, like West Pakistan, East Pakistan was also a lower riparian, less than 1% of East Pakistan's agricultural output in 1947 could be attributed to surface water irrigation from the Ganges, Brahmaputra and Meghna. Furthermore, East Pakistan occupied only 10% of a catchment area, the remaining 90% of which was shared with four other countries — India, Nepal, Bhutan and China.

Unlike the Indus, the Ganges and Brahmaputra and their tributaries crossed increasingly well-watered land until they reached the Bengal delta, one of the wettest regions on Earth. The Bengal delta's major crops at the time, reflecting the flood-prone monsoon-dependent nature of the deltaic environment, were overwhelmingly the early and late monsoon crops of the aus and aman rice, while the dry season boro was grown on under 3% of the land, the remainder being left f allow. The main cash crop, jute, was also a monsoon season crop, grown on the freshly deposited silt of the levees of the major rivers. Thus at independence in 1947, while West Pakistan depended wholly on the Indus tributaries, East Pakistan made little use of the surface waters which passed through it to the sea and dry-season agriculture was insignificant in comparison with the major wet season crops.

Indeed, it is striking that in drawing up the boundaries of Pakistan and India in 1947, one of the few concessions made by Sir Cyril Radcliffe to geographical features was to include the Muslim majority district of Murshidabad in India on the grounds that the three Ganges distributaries, the Bhagirathi, Jalangi and Matabhanga, were vital to Calcutta's (Kolkata) survival as 'a city and as a port'. In contrast to East Pakistan's negligible developed use of the Ganges in 1947, significant use was already made of Ganges water at Independence by India, which as the upper riparian on the Indus made very little use of the pre-Independence river flow, but which as upper riparian on the Ganges already had extensive schemes using the upper reaches of the Ganges and some of its tributaries.

Large-scale irrigation projects had withdrawn water since the mid-nineteenth century in northern India, while Calcutta, with its large industrial, drinking-water and navigation uses, depended heavily on the silt-laden water of the Hugh, the westernmost distributaries of the Ganges as it entered the delta. However, the Bhagirathi-Hugli, a decaying branch of the Ganges, was being progressively cut off by the eastward migration of the main course of the Ganges, during the dry season exposing its population, industries and harbour to increasingly severe shortages of fresh water and siltation.

In this wholly different context, plans to develop water resources in the GBM delta proceeded on a more piecemeal basis and with a far weaker sense of any need for international agreement between the parties than in the Indus basin. The appearance of competitive interests for access to Ganges water gave ample opportunity for the already hostile relationships between India and Pakistan to be expressed through the 1950s and 1960s. For Pakistan, the Ganges offered the opportunity of developing a barrage diversion scheme, the Ganges-Kobadak project, to irrigate 800 000 ha of land in the southwestern districts.

This project was embarked on unilaterally and was seen as conceptually wholly independent of any upper riparian interests, whether in India or Nepal. At the same time, as Crow et al. (1995) have fully documented, India began to bring to fruition its own barrage scheme for diverting dry-season flow from the Ganges into the Bhagirathi-Hugli at Farakka, also without reference to any possible downstream destructive implications — or to any possibilities for mutual benefit. In the event the Farakka Barrage scheme came to dominate relations between India and East Pakistan, and subsequently Bangladesh, from the first notification to the Pakistan government by India in January 1961.

This was 108 years after the first report into the problems of navigation on the River Hugh. In comparison with the Indus Waters Treaty, the provisions of the Farakka Barrage were extremely modest, but from 1951 Pakistan viewed the proposal for a barrage at Farakka with extreme hostility. Concerned to protect its own development on the Ganges-Kobadak, the meetings between India and Pakistan made no effort to move towards an integrated project. Rather the two schemes were seen as inherently competitive, and while the Indus Waters Treaty survived the 1965 India-Pakistan war intact, the talks over Farakka were broken off.

The reasons for this breakdown lie in the contrasting perceived water requirements within the Bengal delta region and the wider catchment area, the almost complete lack of irrigation development before the 1950s in the delta, and the consequent lack of perceived mutuality, and the insufficiently large potential and mutually perceived benefits from cooperation to overcome the still deep-seated distrust between Pakistan and India on a wider political front. These factors were exacerbated by the sense in both Pakistan and India that East Pakistan was of lower strategic importance than West Pakistan.

While the Indo-China war in 1962 raised the security profile of India's northeast, and consequently of East Pakistan, within the South Asian region, East Pakistan was far less strategically significant globally in the West's containment strategy with respect to the Soviet Union than West Pakistan, and the incentive to external parties to get involved in overcoming disagreements over 'relatively minor' matters in the east was proportionately lower. Thus each country proceeded with its own plans either independently or in direct competition with the other. Pakistan's plans for the Ganges-Kobadak pump irrigation scheme originated in 1951, and the project was begun in 1954 and inaugurated in 1968.

This was a clear recognition of the perceived need for extra water in the southwestern districts of East Pakistan. However, the possible advantages of integrate d development were never broached. Indeed, Crow et al. has suggested on the basis of discussions with Arshad Hossein, Pakistan's High Commissioner to India in 1963-8, that an alternative Ganges Barrage, investigated by the commercial TAMS Consultants on behalf of the Pakistan government, was a purely tactical measure, a threat to submerge the Farakka project to prevent its ever coming into operation.

Yet both the actual and the potential significance of the GBM system today cannot be doubted. In total today over 600 million people, 10% of the world's population, live within the catchment area of the Ganges-Brahmaputra-Meghna, substantially more than 350 million living in the Changjiang basin in China. The effective use of its water resources throughout the basin has an essential part to play in tackling poverty, increasing food security and creating a stable and cooperative geopolitical environment.

The Farakka Barrage

The view of the development of the Ganges' water as a competitive zero sum game, which was the hallmark of the Pakistan period, continued after the Farakka Barrage was brought on stream on 21 April 1975. Operations since were widely claimed to have had various adverse effects in Bangladesh. Studies of these have been made, but few are in the public domain. Objectivity is not a major feature of these reports, and there is little attempt to separate out the impacts of freshwater withdrawals at Farakka from other changes that are occurring in the region.

Over-exploitation of fishing and forestry resources is a widespread problem in Bangladesh; water table levels in the dry season are generally lower everywhere where groundwater is being used; and navigation depths are reducing due to polder construction in many rivers. At one stage or another, almost every problem associated with water has been attributed to the impact of Farakka, and estimated as a financial loss. Bradnock and Saunders have shown how global concepts of environmental change, from sea level rise to desertification, have also been pressed into service to add emphasis to the presumed damage being caused by the barrage.

This exaggeration of losses is unfortunate, as it obscures the very real social, economic and environmental problems that have arisen due to withdrawals, but Farakka became the focus of worsening relations between the two countries on a wider front. The inauguration of the barrage coincided with a dramatic deterioration in political relations between India and Bangladesh. The brief detente which had followed the secession of Bangladesh from Pakistan in December 1971, with large-scale Indian political and military help, had been terminated with the assassination of Sheikh Mujib, the pro-Indian 'father of the nation', and the takeover of power by military governments widely seen as hostile to India.

The first diversion of dry season flow from the Ganges at a period of unusually low flows added to profound distrust in Bangladesh of India's intentions, a distrust which coloured their contrasting views of water development for 20 years. The succession of efforts made to find a settlement to the dispute foundered on the rocks of a wider and seemingly more fundamental contrast in each country's perception of its geopolitical interests. Under Mrs Gandhi, India had developed the practice of basing its regional relationship on the principle of bilateralism.

At the geographic centre of the region and sharing borders with each of its smaller neighbours, Mrs Gandhi's India saw bilateralism as a vital strategic mechanism for maintaining its regional security and obviating any risk of being outnumbered by its neighbours. Yet, to India's neighbours, that policy of bilateralism was seen as a policy of achieving and implementing Indian regional dominance. Thus Bangladesh and other neighbours sought ways of widening regional support and seeking multilateral agreement to reduce the power of India in bilateral negotiation.

The inauguration of the South Asian Association for Regional Cooperation (SAARC) in 1983 owed its origin to the initiative of President Ziaur Rahman of Bangladesh, but its highly restricted scope and powers to the determination of Mrs Gandhi not to allow the principle of bilateralism to be overridden in any sphere where India's fundamental strategic interests were held to be at stake. The disputes and negotiations between India and Bangladesh over water resource development from the signing of the Ganges Waters Agreement in 1977 to the Ganges Waters Treaty in 1996 reflected the divergent views of each country of the most effective way of securing their wider strategic objectives.

Under the Ganges Water Agreement of 1977, the two governments deputed the joint Rivers Commission to make recommendations on the augmentation of the Ganges. Although they originally envisaged that the two sides would work together, there was no clear mandate for this, no accepted objective and no agreement on the constraints that should be accepted. Proposals prepared separately by each side were exchanged in March 1 978, then commented upon and rejected by the other.

The process was repeated with updated proposals in 1983. The Government of Bangladesh (GoB) then engaged the services of a technical team, the Expert Study Group financed by the World Bank, to help in the further appraisal of the two proposals, and the criticism received. This team included the normal project evaluation array of expatriate and local design engineers, geologists, hydrologists, environmentalists, economists and other specialists. The team successfully argued with the GoB that it would be more useful to have an objective technical assessment of both proposals, using cost estimates based on Internationally Competitive Bidding procedures, than a 'case for the defence' trying to favour the Bangladeshi proposal over the Indian one.

For the reasons explained below, the team advised against both proposals, and suggested instead that Bangladesh should seek a solution that lay within its territory. The Government of Bangladesh accepted this, and the team then prepared a proposal for what came to be known as the 'new line'. These three proposals are briefly described below. Specific developments in the water and water-related sectors are discussed below.

Ganges Water Treaty

The signing of the Ganges Water Treaty (GWT) in December 1996 was an important demonstration of the willingness of the two countries to find a mutually acceptable solution to the impasse in which they had become locked.

It also provides a useful insight into what both sides found acceptable as a compromise. The Treaty is scheduled to last for 30 years, and Bangladesh will receive at least 90% of the flows agreed upon after that period, until a new agreement is made. The Treaty sets out for each country the share of the incoming flows it will receive in each 10-day period (decade) between 1 January and 31 May each year.

The flows are measured in cusecs at Farakka, and almost all India's share is diverted down the Feeder Canal to the Bhagirathi-Hugli, a mere 200 cusecs being reserved for use in India downstream of Farakka. The sharing arrangement covers flows in three stages, the highest Indian diversion being 40 000 cusecs, equal to the capacity of the Feeder Canal. Under the GWT, India may divert this flow when the incoming flow is 75 000 cusecs, leaving 35 000 cusecs for Bangladesh. The permitted diversion is reduced pro rata as the incoming flow reduces to 70 000 cusecs, and below that the flows are shared equally.

This flow of 70 000 cusecs is exceeded 60% of the time in the dry season, based on the 194 9-88 measurements of flows arriving at Farakka (the flow period used in the GWT to illustrate the effect of its application). Thus for 40% of the dry season period covered by the treaty, the flows are shared equally. If the flow falls below 50 000 cusecs (1418.5m), 'the two Governments will enter into immediate consultations to make adjustments on an emergency basis, in accordance with the principles of equity, fair play and no harm to either party'. Flows less than this figure occur on average for 5% of the time.

The lowest flow on the record used is 1062, in April 1953, which under the GWT would have given India only 107, or 10% of the flow. It is difficult to believe that such a low flow would be acceptable to the concentration of many industries in the belt [the watercourse from Farakka to Calcutta]'. Accordingly, one can reasonably suppose that when flows less than 50 000 cusecs occur, the intent is that the flows will be shared equally, and the clause defining alternating flushing flows suspended. Several factors raise doubts about the sustainability of the Ganges Waters Treaty provisions in the medium to long term.

The GWT states that 'Every effort would be made by the upper riparian to protect flows of water at Farakka as in the 40-years average availability as mentioned above'. This itself may be difficult to respect. The flows arriving at Farakka in the period since 1988, although not used by the negotiators (as they had not been measured by joint teams), indicate there has been a decline in average flow for all decades except the last. These changes in flow are consistent with a general trend over the available flow record 1949-97 for the flows to decline, with the reduction being greatest in March-April.

If these changes were to continue for the duration of the GWT period, the flows would be below 50000 cusecs for 25% of the time, with serious implications for the southwestern region of the delta, both the Indian state of West Bengal and southwestern Bangladesh. What may be deduced from the Treaty? Flows above 75 000 cusecs appear to be in excess of requirements. When flows fall below 50 000 cusecs, each side receives only 15 000 cusecs for a 10-day period, and this is considered an emergency. In view of the changes taking place, the outlook for the Treaty cannot be considered promising. While it may be acceptable for emergency situations to occur 5% of the time, it is unlikely to remain acceptable if they occur 25% of the time.

Although the Treaty makes no specific reference to these concerns, it does refer to the need 'to cooperate with each other in finding a solution to the long-term problem of augmenting the flows of the Ganga/Ganges during the dry season'. Yet the Treaty does not discuss the uses to which the water will be put in each country, a key element in the assessment of demand, nor does it make any provision to share augmented flows. In making allocations, the Treaty makes no reference to the costs to each country of accessing the water, or to any development plans, whether national or cooperative.

Nor does the Treaty make any reservation for flows to be left in the river, as has been discussed on the Teesta. If the records are correct, then these factors alone will make it increasingly difficult for the commitment on Ganges water-sharing to be sustained. If it is sustained, it will be at the cost of diverting from surface irrigation projects in India to Bangladesh specifically to maintain the Treaty commitment rather than to meet development needs in India. This will always be a politically difficult and costly exercise.

It highlights the improbability of Bangladesh ever being in a position to re-negotiate an increase in the total volume it receives, and therefore the present volume of flow is the best it can hope for. Given continuing population increase throughout Bangladesh and sustained increase in water demand in the southwest, already a water-short region, in the absence of major development within Bangladesh current shortfalls can only be expected to increase. If the Ganges alone is unlikely to be able to meet needs of the southwestern region of the GBM delta, can the Brahmaputra be used to augment the total usable supply? In contrast to the decreasing flow of the Ganges, flows on the Brahmaputra are increasing.

The correlation coefficient of the trend (between monthly flow magnitude and year) is low on the Ganges but more significant (absolute value closer to one) on the Brahmaputra. If the rate of change on the Ganges were maintained over the 30-year life of the Treaty, flows at the end of March would decrease by 480m, 27% of their average value, but the gain on the Brahmaputra would be 1200m, more than twice as much.

Per capita Availability

A further indication of the potential utility of Brahmaputra flows is given by a measure of per capita availability of water in different parts of the two river catchments. Such measures are commonly made using annual totals of rainfall and river flow. This is not useful in situations where most of the flow occurs in the form of floods. A more reasonable measure of availability of water resources, and how this might change, can be assessed by looking at the 80% dependable flow in the lowest flow month in each river. Although re-allocating the resources would reduce the imbalance, the flow per capita would still be almost four times higher in the Brahmaputra than the Ganges.

Under the Ganges Waters Treaty, the two Governments agree to conclude water-sharing treaties/agreements with regard to other common rivers according to the same principles used in the GWT. Thus the agreement may be taken as a guide to what might be agreed on the Brahmaputra. Based on the GWT precedent, the most likely outcome on the Brahmaputra will be that, in times of low flow, the countries will agree to share on a 50:50 basis, and no reservation will be made for flows to be left in the river. The shares for each country are likely to vary according to specific requirements.

However, since India has virtually no consumptive demands in its part of the Brahmaputra catchment, it will continue to seek ways to transfer the water to West Bengal, where it can be used. Based on the GWT precedent, the costs of accessing this water will be borne by India alone. These costs are likely to be considerable, and proportional to the quantity transferred. Hence it is unlikely that India would wish to install a conveyance system whose capacity could not be fully utilized for most of the critical period. There is thus a powerful logic behind developing a scheme which increases access to the utilizable flows of the Brahmaputra while minimizing the costs of development to all potential users.

Water Resource Studies in Bangladesh

A further complication in evaluating the long-term sustainability of the Ganges Waters Treaty lies in the cloud which has hung over estimates of groundwater availability in Bangladesh and the secrecy with which all hydrological data in India are kept. The estimation of water demand in Bangladesh is subject to a great deal of political influence. It has become evident from the enormous expansion of Shallow Tubewell (STW) irrigation in Bangladesh that groundwater resources greatly exceed early estimates.

More recent analysis indicates that in much of the delta, sustainable groundwater reserves within the top 20 m of the aquifer are adequate to meet the entire needs of present and future agriculture and water supply. Furthermore, soil moisture and surface water stored in shallow depressions will meet much of the residual demand, thus reducing net demands for surface water resources. The problem with groundwater is one of systemic misunderstanding, a misunderstanding that cannot be resolved by an exchange of information.

An examination of the way in which estimates of groundwater resources were made as part of the National Water Plan (where the technical appendices show that objective estimates were much higher than the figures published in the main report) demonstrates that there has been an important and influential group of people in Bangladesh which has not wanted to believe that there are adequate reserves of groundwater in many regions of Bangladesh, and who would not be persuaded by 'facts' or 'analysis'. Their position has been based on their belief that there is a need to preserve Bangladesh's position in its negotiations with India, and to sustain the arguments in favour of dam and barrage building.

If groundwater reserves are seen to be adequate, then they believe their position will be undermined. This group has been in a position to exert considerable influence over the consultants who were commissioned at various times to assess water resources, and the reports need to be judged accordingly. Yet the Southwest is an exception to the general rule, having very limited groundwater resources in addition to the obvious constraints on existing surface supply. In combination, these constraints are going to place further stresses on the viability of the Ganges Waters Treaty, and demand appropriate policy development now.

Proposed Farakka-Paksi—Mawa Complex

The proposed barrage complex discussed here is the Farakka-Paksi—Mawa Complex (FPMC) proposed in a related paper. Details of the assumptions made, and other technical issues, are not the subject of this chapter, and only the key points are summarized in this section. The FPMC would comprise the existing Farakka barrage, plus two new barrages. One barrage would be constructed on the Padma at Mawa, the site selected for the Padma road bridge crossing, where a combined barrage/bridge could be built. A second barrage would be built on the Ganges at the site of the Paksi Bridge, immediately downstream of the Hardinge railway bridge, completed in 1915, where a second combined bridge/barrage could be built.

Both barrages could also be built immediately downstream of the bridges proposed at each site, with major cost savings, as no guide bunds would be required. The retention level of the Mawa barrage would be set at a level that allows water to flow by gravity into the Dhaleswari river (a distributaries of the Brahmaputra) and hence into the rivers around Dhaka. Water would also flow into the Ganges distributaries from the Gorai to the Anal Khan. The retention level of the Paksi barrage would similarly be set to allow water to flow by gravity into the Ganges distributaries between Farakka barrage and Paksi.

The pond level at Mawa would be above the downstream apron level of the Paksi barrage, sc water from the Brahmaputra could be pumped up into the Paksi pond. Similarly, the pond level at Paksi would be above the downstream apron level of the Farakka barrage, so water from the Brahmaputra could be further pumped up into the Farakka pond. This water could then supply industries on the Feeder Canal. Calcutta itself would be supplied via the

Feeder Canal, the Bhagirathi, Jalangi and the Matabhanga. This combination of barrages would allow Brahmaputra water to supply the surface water needs of North-central and Southwest Bangladesh and West Bengal, without the need for storage or extensive land acquisition.

No Ganges water would need to be released in the dry season from Bihar to West Bengal, apart from that needed to maintain navigation depths and minimum in-stream needs for the maintenance of fisheries and the environment. This flow could therefore be used in Bihar, or any of the upper Indian states on the Ganges where water is available to abstract.

Simulation

Studies of 34 years of simultaneous flows for the Ganges at Farakka and the Brahmaputra at Bahadurabad were made for the period January to May each year, to simulate how the FPMC would have performed, had the complex been in place.

Future Development

While this complex of barrages would be freestanding and independently v viable of any other development upstream, any augmentation from dams built in the headwaters of the Ganges or Brahmaputra could be utilized wherever most needed in the river system.

Flow Sharing

In order to examine the shares of water going to each country, Brichieri-Colombi's study (2001) introduced the concept of utilizable flow. It argued that dry season flows in excess of requirements should not be considered, and compared the shares on the Ganges under the GWT with those on the Ganges and Brahmaputra combined with the FPMC.

The utilizable flows for both countries were considered to be the entire flow diverted into the various distributaries in each country. In addition, for India, the Bihar abstraction was included and for Bangladesh, flows up to 2000 for salinity control. Any excess flows into the Lower Meghna were ignored. The shares of utilizable flow of the Ganges under the GWT were 52% for India and 48% for Bangladesh. Those of the Ganges-Brahmaputra under the FPMC combined 50% each.

The geopolitics of the Farakka-Paksi-Mawa Barrage Complex

Large-scale river barrage diversion schemes today, especially those on successive rivers, have geopolitical ramifications ranging from the global to the local. While Bangladesh and India have a dominant interest in the FPMC proposal, global concerns at large dam development which gave rise to the World Commission on Dams (WCD) IUCN report have ensured that all large river diversion schemes come under international scrutiny, especially with respect to their putative environmental consequences.

Thus in addition to the development and political implications of the proposal for India and Bangladesh, it is necessary to examine the possible relationship between the proposed scheme and wider environmental issues in the southwestern region of the Bengal GBM delta system. Politically, the FPMC would achieve some key objectives for both Bangladesh and India.

The scheme would allow Bangladesh to realize its long-expressed wish to harness the flows of the major rivers, including the Brahmaputra, and to retain control of all the headworks of such development within its own borders. At the same time, it would allow India to realize its equally long-expressed desire to access a share of the Brahmaputra water for use in West Bengal, and so free up Ganges water for use in drier parts of the catchment.

Objections to the FPMC

Both parties may have difficulties with some aspects of the proposed scheme. India may have reservations about the controls lying within Bangladesh, as it would be a relatively easy matter for Bangladesh not to pump the water up to the Paksi barrage. India's obvious response, to divert all Ganges flows at Farakka, would penalize only a relatively small part of Southwest Bangladesh. This, however, is merely a reversal of the present situation, where the controls (Farakka) lie in India. The situation is common in water resource agreements and is managed, as now at Farakka, by having joint teams measuring discharges.

A similar situation exists on the Nile, where Egyptian engineers monitor releases from Lake Victoria under the Owen Falls agreement, and under the terms of the Indus Waters Treaty. There may also be concerns about making flows into West Bengal dependent on the operation of a pump station and the reliability of the electrical supply at Paksi. Generation facilities could be built there, and the FPMC shows that this would be economic, provided it could sell into the local market in the wet season. Calcutta, as any large industrial centre, is already dependent on reliable electricity supplies, and to be competitive these must be provided.

The dependency of water supply on electricity would add to pressures to ensure improved reliability. Some in Bangladesh may see the FPMC scheme as a variant of the original Indian proposal to transfer water from the Brahmaputra, and a loss of the Brahmaputra as well as the Ganges. In the light of the current debate in Bangladesh over the sale of natural gas to India, it can be expected that some will see any transfer of water to India as the loss of a birthright.

A further concern for Bangladesh could be that by coming to agreement with India on the allocation of flows, options to use the water to cover unforeseen events are restricted, such as measures to deal with arsenic, should this prove to be an issue for agriculture (quantities needed for drinking water are too small to be of significance), or measures to provide for irrigated agriculture, should estimates of groundwater reserves prove erroneous. The

FPMC proposal goes a significant way to meeting both difficulties.

Vulnerability

A measure of the potential advantages of the proposed FPMC scheme can be obtained from applying the concept of vulnerability. The simplest indicator of vulnerability is perhaps the proportion of the basin population that lives upstream of a vulnerable state. The proportion of the total basin population living upstream of Bangladesh on the Brahmaputra is 43%, compared to the 92% upstream on the Ganges. For West Bengal, the proportion living upstream is 73%. Bangladesh and, to a slightly lesser extent West Bengal, are thus both highly vulnerable to upstream developments on the Ganges. If the population of Bangladesh and West Bengal were, as a result of the FPMC scheme, to become dependent only on the Brahmaputra for surface water, then the vulnerability would change.

The vulnerability for Bangladeshis now living in the Brahmaputra Dependent Area would reduce from 43% to 18%, while for those now living in the Ganges Dependent Area would reduce from 92% (based on the Ganges) to 18% (based on the Brahmaputra). For the population of West Bengal, vulnerability would also be reduced, from 73% (based on the Ganges) to 59% (based on the Brahmaputra). In effect, Bangladesh and West Bengal both become less vulnerable to upstream developments on the Ganges, where their views carry relatively little weight because of the large population living there.

They become vulnerable to upstream developments on the Brahmaputra, but their combined populations are relatively large in relation to the basin total. Population is, of course, not the only factor. As demonstrated on the Nile and the Tigris, economic power is an even greater factor in the control of international rivers. If the population numbers quoted above were weighted by per capita GDP, the current vulnerability would be even greater.

Equity

Equity is another important consideration in the presentation of any scheme to develop resources. Most people appreciate that resources have to be shared, and it is notable how several of the treaties referred to above include concepts of equality, rather than a larger allocation to India due to its greater size and economic strength. The Mahakali Treaty between India and Nepal allocates border flows on a 50:50 basis.

The Ganges Water Treaty allocates the water on a 50:50 basis in times of stress, and it appears that the Teesta flows will be negotiated on a similar basis. It can be presumed that a Brahmaputra Water Treaty, if negotiated separately, would also end up with similar shares. A key element of the proposed development is that the overall sharing arrangement under the FPMC as set out in the study would be a 50:50 split that has proved acceptable to both sides on in the GBM.

Cost sharing and affordability

The costs of the FPMC, estimated at $3600 million, are high in absolute terms but not large in the context of the water development debate in the region. Verghese suggested that the first phase of the Chisapani Dam project in Nepal would cost $6000 million in 1989, equivalent to $7700 million in today's prices. The 1984 Bangladesh proposal envisages, at a minimum, six such dams. India has continued to press ahead with the huge Narmada scheme, and Bangladesh has recently completed the $950 million Jamuna Bridge. Both countries are obviously ready to expend large sums for infrastructure development. The more pertinent question is how the costs of the scheme should be divided.

For India, the net benefit is the water diverted upstream of Farakka and the flow diverted into West Bengal in excess of that provided under the GWT. For Bangladesh, the benefits would be the flow diverted into the South West

Region upstream and into the Dhaleswari, since at present the dry season flows into these distributaries are negligible. The flows into the Anal Khan are unchanged, and those down the Lower Meghna are reduced to the minimum acceptable level. The net gains, in terms of water supplied.

However, the value of a dependable supply of water is different in different parts of the catchment, and may be expected to be much higher upstream of Farakka, and for urban use in Calcutta, than for agriculture and environmental use in Southwest Bangladesh. The FPMC paper made various assumptions about values and proportions in different uses and suggested the relative values were 2.50cm in India and 0.67cm in Bangladesh, a ratio of 3.71. This would indicate an 86% share for India. Thus, the Bangladesh share of the works would probably be between 15% and 23% of the works.

If the total cost were around $3.6 billion, the cost to Bangladesh for a 20% share would be $720 million, less than the cost of a single barrage. Over a seven-year period, the cost of $100 million per year would be 20-25% of the annual investment budget in the water sector of $360 million per year, rising to $500 million year over the period 2001-10. The costs to India would be six times as much, but with an economy eight times as large, the affordability would be greater. That Bangladesh would be willing to invest so much in a single project is indicated in the provisions for capital spending in the water sector in the Fifth Five-Year Plan, where $354 million, 23.4% of the budget, was assigned for the Ganges Barrage. It is unclear whether India still accords such a high priority to the sector.

Sharing, pumping and pricing

One of the more interesting aspects of the FPMC is that the costs of pumping (capacity plus energy costs) are 32% a significant proportion of total costs. The more water India wishes to take from the Brahmaputra, the more expensive the project. There is, thus, an incentive to minimize demands rather than maximize them. However, if either side reduces its share, prices per metre of water will have to rise to make the scheme economically viable. This will tend to make both sides review critically their needs, and try to make an objective assessment, to reduce as far as possible their proportion of scheme costs while obtaining the supplies they need. Such assessments have not been a feature of past negotiations.

There is likely to be some vigorous debate about the relative value of water to each side, as this also has a major effect on the share of cost each would pay. The cost of pumping up to the Paksi pond is quite low (0.5 c compared with the average cost of 2.5 c for India. When the additional costs of pumping to Farakka are added, they become .2 c almost half the total cost. This will tend to make India consider whether it would be better to take more water through the Bhagirathi rather than Farakka, and further reduce the cost of the scheme.

These features of the FPMC are likely to improve the allocative efficiency of the water supplied through the scheme, which should make it more attractive to Governments and donor agencies alike. It should also make it easier for a joint team to study the project, as both sides gain from minimizing costs.

Other factors Influencing Decisions

While the above analysis of costs and benefits is illustrative rather than technical, it is sufficiently strong to suggest powerful arguments for taking the proposal further. Two further arguments may also be entered. As described above, much has been made in the past of the adverse effects of Farakka, centred on the increased salinity and the drainage of the aquifer adjacent to the Ganges and Gorai. Whether accurate or not, both effects would be reversed by the scheme, as water levels in the Paksi pond would be close to bank-full level, and hence recharge rather than drain the aquifer, while flows down the Gorai would be greater than those pre-Farakka, and hence reverse salinity intrusion.

Secondly, proposals have recently been made to create a navigable waterway around Dhaka. The proposal would be greatly enhanced if there were significant freshwater flow in the system instead of tidal ebb and flow of the same polluted water. The flows into the Dhaleswari would create year-round navigable depths for much larger vessels, and could permit barge traffic to Chittagong. Further studies would be needed to ascertain whether sea-going ships would be able to sail directly from Dhaka, but if so the direct benefits of the scheme would reach a still wider proportion of Bangladesh's population.

The Report of the World Commission on Dams

If Bangladesh and India wish to receive international assistance to construct the scheme, they will need to take into consideration the attitudes among multi-lateral and bi-lateral agencies following the recent publication of the World Commission on Dams. Although barrages seldom meet the definition of large dams (a height greater than 15 m or a retention volume greater than 3 [Mm]), they are often confused with dams, and are viewed with the same suspicion. They are likely to be subject to the same kind of scrutiny that the WCD applied to high dams.

The WCD suggest five tests be applied to any proposal for high dam construction, of which the first two relate to planning and the selection of the preferred development plan:

    (a) Needs assessment — validating the needs for water and energy services.

    (b) Selecting alternatives — identifying the preferred development plan from among the full range of options.

Where a dam emerges from this process as a preferred development alternative, three further critical decision points occur:

(a) Project preparation — verifying that agreements are in place before tender of the construction contract.

(b) Project implementation — confirming compliance before commissioning.

(c) Project operation — adapting to changing contexts.

Validating the needs for water and energy services

The FPMC is designed to provide water, not energy, as the latter would be largely for internal consumption by the complex. The question therefore is whether the water is needed, and in how large a quantity. Could other sources be used, and could demand be managed to match supply and demand at a lower level of consumption? The needs to be assessed are those arising upstream of Farakka; those in West Bengal, and those in Bangladesh.

Of these three, recent estimates are available only for Bangladesh. BrichieriColombi (2001) notes that there may be difficulties in Bangladesh in accepting the estimates contained in the Draft Development Strategy. He also acknowledges the weakness of the assumption that the demand exists in India merely because the Government of India have made expensive proposals to transfer water to the Ganges from the Brahmaputra.

Chapman discusses future demand in the Ganges Plains. He makes the point about the absence of data: ... for many seemingly important issues, either there are no data, or there is data but they are not centrally collected and no-one knows who has them, or there are data but they are withheld from the public domain for political reasons. In other words ... a book such as this is floating in a sea of uncertainty and ignorance.

There appears to be no available analysis of how the water released at Farakka is used, but some indications are given by the Centre for Policy Research (1999), where it is suggested that 15 000 cusecs is used for flushing the Port of Calcutta and 6000-8000 cusecs is used for irrigation in fields adjacent to the Bhaghirathi. Some 15m is abstracted for municipal water supply. If the capacity of the Feeder Canal represents the maximum demand, this leaves a balance of 460 unaccounted for.

The 1978 Indian Proposal claimed that 40 000 cusecs was needed for Calcutta Port. In his analysis of whether Farakka has solved the problems of Calcutta Port, Crow quotes Sau, who shows that, although the draught available for shipping to the Calcutta—Haldia complex has improved since Farakka started operating, this has not stopped Calcutta's decline as a port. Although this analysis shows increased flows are not sufficient to solve the problems, they may still be a necessary part of the solution, together with other measures to improve productivity.

Studies in Bangladesh cannot properly assess Indian needs upstream or downstream of Farakka. It is inappropriate that they should attempt to do so, as only a joint study can do this. However, it is evident that much work needs to be done to establish without doubt that the water is needed. As noted in relation to debates over water in South Asia: 'That debate has clearly to begin by reviewing the key features of demand, before going on to explore alternative ways in which that demand can be met'.

Selecting Alternatives

The main alternatives for meeting the demand, if established, have been identified in the proposals by the two sides, and in this chapter. Already Bangladesh is tacitly accepting that constructing high dams in the Himalaya is unlikely, being 'too big, too costly, and too far off in the future'. India has now accepted that the Assam—West Bengal Link Canal is 'no longer on the table', although smaller variants are under consideration in some quarters. The World Commission on Dams report will further undermine the prospects of either of these proposals being implemented. The FPMC proposal set out in this chapter would appear to be the last option worthy of consideration.

Project Preparation and Implementation

Within Bangladesh, where most of the work would be carried out, important precedents were set with regard to the protection of the interests of all project-affected persons (PAPs) when the Jamuna Bridge was constructed. These are now being implemented on the Bhairab Bridge. These practices, together with lessons learned from their application, could be extended to all people affected by barrage construction. Great attention will need to be paid to environmental issues, and some of these will undoubtedly lead to differences of technical opinion. In annual terms, the volume of water abstracted would be only a small proportion of the volume entering the Bay of Bengal, but the seasonal distribution may well be important.

All barrages affect fisheries, but in this case the minimum through-flow of 1800m should be enough to allow major passageways for fish. The impact of increased salinity in the Lower Meghna will be the subject of much debate. One of the biggest uncertainties will be the prediction of morphological changes, as this is an area where science is least developed.

Project operation — adapting to changing contexts

The major advantage of the proposal is its flexibility. The several contexts — political relations, social development and urbanization, economic relations, global warming — in which the complex would be set are likely to change and evolve quite rapidly over the next 50 years. One of the tests against which this proposal needs to be evaluated against is how flexibly it could be operated under a variety of changed circumstances.

The indications are that it would do well, offering the opportunity to redistribute flows among the different potential demands. Both the perception and reality of water demand in the Ganges—Brahmaputra—Meghna delta have changed radically since India and Pakistan became independent in

1947. With over 200 million people, the delta has experienced more than doubling of water demand in the period.

Despite the huge increase in the development and use of groundwater, southwestern Bangladesh and southern West Bengal have experienced increasing water shortages. The predicted increase in demand in the upper catchment of the Ganges as well as in the GBM delta puts the sustainability of the current Ganges Waters Treaty in serious doubt, and makes urgent the search for further appropriate development of water resources. The proposal set out here for bringing into use water from the Brahmaputra which currently flows out to sea is speculative.

The review above sets the context, and some of the issues, which will be associated with any engineering solution to augment dry season flows in the region. Any such solution will be seen by some as sacrificing more narrowly defined self-interest, and hence meet objections. Such objections are unlikely to be set out overtly, however, but couched in the current rhetoric of sustainable development, a language that is learned as fast by people in the government departments of developing countries as it is within the aid institutions. The proposed scheme is not the only possible form of adaptation to diminishing water supplies.

Dawkins' powerful concept of adaptive evolution is at work at present in the dynamic water balance of the delta. For over two decades, the two countries have adapted to the declining regime of water supply at Farakka, and they may well continue to adapt. Economic life in Southwest Bangladesh has adapted, with brackish-water shrimp production has become a major industry and export earner. The poor, and the environment, have suffered enormously, but they are seldom seen as beneficiaries of major water resource development projects.

The rural poor will continue to migrate to the cities, and the environment to deteriorate, and there is little political imperative to change this. The key to the proposal put forward above lies in realizing the potential for cooperation without which the scheme is unviable. Without cooperation, the waters of the Brahmaputra are unlikely to be used. Bangladesh is unlikely to get funding for the Ganges barrage, as the proven needs of the region it serves are too low to attract investment. Equally, India is unlikely to be able to find a way of transferring water from Assam to West Bengal as the technical problems are too great and the social upheaval unacceptable to Bangladesh. Only by cooperating and using the natural watercourses of the two great rivers can a solution be found.

6

India and Pakistan Water Disputes: The Indus Water Dispute

The water wars rationale forecasts war between countries dependent upon a shared water resource if there is water scarcity, competitive use and the countries are enemies due to a wider conflict. Following this rationale, a war should have occurred between India and Pakistan over the Indus basin waters. Instead, the countries negotiated an international water treaty and have maintained it for over 40 years through two wars and the nuclear era. In trying to explain India and Pakistan's successful cooperation over water, as recommended by Biswas, the author has had unique access to the Indus basin files in the World Bank's archives. The Indus Waters Treaty is a water-sharing treaty between the Republic of India and Islamic Republic Of Pakistan, brokered by the World Bank (then the International Bank for Reconstruction and Development).

The treaty was signed in Karachi on September 19, 1960 by Indian Prime Minister Jawaharlal Nehru and President of Pakistan Mohammad Ayub Khan. The treaty was a result of Pakistani fear that since the source rivers of the Indus basin were in India, it could potentially create droughts and famines in Pakistan, especially at times of war. However, India did not revoke the treaty during any of three later Indo-Pakistani Wars. The Indus System of

Rivers comprises three Western Rivers the Indus, the Jhelum and Chenab and three Eastern Rivers - the Sutlej, the Beas and the Ravi; and with minor exceptions, the treaty gives India exclusive use of all of the waters of the Rivers and their tributaries before the point where the rivers enter Pakistan.

Similarly, Pakistan has exclusive use of the Western three Rivers. Pakistan also received one-time financial compensation for the loss of water from the Eastern Rivers. The countries agree to exchange data and co-operate in matters related to the treaty. For this purpose, treaty creates the Permanent Indus Commission, with a commissioner appointed by each country. The waters of the Indus basin begin in the Himalayan mountains in the state of Jammu and Kashmir. They flow from the hills through the arid states of Punjab and Sindh, converging in Pakistan and emptying into the Arabian Sea south of Karachi.

Where once there was only a narrow strip of irrigated land along these rivers, developments over the last century have created a large network of canals and storage facilities that provide water for more than 26 million acres - the largest irrigated area of any one river system in the world. The partition of British India created a conflict over the plentiful waters of the Indus basin. The newly formed states were at odds over how to share and manage what was essentially a cohesive and unitary network of irrigation.

Furthermore, the geography of partition was such that the Source Rivers of the Indus basin were in India. Pakistan felt its livelihood threatened by the prospect of Indian control over the tributaries that fed water into the Pakistani portion of the basin. Where India certainly had its own ambitions for the profitable development of the basin, Pakistan felt acutely threatened by a conflict over the main source of water for its cultivable land. During the first years of partition the waters of the Indus were apportioned by the Inter-Dominion Accord of May 4, 1948. This accord required India to release sufficient waters to the Pakistani regions of the basin in return for annual payments from the government of Pakistan.

The accord was meant to meet immediate requirements and was followed by negotiations for a more permanent solution. Neither side, however, was willing to compromise their respective positions nor negotiations reached a stalemate. From the Indian point of view, there was nothing that Pakistan could do to prevent India from any of the schemes to divert the flow of water in the rivers. Pakistan's position was dismal and India could do whatever it wanted. Pakistan wanted to take the matter to the International Court of Justice but India refused, arguing that the conflict required a bilateral resolution.

By 1951, the two sides were no longer meeting and the situation seemed intractable. The Pakistani press was calling for more drastic action and the deadlock contributed to hostility with India. As one anonymous Indian official said at the time, "India and Pakistan can go on shouting on Kashmir for all time to come, but an early settlement on the Indus waters is essential for maintenance of peace in the sub-continent". Despite the unwillingness to compromise, both nations were anxious to find a solution, fully aware that the Indus conflict could lead to overt hostilities if unresolved.

In this same year, David Lilienthal, formerly the chairman of the Tennessee Valley Authority and of the U.S. Atomic Energy Commission, visited the region to write a series of articles for Colliers magazine. Lilienthal had a keen interest in the subcontinent and was welcomed by the highest levels of both Indian and Pakistani governments. Although his visit was sponsored by Colliers, Lilienthal was briefed by State Department and executive branch officials, who hoped he could help bridge the gap between India and the United States and also gauge hostilities on the subcontinent.

During the course of his visit, it became clear to Lilienthal that tensions between India and Pakistan were acute, but also unable to be erased with one sweeping gesture. In his journal he wrote:

"India and Pakistan were on the verge of war over Kashmir. There seemed to be no possibility of negotiating this issue until tensions abated. One way to reduce hostility . . . would be to concentrate on other important issues where cooperation was possible. Progress in these areas would promote a sense of community between the two nations which might, in time, lead to a Kashmir settlement. Accordingly, I proposed that India and Pakistan work out a program jointly to develop and jointly to operate the Indus Basin river system, upon which both nations were dependent for irrigation water. With new dams and irrigation canals, the Indus and its tributaries could be made to yield the additional water each country needed for increased food production. In the article I had suggested that the World Bank might use its good offices to bring the parties to agreement, and help in the financing of an Indus Development program."

Lilienthal's idea was well received by officials at the World Bank, and, subsequently, by the Indian and Pakistani governments. Eugene R. Black, then president of the World Bank told Lilienthal that his proposal "makes good sense all round". Black wrote that the Bank was interested in the economic progress of the two countries and had been concerned that the Indus dispute could only be a serious handicap to this development. India's previous objections to third party arbitration were remedied by the Bank's insistence that it would not adjudicate the conflict, but, instead, work as a conduit for agreement.

Black also made a distinction between the "functional" and "political" aspects of the Indus dispute. In his correspondence with Indian and Pakistan leaders, Black asserted that the Indus dispute could most realistically be solved if the functional aspects of disagreement were negotiated apart from political considerations. He envisioned a group that tackled the question of how best to utilize the waters of the Indus Basin - leaving aside questions of historic rights or allocations. Black proposed a Working Party made up of Indian, Pakistani and World Bank engineers. The World Bank delegation would act as a consultative group, charged with offering suggestions and speeding dialogue.

In his opening statement to the Working Party, Black spoke of why he was optimistic about the group's success:

One aspect of Mr. Lilienthal's proposal appealed to me from the first. I mean his insistence that the Indus problem is an engineering problem and should be dealt with by engineers. One of the strengths of the engineering profession is that, all over the world, engineers speak the same language and approach problems with common standards of judgment. Black's hopes for a quick resolution to the Indus dispute were premature. While the Bank had expected that the two sides would come to an agreement on the allocation of waters, neither India nor Pakistan seemed willing to compromise their positions.

While Pakistan insisted on its historical right to waters of all the Indus tributaries, and that half of West Punjab was under threat of desertification the Indian side argued that the previous distribution of waters should not set future allocation. Instead, the Indian side set up a new basis of distribution, with the waters of the Western tributaries going to Pakistan and the Eastern tributaries to India. The substantive technical discussions that Black had hoped for were stymied by the political considerations he had expected to avoid.

The World Bank soon became frustrated with this lack of progress. What had originally been envisioned as a technical dispute that would quickly untangle itself became an intractable mess. India and Pakistan were unable to agree on the technical aspects of allocation, let alone the implementation of any agreed upon distribution of waters. Finally, in 1954, after nearly two years of negotiation, the

World Bank offered its own proposal, stepping beyond the limited role it had apportioned for itself and forcing the two sides to consider concrete plans for the future of the basin. The proposal offered India the three eastern tributaries of the basin and Pakistan the three western tributaries.

Canals and storage dams were to be constructed to divert waters from the western rivers and replace the eastern river supply lost by Pakistan. While the Indian side was amenable to the World Bank proposal, Pakistan found it unacceptable. The World Bank allocated the eastern rivers to India and the western rivers to Pakistan. This new distribution did not account for the historical usage of the Indus basin, or the fact that West Punjab's Eastern districts could turn into dessert, and repudiated Pakistan's negotiating position.

Where India had stood for a new system of allocation, Pakistan felt that its share of waters should be based on pre-partition distribution. The World Bank proposal was more in line with the Indian plan and this angered the Pakistani delegation. They threatened to withdraw from the Working Party and negotiations verged on collapse. But neither side could afford the dissolution of talks. The Pakistani press met rumors of and ends to negotiation with talk of increased hostilities; the government was ill-prepared to forgo talks for a violent conflict with India and was forced to reconsider its position.

India was also eager to settle the Indus issue; large development projects were put on hold by negotiations and Indian leaders were eager to divert water for irrigation. In December of 1954, the two sides returned to the negotiating table. The World Bank proposal was transformed from a basis of settlement to a basis for negotiation and the talks continued, stop and go, for the next six years. One of the last stumbling blocks to an agreement concerned financing for the construction of canals and storage facilities that would transfer water from the eastern Indian rivers to Pakistan.

This transfer was necessary to make up for the water Pakistan was giving up by ceding its rights to the eastern tributaries. The World Bank initially planned for India to pay for these works, but India refused. The Bank responded with a plan for external financing supplied mainly by the United States and the United Kingdom. This solution cleared the remaining stumbling blocks to agreement and the Treaty was signed by the Prime Ministers of both countries in 1960. The agreement also set up a commission to adjudicate any future disputes arising over the allocation of waters.

The Permanent Indus Commission has survived two wars and provides an on-going machinery for consultation and conflict resolution through inspection, exchange of data, and visits. The Commission is required to meet regularly to discuss potential disputes as well as cooperative arrangements for the development of the basin. Either party must notify the other of plans to construct any engineering works which would affect the other party and to provide data about such works. In cases of disagreement, a neutral expert is called in for mediation and arbitration.

While neither side has initiated projects that could cause the kind of conflict that the Commission was created to resolve, the annual inspections and exchange of data continue, unperturbed by tensions on the subcontinent. The Indus Waters Treaty is the longest agreement that has been faithfully implemented and upheld by both India and Pakistan. There have, however, been concerns that disputes over water supplies could become a problem in the future due to the fragile nature of Indo-Pakistani relations and India's commencement of a number of ambitious water projects.

Objections

According to Kashmiri Separatists, Indus water treaty has deprived J & K state to use its own water resources and became one of the reasons for the alienation of people and has severely affected the economic development in the state. The state incurs losses estimated at Rs 6500 crore annually by the dint of Indus Water Treaty. There are losses in agricultural sector as well as in the generation of hydro-electric power which has otherwise an estimated potential of 20,000 MW. India is planning to construct Swal Kot Dam on river Chenab near the district Doda and Udham Pur which is just 70 miles away from Pakistan. Swal Kot Dam is expected to be higher than Tarbela Dam and Mangla Dam.

The height of the Swal Kot Dam is 646 feet and the storage capacity of Swal Kot Dam is expected to be 13 times higher than the disputed Baglihar Dam. In comparison, the height of Tarbela is 485 feet while Mangla is 453 feet high. The project would cost $2 billion dollars and would produce 1200 MW of electricity. While Pakistan objected that it would dry up the river Chenab, which was given to Pakistan and to which it has all the rights.

The water wars rationale

Drawing heavily on the situation in the Middle East, the water wars rationale reasons that given water's critical role in a country's survival if there is water scarcity amidst a wider conflict, and enemy states depend on same shared resources, each country will try to ensure that it has the access to water that it needs. Controlling access to water is vital for national security and, therefore, highly political.

Under a wider conflict, the spectre of an enemy controlling another country's water supply is untenable. This means that each country might wage war to safeguard its supply. In other words, because water is scarce, vital, a security issue and demand is outstripping supply, states will go to war with their competitors to secure supplies. This implies that "'[w]ater [w]ars" are, unfortunately, likely to be of more and more common occurrence in the future'.

Water wars are understood to be international wars between states triggered and sustained solely over issues arising from access to water. This is to distinguish them from water-related conflicts within countries, and water used as a weapon. The concept derives from the Middle East's increasing demand for water due to urbanization, industrialization, increasing populations, consumerism and irrigated agriculture, and the political nature of water use in the region.

Expecting a water war in the Indus Basin

Following the water wars rationale, India and Pakistan should have gone to war over the Indus waters. All the ingredients were present — two enemies engaged in a wider conflict; a riparian completely dependent upon the Indus waters; water scarcity despite large average runoffs; and poverty preventing the construction of infrastructure to offset this scarcity. The enmity between India and Pakistan has its roots in the movement to gain independence from Great Britain. The principal fault line ran along religious lines and placed Hindus against Muslims.

The process by which the British partitioned the Indian sub-continent in 1947 into independent India and Pakistan helped to fuel this animosity. In particular, the issue of Kashmir has persistently aggravated Indo-Pakistan relations. Partition led to a number of disputes between the countries, for example, over refugee property and currency exchange rates. Over the latter issue, Pakistan even spoke of an economic war fuelled by the belief that 'there is a large element in India that does not accept the partition of India, that is still talking and planning to undo what they insist was a mistake'.

Another source of Indo-Pakistan tensions was the Indus waters dispute. Critical to understanding the water dispute's origins is the role of irrigated agriculture in the basin. With a semi-arid climate, agriculture in the Indus basin is heavily dependent upon irrigation. This is reinforced by the large seasonal and annual variability in water availability which is masked by large average annual runoff, 150-200 [km]. For example, the Indus River measured at Kalabagh can change from 70 [km] during the summer to 12 [km] during the winter.

With irrigation important to an agrarian economy in the basin, irrigation was extended under the British in the provinces of Punjab and Sindh. The most cost-effective developments were along the Sutlej and Indus rivers, and therefore, each province concentrated its irrigation canals and supporting infrastructure on those rivers. In Punjab this meant that the works were primarily in the west of the province using the Sutlej River.

Partition in 1947 divided the province of Punjab between India (East Punjab) and Pakistan (West Punjab) and the province's irrigation infrastructure, with headworks (structures controlling water flow) in upstream India, and the dependent canals in downstream Pakistan. Pakistan's geography makes it completely dependent upon the Indus basin for its agricultural and municipal uses. Unlike India, which has a number of river systems including the Ganges-Jumna system in the north, or the Cauvery River in the south, Pakistan only has the waters from the Indus basin. Moreover, Pakistan's agricultural products which are its primary economic income are heavily dependent upon irrigated agriculture in, firstly, the Punjab and secondly, Sindh.

As Iliff pointed out, 'if Pakistan was deprived of her canal water from the Indus system, the whole of West Pakistan would really become a desert' (1961). Partition left Pakistan heavily dependent upon canals that were controlled by India. Initially, temporary agreements were signed by East and West Punjab to ensure continued water supply to Pakistan's canals after partition. However, the agreements expired on 31 March 1948, and on 1 April 1948, East Punjab stopped the water flowing across the international border. For Pakistan the timing could not have been worse. Farmers in the Punjab plant two crops per year.

The water shortage threatened both the winter crop that was about to be harvested, and the summer crop which would be sown immediately afterwards. Without water, both seasons' crops would be lost. In addition, the sectarian violence in India and Pakistan that surrounded the transition to independence had led to a social and economic upheaval. The displacement of people escaping this violence also disrupted food production in the Punjab (the bread basket of British India) just as there were millions of refugees to feed. As Wescoat et al. Describe, [v]iolence disrupted cultivation and destroyed local irrigation channels and wells. Waterborne disease out-breaks occurred in metropolitan areas that swelled with millions of refugees.

The water stoppage woke Pakistan's leadership up to the country's dependence upon the Sutlej River and India's control over this supply. The headwaters of all these rivers were in India, or in territory not subject to Pakistan, and the consequences of possible aggressive intentions on India's part soon loomed large before Pakistan.

The Prime Minister of Pakistan, Liaquat Ali Khan, proposed an inter-dominion conference to settle the dispute, and asked for the 'immediate restoration of the water supply'. The Prime Minister of India, Jawaharlal Nehru, had to intervene personally to have the Provincial Government of East Punjab restore water to West Punjab's canals. In early May, India and Pakistan met in New Delhi to discuss the dispute.

The Inter-Dominion (Delhi) Agreement was signed on 4 May 1948, documenting the countries' agreement that each had needs to be met from the Sutlej River, and to continue bilateral talks. Over the next three years, as the wider conflict raised tensions and positions became more entrenched, bilateral attempts to resolve the Sultej River dispute failed, including Pakistan's proposal to submit the dispute to the International Court of Justice (ICJ) which India refused. The Sutlej River dispute was heightened by differing interpretations of the Delhi Agreement and the resultant water use allowed to India and Pakistan.

Hirsch suggests India's refusal to submit the case to the ICJ stemmed from a 'feeling that a purely legal evaluation of the situation would favor Pakistan'. Pakistan believed that India was unwilling to 'test its unilateral interpretation' of the Delhi Agreement which it saw as allowing it to diminish water to Pakistan. The enormity of the situation struck observers as potentially catastrophic — a powder keg waiting to explode. American diplomats stationed in Pakistan and India stressed the importance of a final and bindin8 settlement of water rights. In their view the control of Indus waters by India threatened to return the entire Punjab to a desert.

Seeing cooperation instead despite indications to the contrary, India and Pakistan were to cooperate over the Sutlej River dispute, and eventually, sign an international water treaty in 1960. Critical to the dispute's resolution was the intervention of the World Bank. In the period following the 1948 Delhi Agreement, while inter-dominion talks continued on the Sutlej River dispute, India and Pakistan were also developing their water resources. Both countries had applied to the World Bank for development loans. Despite the apparent economic viability of these projects, the Bank had to refuse the loans as the projects planned to use the disputed Sutlej River (IBRD 13/4/49 2/6/49 3/6/49 28/9/49 9/1/50 11/1/50 2/3/50 22/6/50 31/1/51).

As tensions continued to rise, and India and Pakistan's competitive development of the Sutlej River threatened to not only obstruct socioeconomic development but also become a potential flashpoint, the World Bank offered its 'good offices' in September 1951. Contrary to expectations, both India and Pakistan accepted the offer. Pakistan pointed out that the Bank's proposal would 'seriously compromise the Pakistan position if the talks failed'. The Bank's offer was based upon three principles.

First, that the Indus basin had enough water for both countries. Secondly, that in resolving the Sutlej River dispute, the basin would be treated as a single unit implying all the rivers were to be discussed. Finally, that the negotiations would put aside past grievances and retain a technical rather than a political focus. The Indus Mediations started in May 1952 at the Bank's headquarters in Washington DC. In October 1953, after field trips for data collection, the Indian and Pakistani delegations submitted their plans for the comprehensive development of the Indus basin. To address the gap between these plans, the World Bank presented its own plan in February 1954.

The Bank's 1954 plan proposed to divide the Indus basin. India would receive the three eastern rivers (the Sutlej, Beas and Ravi) or approximately 20% of the Indus waters, and Pakistan would receive the three western rivers (the Chenab, Jhelum and the Indus) and approximately 80% of the total surface waters. The infrastructure needed to divide the basin would be paid for by the party benefiting under the beneficiary pays principle. Pakistan felt the 1 954 Plan left it insufficient water to meet its needs. Since Pakistan could not afford, politically, to give away water nor did it have the finances to build storage facilities unilaterally, it refused the 1954 Plan. A combination of geography, financial concerns deriving from the potential loss of the eastern rivers, and political instability made Pakistan extremely cautious in its negotiations.

Pakistan succeeded in persuading the World Bank that it needed storage facilities to meet its needs, and having the 1954 Plan amended with the 1 956 Aide-Memoire which envisaged storage facilities on the western rivers for Pakistan. Whereas India had accepted the 1954 Plan, it objected to the Aide-Memoire because it was concerned about incurring additional financial obligations to Pakistan. Further negotiations separated discussions on the technical need for infrastructure from their funding. Parallel to the main negotiations were discussions to have ad hoc agreements under which India would supply water to Pakistan for six or 12 months. Successions of agreements were signed, each of which were negotiated separately, starting on 1 April 1955 and lasting until 31 March 1960.

The only period for which India and Pakistan were unable to agree on an ad hoc agreement was 1 October 1957-30 September 1958. Following a coup d'etat in October 1958, the Government of Pakistan unconditionally accepted the 1954 Plan (the division of the basin) and the 1956 Aide-Memoire (storage facilities on the western rivers) in December 1958. Though India had already accepted these documents, it took two years to draft the treaty.

The Indus Waters Treaty was signed on 19 September 1960 by India, Pakistan and the World Bank (World Bank 1960), and ratified by the countries in January 1961. India received the three eastern rivers (the Sutlej, Beas and Ravi) or 20% of the basin's waters, and Pakistan received the remaining 80% or the three western rivers (the Chenab, Jhelum and Indus).

The characteristics of Indus Basin Cooperation

Amidst the broader conflict that saw intermittent clashes along the Line of Control within Kashmir, strong rhetoric on both sides, alliance forming amongst the international community, such as Pakistan's joining of the SEATO Pact in 1954 and the Baghdad (later CENTO) Pact in 1955, India's closer relations with China, the two countries were cooperating specifically over water. Yet, the Indus Waters Treaty is seen by some as sub-optimal due to the division of the basin.

The agreement is at best a compromise and India should have had a better consideration specially in respect of Chenab valley, where a large amount of power potential exists but cannot be developed fully due to restriction on storages.

Others also recognize that, given Indo-Pakistan relations, the Treaty and the basin's division was the most feasible politically. Resolving the Sutlej River dispute was seen by outside observers as a way of lessening Indo-Pakistan tensions to the point of resolving the issue of Kashmir. In 1951, the US Assistant Secretary of State, George McGhee, pointed out, a settlement of the canal waters question would signify those basic reversals of policy by the Governments of both India and Pakistan without which there can be no political rapprochement. Thus, the canal waters question is not only a functional problem, but also a political one linked to the Kashmir dispute.

In 1956, the Bank was advised that the British Prime Minister, Anthony Eden, had spoken at length with the Indian

Prime Minister on Kashmir, but to no avail. Eden thereupon had had the bright idea that if the canal waters situation could be pushed fairly quickly in the right direction it might take some of the heat off the Kashmir issue.

However, the Prime Minister of India had explained from the outset the specific nature of the Bank's intervention: I might make one point clear. The Canal Waters dispute between India and Pakistan has nothing to do with the Kashmir issue; it started with and has been confined to the irrigation systems of East and West Punjab.

The Pakistani Prime Minister, Liaquat Ali Khan, concurred, stating that the parties should 'refrain from using the negotiations in one dispute to delay progress in solving any other' (IBRD 25/9/51a). Moreover, the cooperation appeared to be reluctant, with suspicions remaining on both sides despite the Bank's efforts to build trust. The delegations remained sensitive to the merest rumour of not receiving information equally, as expressed by one delegate who 'wanted to know if there were any secrets that he hadn't heard about'. Caveats were also used in agreements to limit the consequences on each country. For example,

[t]he acceptance by either Government of the above Heads of Agreement, or any one of them, as a basis for an approach to an international water treaty, shall not, in the event of failure to conclude such a treaty, be invoked by the other Government in support of any of its legal rights of claims.

The parallel ad hoc agreement negotiations fared no better. For example, at a joint meeting in May 1955, '[a]fter much bickering', India and Pakistan agreed that there was 'no difference' between their data, only in the principles upon which these figures were based. On another occasion, the Bank representative was forced, 'almost in exasperation', to remind India and Pakistan that it was absurd to spend so much valuable time over a few hundred cusecs when there are thousands in the Indus basin to agree upon.

Using strong language by the standards of international diplomacy, the Bank representative said, 'that he was completely out of sympathy with both India and Pakistan in their attitude over this whole issue', and added that 'considerably more reasonableness will have to be shown if any progress is to be made'. As late as March 1960, India and Pakistan had to be reminded that the negotiations' purpose was 'to find a solution acceptable to both India and Pakistan'. But mistrust continued. Pakistan had agreed to Indian withdrawals from the western rivers for use in Indian-controlled Kashmir but demanded an inspection system to ensure India did not withdraw more water than it was entitled to. India refused:

certainly not. We've put our name to a treaty, you got to accept that we are going to carry out that treaty, and we're not going to have any action of the Government of India policed by Pakistan.

Each side proposed plans they regarded as the only solution to the dispute:

strong value differences mean that parties are reluctant to give away too much for fear of offering a fatal compromise, or of being accused by their constituencies of "selling out" their water rights. Lamb and Taylor (1990)

For example, the 'Indian Plan' was 'in the Indian view the only practicable Plan for a solution of this dispute' (IBRD 9/12/58, emphasis in original). However, in Pakistan's view the Indian Plan was unacceptable because it was politically undesirable and [t]here are important major issues like the control of the Chenab by India, Pakistan's dependence on India for deliveries etc. which are not acceptable to Pakistan under any circumstances.

Negotiations were not just held between India and Pakistan, but also internally within Pakistan's delegation. The provinces of Punjab and Sindh continued to compete for water, and each needed to ensure that any agreement with India accounted for its needs. Therefore, each province had strong representation within the Pakistan delegation. In particular, Sindh was concerned that its planned uses on the Indus River would be lost to replacement works that would mainly benefit Punjab, and therefore pushed for development works to be included in the negotiations with India.

At times these provincial differences hampered progress in the negotiations with India. Internal negotiation within the Bank was also needed as senior management began to question its involvement in the negotiations, given the slow pace, India and Pakistan's wavering commitment to finding a resolution and the costs involved (approximately US$1 million at 1950s prices).

Explaining Indo-Pakistan cooperation over water

Given the water wars rationale and its expectation of enemies such as India and Pakistan who depend upon a shared water resource to go to war to safeguard their supply, how can India and Pakistan's specific cooperation over water be explained? How can their decision to not only negotiate for a comprehensive agreement for the Indus basin, but to repeatedly negotiate the ad hoc agreements be explained? Why did they sign an agreement over a resource that affects their national security, ratify and implement it over a decade and maintain their obligations under the Treaty despite two wars in 1965 and 1971?

The most common explanation for India and Pakistan's specific cooperation over the Indus waters is the financial support they received: over US$1000 million (in 1960 rates) through the Indus Basin Development Fund (IBDF). Afroz (1983) even attributes the Indus Waters Treaty to the USA, as it was the largest donor to the IBDF. Undoubtedly, the availability of finances played an important role in concluding the negotiations once agreement was reached by India and Pakistan, especially since the agreement was to divide the waters of the Indus basin. To implement this agreement, Pakistan would need extensive infrastructure such as storage facilities and link canals to replace the loss of the eastern rivers to India. However, as the downstream riparian, Pakistan had clearly stated its position to the Bank:

India has other systems from which water would be available. Pakistan has not. Money for water is no proposition — not a question of sentiment or principle.

There are also a series of questions that remain unanswered by the financial explanation. The Bank had promised in 1951 to 'consider any financing proposals that might develop as a result of joint planning' and make available any technical help needed to get a settlement. So why did India and Pakistan take nine years to reach agreement on a comprehensive plan, if all that was needed for agreement was the financing of an implementation plan? Financing was only available for the comprehensive plan and not for the ad hoc agreement negotiations; therefore, why did India and Pakistan hold repeated negotiations for these interim agreements?

Why did the negotiations come close to breaking down in 1954? Commentators, including a member of Pakistan's delegation, placed the October 1958 coup d'etat in Pakistan at the centre of getting the government's agreement, which in turn led to the drafting of the treaty. If this is the case, how does the financial explanation address the coup's role? An alternative explanation for India and Pakistan's specific cooperation over water is because it was 'water rational'. Water rationality. Water rationality is any action taken by a state to secure its water supply in the long-term, both in quantity and quality. This implies that, nationally, a state manages its water prudently, and internationally, it maintains relationships with its co riparian countries that are conducive to ensuring long-term access to the shared water.

Both countries needed water urgently to maintain existing works, and tap the irrigation potential in the Indus basin to develop socio-economically. Pakistan felt that India's upstream developments on the Sutlej River would damage its existing uses, and therefore threaten its very livelihood. India, in turn, planned to develop its irrigation potential to offset poverty in the country. By signing the Indus Waters Treaty, both countries were able to safeguard their long-term water supplies from the Indus basin.

As a Bank official reported, [i]n the course of my conversations with the Government of India and the Government of Pakistan during my visit to the Sub-Continent, I have been repeatedly assured of the desire of both Governments to reach an agreed solution of the Indus Waters question.

It would appear that Indo-Pakistan cooperation occurred because water is scarce, vital, expensive, a security issue, demand is outstripping supply and a war would not guarantee future resources — neither water nor international finance — to build the infrastructure needed to use the water.

[T]he more valuable lesson of international water is as a resource whose characteristics tend to induce cooperation, and incite violence only in the exception.

Questioning the water wars rationale Following on from the water wars rationale as voiced by World Bank Vice-President Ismail Serageldin in 1995, '[t]he wars of the next century will be over water', India and Pakistan's cooperation over the Indus waters seems to be an anomaly. But there is growing evidence that such international cooperation over shared waters is, in fact, the 'norm', and that water wars may be the exception. This is not to suggest a utopia of unhindered cooperation. The dispute and its surrounding interests remain real, but the preferred resolution process becomes one of cooperation rather than war.

The water wars rationale comprises three principal building blocks — water scarcity, a wider conflict and bellicose public statements. The first two blocks — water scarcity and a wider conflict — have been questioned already. The last block — bellicose public statements by key decisionmakers — is examined here. Amongst the most commonly cited as evidence of forthcoming water wars in the Middle East are:

(a)   The only matter that could take Egypt to war again is water. President Anwar Sadat of Egypt

(b)   The next war in the Middle East will be fought over water, not politics. Butros Butros-Ghali, while

Egyptian Minister of State for Foreign Affairs

Neither Syria nor Iraq can lay claim to Turkey's rivers, any more than Ankara could claim their oil ... We have a right to do anything we like. The water resources are Turkey's, the oil resources are theirs. We don't say we share the oil resources, and they cannot say they share our water resources. President Suleyman Demirel of Turkey

Politicians from India and Pakistan also made bellicose statements in public, as negotiations continued between their countries over the Indus basin. If the public statements were to be believed, a war was imminent between the two countries. However, information held in the World Bank's Indus basin files questions how representative the political rhetoric was compared to the actions of the governments, and highlights the Bank's view that such statements could destabilize actual cooperation. For example, in July 1957, while the negotiations were continuing, the Pakistani Prime Minister, Hussain Suhrawardy (October 1956-October 1957), commented in public on the threat posed by India's development of the Indus waters:

There are, as you know, six rivers. Most of them rise in Kashmir. One of the reasons why, therefore, that Kashmir is so important for us, is this water, these waters which irrigate our lands. They do not irrigate Indian lands. Now, what India has done — it is not threatening — it has actually, it is building a dam today, and it is threatening to cut off the waters of the three rivers for the purpose of irrigating some of its lands. Now, if it does so without replacement, it is obvious that we shall be starved out and people will die of thirst.

Under these circumstances I hope that contingency will never arise — you can well realise that rather than die in that manner, people will die fighting. Because that will be the very Worst form of aggression. But I think before any such situation can arise, those countries of the worlds that undertake and have undertaken to insure that peace exists and that matters between countries of our type are adjusted, will step in to see that India does not perform any such barbarous action.

The Indian government protested to the Bank 'against the general tenor' of Prime Minister Suhrawardy's remarks, and also pointed out that there was total omission of any reference to the fact that discussions are still proceeding between India and Pakistan, with the good offices of the Bank, designed to work out an agreed solution of the question and that meanwhile India has not increased her withdrawals from the Eastern Rivers beyond Pakistan's replacement capacity.

'The Indian Ambassador felt that when the transcript was read in Delhi, there was bound to be a sharp reaction from the Government of India'. Though the Bank refused to issue a public statement, it was felt these remarks can only add to the difficulties facing the Bank in bringing about an agreement and that public statements of this nature, apart from any other considerations, might well lead to a situation where the Bank might find it impossible to continue to use its good offices.

In another instance, in a meeting between the Bank and Pakistan, the Bank official noted that:

the Prime Minister made an opening statement summarizing in somewhat less intemperate form his views about the Government of India and Mr. Nehru. (This, I suppose, was for political motives and in order to convince his chaps that the interests of Pakistan were safely left in his hands to be cared for) ... Just before the meeting broke up, I asked the Prime Minister if he would be good enough to warn all his people who were present about the necessity for extreme reticence about the matters which had been discussed in the course of these conversations, as there already had been serious embarrassment caused to the Bank in the exercise of its good offices by intemperate and sometimes inaccurate statements that had appeared in the

press and which could obviously only have come
from informed sources. The Prime Minister then
gave quite an emphatic exhortation to those present
at the meeting to refrain from any comment and to
exercise the utmost discretion.

In 1953, the Indian Prime Minister wrote to his Pakistani counterpart protesting at the intensive propaganda being carried on in Pakistan on the canal waters issue accusing India of deliberately following a policy to cause deep injury to Pakistan by withholding canal waters. Charges have been made not only in the public press but also by responsible ministers that we are cutting off canal water supply to Pakistan.

On another occasion the Bank wrote to Pakistan that it was concerned that publication of a 'White Paper' by the Government of Pakistan at this point of time might lead to a counter-publication by the Government of India and hence to a situation in which the merits of the Indus Waters question would become the subject of a battle of propaganda. Such a development could create an atmosphere in which the exercise of the Bank's good offices might be seriously prejudiced and the prospects of an agreed solution given a regrettable set-back.

Therefore, the Bank asked the Pakistani delegation to inform the Government of Pakistan that the Bank would regard it as most unfortunate if any action by either Government should drag the Indus Waters question into the realm of public or press controversy. In October 1957, the Indian Minister of Irrigation and Power commented publicly on whether the President of Pakistan, Iskandar Mirza, had 'threatened to attack India if river waters to Pakistan were stopped by India', and how the Government of India would respond. The minister stated:

According to the reports appearing in the Pakistan Press, the Pakistan President, in a speech delivered on the 7th October, 1957, is reported to have said that any action by India calculated to cut off waters flowing to

Pakistan would be considered as an act of aggression and that Pakistan would meet aggression by aggression. In order to maintain a favourable atmosphere for the negotiations which are now going on between the two countries through the good offices of the World Bank, the Government of India does not propose to take any notice of the speech, at this stage.

In March 1958, the same Indian Minister for Irrigation and Power stated in parliament that India was not prepared to wait for a day longer than 1962 to withdraw water she was now supplying to Pakistan. He stated that this is 'last word so far as Government of India is concerned.' Mr. Patil also implied that proposed action was in accordance with the division proposed by the Bank and that India was prepared to pay for links to be constructed in Pakistan.

Political rhetoric in itself is also seen as a potential destabilizer. Especially since [c]ommunication is extremely delicate. Public pronouncements, especially those aimed at one's constituency and other third parties, tend to obscure rather than clarify intentions.

In Pakistan, for example, the political situation was a fragile balance between different interest groups which put 'conflicting demands and pressures on the central government' all of which produced 'a political climate of confusion and conflict'. Consequently politicians needed to shore up their domestic constituency to remain in power. Though, by the 1958 coup d'etat, Pakistan had had seven prime ministers, and one chief of staff — Ayub Khan who led the 1958 coup, in contrast India had one Prime Minister — Jawaharlal Nehru — and seven chiefs of staff.

Therefore, to create space for the negotiations to occur, the Bank had pressed for confidential negotiations, since it was concerned that any leaks 'might endanger all chances of progress'. Since there had been '[m]any articles press subject water shortages with high level Pakistan charges and Indian denials'. The concern was that publicity would provoke repercussions in India and Pakistan that would have an 'unfavourable' effect on the negotiations such as happened with a broadcast of the Information Service of India: 'The broadcast kept pretty well to the facts but put a very tendentious and highly controversial interpretation on the facts which greatly annoyed the Pakistanis'.

Though the Government of Pakistan refrained from any official comment, the Pakistani press was in uproar, and attacked India bitterly. Therefore, the Bank had stated that, publicity should be avoided at least until an agreement on procedure has been reached by the working party at the initial meeting. Whether any public statement should be made after a working procedure has been decided upon would be a matter for discussion between the two Governments and the Bank.

A neutral location was also needed 'to avoid delegates being subjected to political pressure all the time and to avoid tendentious press propaganda in the subcontinent'. This was reflected by the countries themselves. 'Both sides extremely anxious [to] avoid publicity at this time. Fear local press clamor which might force engineers take intractable positions at conference'. Despite bellicose statements, even at the highest levels, India and Pakistan persisted in negotiating over the Indus basin. This suggests that though statements made by key decisionmakers in public may suggest a move towards war, the statements are used to generate domestic support for a political position.

As seen in the Indus basin, the political rhetoric did not match the governments' actions which sought to resolve an international water dispute through cooperation. In winter 2001-2002, against a backdrop of deteriorating Indo-Pakistan relations, notably the attack on the Indian parliament in December 2001, statements were made in India that it would unilaterally abrogate the Indus Waters Treaty.

Despite considerable discussion within the Indian and Pakistani press, the Permanent Indus Commission, set up as part of the Treaty, met for the 37th time in New Delhi on 29 May 2002 for three days.

This can be seen as a clear indication of the countries commitment to the Treaty despite statements by senior decisionmakers and speculation in the press. The experience from the Indus basin, therefore, throws into question whether public statements made for a domestic audience are truly indicative of a country's intent to go to war over shared waters. The water wars rationale would suggest that India and Pakistan should have gone to war over the Indus basin. Despite water scarcity, competitive use, Pakistan's absolute dependency upon the basin and the wider dispute involving a series of issues including Kashmir, the two countries cooperated instead.

With the good offices of the World Bank, India and Pakistan negotiated the Indus Waters Treaty over a period of nine years, signing it in September 1960. The principal explanation for this Indo-Pakistan cooperation is based upon the finances that the Treaty brought with it in the Indus Basin Development Fund. However, the financial explanation is inadequate, as it does not explain why the countries cooperated over nine years so that there was a treaty to finance.

Nor does it explain the repeated negotiations for the temporary ad hoc agreements that supplied water to Pakistan during the larger negotiations for a comprehensive agreement. An alternative explanation is that India and Pakistan cooperated because it was water rational. In other words, cooperation was needed to safeguard the countries' long-term access to shared water. This suggests that the issues of water scarcity, competitive use and a wider conflict do not necessarily lead to war, since war cannot guarantee a country's water supply in the long term. However, the nature of the Indo-Pakistan cooperation was shaped by the wider tensions between the two countries.

Therefore, it was specifically over water and did not lead to an easing of tensions over other areas of dispute such as Kashmir, and at times the negotiations were tense, with the delegations showing their reluctance to move from their established positions. That India and Pakistan did not wage war over the Indus waters, despite their prime candidacy for a water war, leads to a questioning of the water wars rationale. The rationale is based upon three principal building blocks — water scarcity, a wider conflict and bellicose public statements.

The first two blocks — water scarcity and a wider conflict — have already been brought into question elsewhere. The use of the last building block — bellicose public statements by key decisionmakers — to forecast a war over water is also found wanting. From the Indus basin experience, the disconnection between political rhetoric and action by governments is highlighted. India and Pakistan have during the negotiations in the 1950s, and more recently in 2002, shown their commitment to cooperating over the Indus basin despite public statements made by senior decisionmakers in government.

7

India with China over Water

"Water issues play a crucial role in Central-South Asia, both in the quantity of water available and its quality. Access to clean drinking water is a major, though largely unmet, objective. While much of the region is experiencing water shortages, poor water management lies at the heart of many problems. Climate change — in the form of glacier melt, drought, rising temperatures, and changes to the monsoon cycle — will increasingly exacerbate water scarcity. Even as India and China are yet to resolve their decades-old territorial dispute, another conflict is looming.

China's diversion of the waters of a river originating in Tibet to its water-scarce areas could leave India's northeast parched. This is expected to trigger new tensions in the already difficult relations between the two Asian giants. Prime Minister Manmohan Singh is reported during his recent Beijing visit to have raised the issue of international rivers flowing out of Tibet. Chinese Prime Minister Wen Jiabao has said that water scarcity threatened the very "survival of the Chinese nation". The river in question is the Brahmaputra, which begins in southwestern Tibet where it is known as the Yalong Tsangpo River.

It flows eastwards through southern Tibet for a distance of about 1,600 kilometers and at its easternmost point makes a spectacular U-turn, known as the Shuomatan Point, or the "Great Bend". This is just before the river enters India, where it is joined by two other major rivers; from this point of confluence it is known as the Brahmaputra.

It then snakes into Bangladesh, where it is joined by the Ganges River to create the world's largest delta before emptying into the Bay of Bengal. Given rising tensions across a number of fronts including dominion of the far eastern Arunachal Pradesh state, which China calls Southern Tibet, Delhi is concerned about China's deepening role in Pakistan's hydro projects in particular and infrastructure projects in general.

In 2009, the Chinese government blocked a US$60 million Asian Development Bank loan to India for flood management, water supply and sanitation in the Arunachal Pradesh area. India's foreign ministry has said that China has been informed of New Delhi's apprehensions and has asked Beijing to consider the long term view of Indian-Chinese relations and cease activities in Pakistan Kashmir. China, however, has persisted with its plans, couching its words in diplomatic niceties. The Chinese foreign ministry has been quoted as saying: "The Kashmir issue is a matter left over from history. It should be settled properly through dialogue and consultation between India and Pakistan, and China's position has been consistent."

The Chinese have considerable experience in building dams due to massive developments such as the Three Gorges Project on the Yangtze River. India fears that the involvement of efficient Chinese companies will extend to other spheres such as better roads and connectivity, which could offer a military advantage to Pakistan, such as rapid troop movements. China's presence in the region has become a touchy issue with India, whether it is winning energy blocks in Myanmar, looking at gas in Bangladesh or setting up ports and naval bases in Sri Lanka, Myanmar or Pakistan and buttressing its navy to patrol the waters of the Indian Ocean.

Apart from hydro, Pakistani and Chinese companies have signed many agreements in thermal and renewable energy projects, highways, irrigation and fisheries and mobile networks. China is closely involved with Pakistan's missile and nuclear program as well. Late 2009, India also reacted strongly to reports that the Chinese are building a dam over the Brahmaputra River, or the Tsangpo as it is called in the 1,700 km Chinese stretch. The reports have touted it as the world's largest dam, with 26 turbines.

The Tsangpo Canyon is believed to be the deepest in the world and is about 150 km long before the river enters Arunachal Pradesh and eventually becomes the Brahmaputra. As with the rest of the gigantic water system that serves both countries, the Brahmaputra is the lifeline of the Northeastern states of India, West Bengal and Bangladesh. The Tibetan plateau gives rise to the biggest river system by far in the world. Water from the region flows to 11 different countries via 10 major rivers, bringing fresh water to as much as 50 percent of the world's population.

Though China has denied any such plans as "unnecessary, unfeasible and unscientific," and completely lacking government backing, New Delhi is not taking chances and has said that it would like to verify the claims independently. There was a possibility that Pakistan and India could be more accommodating to each other's requirements, but the suspicions post the November Mumbai terror strikes in 2008 have spoilt any such scenario. In the poisonous atmosphere between India and Pakistan, Kashmir has become a convenient arena for finger pointing and gaining points in the eyes of the western world.

Pakistan has been playing up alleged "human rights violations by security forces" in Indian Kashmir in foreign forums for long to gain the sympathy of America and the military and civilian aid that follows. A bit of the jihadi terror against India has been fuelled by such assertions. India, which has in the past defended its position in Kashmir, including holding of free and fair elections, has opted for a more aggressive posture in the recent past, highlighting the lack of basic development, absence of democratic rights in Pakistan Kashmir and the proliferation of terrorist training hideouts in the region.

The option of hot pursuit or Indian troops taking out terror dugouts in Pakistan Kashmir was hotly debated in the aftermath of the Mumbai attacks. The people of Kashmir, on both sides, meanwhile continue to be caught in the cross fire even as the fear of terror and violence has decimated the once thriving tourism sector in Indian Kashmir. It is at the Great Bend that China plans to divert water, in addition to its hydroelectric power project that is expected to generate 40,000 megawatts of power. The diversion of the waters is part of a larger hydro-engineering project, the South-North water diversion scheme, which involves three man-made rivers carrying water from the icy Tibetan plateau to the arid north.

This water diversion scheme will draw from the waters of the Yalong, Dadu and Jinsha rivers, which rise in the Tibetan plateau, and channel them to the Yellow River. The aim of the project is to provide water for human use, including farming and industry in China's water-scarce areas in the north and northwest. This water diversion project involves three diversion routes - the eastern, central and western routes. The diversion of the Yalong Tsangpo at the Great Bend is the western route of the project - the most technologically challenging and controversial of the three routes. For Beijing, the argument in favor of the water diversion project is simple.

More than a quarter of China is classified as desert. Its north and northwest areas are water scarce. Increasing consumption of water, rapid industrialization and pollution have rendered the waters of many of China's rivers unusable. Besides, sections of the Yellow River run dry. In contrast, rivers that rise in the Tibetan plateau's glaciers have much water.

Once completed, the water diversion scheme is expected to transfer over 40 billion cubic meters of water annually to China's water scarce areas, relieving China's thirst to a significant extent. It is true the Tibetan plateau is a source of much water.

It is Asia's principal watershed and the source of 10 of its major rivers, including the Yalong Tsangpo/Brahmaputra, the Sutlej and the Indus. China, India, Bangladesh, Nepal, Pakistan, Thailand, Myanmar, Laos, Cambodia and Vietnam, indeed 47% of the world's population, are dependent on water rising in the Tibetan plateau. But while rivers with sources in the icy Tibetan plateau are rich in water, critics of the water diversion project say they are not inexhaustible, as Chinese officials claim. The Tibetan plateau is ice-covered but it is an arid desert with very little rainfall. The source of much of its water bodies and rivers is glaciers, which are melting due to global warming.

If, alongside the impact of rising temperatures on glaciers, China diverts water from its natural course, Tibet will be a water-scarce region in a few decades. Critics also point to the environmental and ecological destruction it is likely to cause. The water diversion project at the Great Bend spells disaster not only for the Tibetan plateau but also for the lower riparian countries - India and Bangladesh. These countries view the project with some concern as it represents a direct threat to the lives and livelihoods of millions of people living downstream.

With the Yalong Tsangpo's waters being diverted, the amount of water in the Brahmaputra will fall significantly, affecting India's northeast and Bangladesh. It will severely impact agriculture and fishing there as the salinity of water will increase, as will silting in the downstream area. A shortage of water in the Ganges has already affected the lives and livelihoods of millions in Bangladesh, pushing them to migrate to India, especially to its northeast. This migration of Bangladeshis has changed the demographic composition of vast tracts in the northeast (especially in Assam) and triggered serious ethnic conflicts there.

A shortage of water in the Brahmaputra will accentuate these problems to dangerous levels. There is concern too that with the water diversion project taking off, China will acquire great power and leverage over India, worsening tensions between these two countries. Analysts have drawn attention to incidents in the past to show how vulnerable downstream areas are to what takes place upstream in Tibet. In June 2000, for instance, the breach of a dam in Tibet led to floods and left over 100 people dead or missing in Arunachal Pradesh. In August that year, swollen lakes in Tibet caused severe flooding of the River Sutlej in the northern Indian state of Himachal Pradesh, sweeping away around 100 bridges and killing scores of people.

If floods upstream have a serious impact on downstream areas, the diversion of waters will have "even more devastating consequences", an India-China watcher in India, Claude Arpi, warned. Underscoring the implications of the project, Arpi said that issues of concern "not only pertain to the environment but also to national and international security. If Beijing goes ahead with the Tsangpo project it would practically mean a declaration of war against South Asia." India is watching the water diversion project with concern. It does not have a water sharing treaty with China, so it is at Beijing's mercy with regard to the Brahmaputra's waters.

China's reluctance to pay heed to concerns of lower riparian countries is evident from the fact that it is unwilling to share even hydrological data on flood waters with India; this despite the fact that it is obliged under an agreement with India to do so, with regard to flood waters of the Sutlej. The two countries had also agreed to set up a joint expert-level mechanism on interstate river waters, but it has not showed any enthusiasm about moving forward on that either. It seems that India can only watch helplessly as China steams ahead with its water diversion ambitions.

China's building of the port of Gwadar at the mouth of the Persian Gulf in fact is meant to blockade the oil supplies of the world. Its military diplomacy is on display at the Tibet-India border, where for the last ten years it has strengthened its military infrastructure to intimidate India. In its blockage diplomacy, it is planning to divert the flow of the River Brahmaputra, also called the Tsandpo in Tibet, toward China's northeast, hence in the process starve 100 million people in India.

With a US$2 trillion economy, 1.3 billion souls and a $1,600 per capita GDP, the Chinese consider themselves wealthy. To them India is a poor rival, although India has a US$1 trillion economy, $1,000 per capita GDP and a superior and faster-growing technological sector than China. The Chinese think of India as a minor opponent. Their friendship with Pakistan is a Machiavellian tactic to checkmate India. The scheme to block and divert the River Brahmaputra shows the Chinese do not care about others, only about themselves.

The scheme is foolhardy to begin with. Its environmental impact on Tibet's economy, ecology and culture is of no consequence to them, however. All they need is additional water to flush the rapidly silting Three Gorges Dam and provide water to the parched northeast. The net consequence on India will be a manmade disaster. If 50 percent of the river's water, which flows through the center of India's northeastern state of Assam, is taken out, the river will become a seasonal ditch. One hundred million souls in India and Bangladesh will lose their livelihood. It will surely start a big new dispute between the two rivals and could eventually lead to a shooting war.

The river begins its journey in the glacier country of western Tibet in close proximity to the sources of other mighty rivers — the Indus and Sutlej. Its origin is not far from the Indian border in Tibet, in the holy land of Lake Mansrovar and Mount Kailash. The Tsandpo-Brahmaputra travels west for 1,500 kilometers, hugging the northern slopes of the Himalayas through Tibet. All along its journey it gathers more water and sustains life in Tibet. Because of its remoteness, it has long gone unexplored. The river skirts the last of the Himalayan ranges and turns south into India into Arunachal Pradesh.

It later turns west into the plains of the Indian state of Assam. Multiple smaller rivers join it in Arunachal Pradesh to make it into a huge water resource. At about this place the pre-rainy season flow averages well above 120,000 cubic feet per second, rising to 1million cubic feet per second during the heavy monsoon rains. The Tsandpo begins its long journey at about 13,000 feet and drops to about 5,000 feet in eastern Tibet, before it enters India. Through a series of mysterious falls and gorges, the river manages to drop to about 1,000 feet and then to 500 feet in Assam state.

The water flow before the river enters Arunachal Pradesh is about 60,000 cubic feet per second. It is mostly fresh glacial water. As the river meanders thru Arunachal Pradesh it receives additional water from its tributaries and then in Assam from the discharge of other streams. The 1 million cubic feet per second flow of the Brahmaputra during the rainy season is due to the topography of the land. All the rainfall in the Assam hills is discharged into this river, making it at places 10 kilometers wide.

This area is known for the highest rainfall in the world, leading at times to massive flooding in Assam and Bangladesh. Flooding brings misery, but it is also welcomed as it deposits rich nutrients for better crops the following year. Ever since they occupied Tibet, the Chinese have viewed the Tsandpo-Brahmaputra River as a source of hydroelectric power and a new source of water for the Yangtze River and parched northeast China. Numerous rafting expeditions by the Chinese military were mounted to explore the river, prior to its entry into the deep gorges in India. They were looking for a suitable site to divert the river.

The first hint of this scheme came out in official Chinese newspapers in the 1990s, confirming its intent. A Chinese-inspired paper in Scientific American in June 1996 also confirmed it. The Chinese wished to use the tremendous drop in elevation of about 8,000 feet to generate electricity. According to the Chinese account, 40,000 megawatts could be generated. Just before it enters India, the river would be diverted through a network of canals, tunnels and pipelines to

China's parched mainland. All the electricity generated would be needed to pump the river into the new system. The advantage to the Chinese would be that the parched northwest may become fertile. Any remaining water could join the Yangtze River to inhibit silting in the Three Gorges Dam.

This scheme is twice as big as the Three Gorges Dam. About half the total capital of about US$40 billion will go to power generation and the rest into dams, diversion canals, pipelines and tunnels. The power generation capital is a net waste, as not 1 kilowatt will benefit the Tibetan populace. All of it will be needed to pump the water through the system. The Chinese do not undertake any environmental or socioeconomic studies on large projects, lest they discover any negative impact on the environment and people. That is how they built the Three Gorges Dam, against the advice of environmentalists on locating it in a high seismic region. A major earthquake could knock this dam down or damage it. The floods that would follow could bring death and destruction to 200 million people.

The Tsandpo project could bring similar damage to the ecology and people, as well as possible confrontation with India, making it not worth the effort. But the Chinese do not care. The impact on India and Bangladesh would be tremendous. Assam and part of Bangladesh would lose the capability to grow food. A massive migration toward the rest of India would follow. A wave of 100 million homeless people moving toward India would overwhelm it. India would surely move to prevent this from happening, and a military confrontation could begin.

In this foolhardy scheme the Chinese have counted on their financial and military muscle. They regard India, as stated above, as a poor rival. But with the livelihood of 100 million people impacted, India would muster its own financial, technological and commercial muscle and come out fighting with vigor. This confrontation could be far bigger than the present India-China territorial dispute over the possession of the Tawang tract. In this scenario, India would have many supporters of its cause. In general, the blocking of naturally flowing rivers has not been taken kindly in human history. The world will support India.

China will have a lone supporter in Pakistan. Today's Chinese leadership is obstinate, headstrong and overconfident of its prowess. This confidence will have to be tested, if necessary, militarily. A shooting war may follow an attempt to divert the river. In a war of short duration China would have the advantage of better infrastructure close to the border. In a broader, drawn-out war, China would be at a disadvantage as its Tibet rail and road links could be interdicted and the Tibetan population inflamed to expel the Chinese from their land. It may become a lose-lose situation for China.

Before a shooting war began, India could make its intentions known by a display of its own military prowess in the border region and in the Indian Ocean. India would have international law on its side. U.S. and Russian support would be critical in this situation. The United States could tie down Chinese forces on their eastern seaboard opposite Taiwan, and the Russians along the Ussuri River border. As far as Pakistan is concerned, it would have to be prevented from making mischief along India's western border. U.S. support would be needed to keep Pakistan in check.

8

Kosi Canal Waterway

Nepal says the Kosi flooded because India ignored its suggestion on constructing an upstream barrage on the river at Chatra. Point of contention: A file photo of the Kosi barrage at Bhimnagar which was built by India in 1954. Chatra, in Nepal, is around 50km from Bhimnagar, where India built a barrage in 1954. The Kosi River flows through Nepal. On one side of the river is the East Bihar. The 12 km long Kashua dam serves to retain the water & guide it to flow through river protecting the areas of Bihar from getting inundated.

The asters serve the dam band orthogonally to keep the water flow off the Kashua dam band body. The asters were seen damaging long before but the officers did not take a serious not of those damages & condoned the lacking strength of the dam guides/bunds. The water of the river got access to touch the dam body imparting its water pressure in to the dam consequently; the dam yielded & started disintegrating @ 4 feet per hour. The material to maintain yearly upgradation by strengthening was already brought by the contractor prior to the aster damage but it was not put in place.

There was a dispute between the labour workers & the contractor. The contractor & the engineers intended to pay lesser wages to the workers. The workers refuted the wages & refused to work on those wages. The workers did not agree & the work of strengthening of aster & the dam was delayed for long. The breaking of the dam continued &

2 km long stretch broke. The river water diverted into the East Bihar portions & the 7 districts were gradually under water. Floods have been a consistent feature in Bihar but the floods in 2008 have been the most terrifying and disastrous. The damage in terms of loss of lives, loss of agriculture lands, crops, livelihoods, and animal capital has been unprecedented.

The Kosi River known as Sursar and Sunsari in Nepal has been known as the Sorrow of Bihar. Now with the destruction of Kusaha embankment hundreds of villages and its fertile lands have come under the new path that Kosi has created for itself. The destruction wrought by the floods caused the UPA government to declare the flood as a national tragedy. More than 35 lakh people were displaced. Millions lost their crops worth billions. Landless poor have been reduced to penury. For millions of households, the future is bleak. Adults are forced to migrate to big cities for livelihoods leaving their women and children behind.

A group of individuals and organizations have formed a group called Kosi Andolan for advocating on the course corrections for minimizing the uncertainties of the Kosi River and for eliminating the uncertainties in the lives of people living in the more than 1000 villages that have come under the course of Kosi River. This includes around 800 villages under the new course and around 300 villages under the old tracks. Kosi Andolan seeks to address the root cause of the flood and eliminate suffering in the lives of people living in the villages where people have lost their animal capital, crops, and farmlands and continue to fear floods.

There are millions of stories of suffering, hunger, malnutrition that are being narrated each day as one visits the villages and relief camps. Tragedy unfolds in disparate responses from the villages where relief materials are looted, distribution disrupted and creation of distribution lists disputed. Parents specially belonging to landless families are finding it difficult to feed their children. People living on the embankments in Sursar have not yet found hope for going back to their homes that continue to be wet even after more than one month of floods. Kosi Andolan has traveled to several villages in the flood affected districts of Madhepura, Supaul, Purnia, Katihar, Araria, & Bhagalpur.

It has witnessed the destruction of the farms and lives of the men, women, children, animals and all the lives that came in the way of the water. As late as on 28 September, dead buffalo calves were seen flowing downstream at Sursar. According to an account more than 5000 villagers including children, women and elderly were drown in the river as Kosi River created its course through the sandy layer of the foundation of the embankment that had been place for safety in the Balua village, birth place of the former chief minister Jagannath Mishra. There are thousands who have no home left as that has gone under the Kosi River.

Now the Kosi Andolan has decided to travel from Kusaha[Nepal] to Kursela[Bihar]. The journey will be by boats for recording the evidences of destructions. It has been named "Tabahi ki Gawahi: Naav Yatra Kusaha se Kursela". The Naav Yatra has started on 11th Oct and concludes on 23 October 2008 at Kursela. The team of Kosi Andolan leaders and volunteers will visit the villages, record stories, document evidences and share the vision of Bihar that is floodless while seeking solutions at the grassroots through conducting meetings, discussions with the people and the opinion leaders, panchayat representatives. The key strategies will include observation, discussion with the affected.

As the members of the Core Group include people who have lost crops, there is a deep interest in seeking permanent solution to the problem of floods in Bihar. The strategy include detailed observation, documentation, discussion, deep interviews, analysis of the literature on flood control measures, analysis of international agreements, meetings with the international and national agencies involved in seeking a permanent solution to floods in Bihar and advocating on the solutions with the concerned government. Kosi Andolan believes that India, Nepal and Bangladesh together need to work for solution.

In Janakpur, capital of the Mithilanchal region that now falls in Nepal, people say a girl from the area should never marry a boy from the west (which, in this case, would be Uttar Pradesh in India). The reference of course is to the tribulations faced by Sita, daughter of Janak in the Ramayan, after her marriage to Ram from Ayodhya in Uttar Pradesh. That negative opinion of India, which flares up every now and then in India's relationship with Nepal, surfaced again after the Kosi river broke through its embankments in the last few days, breaching the Bhimnagar barrage located a mere 12km within Nepal, wreaking havoc in parts of Nepal and across the border in Bihar.

The floods created a wave of anti-India feeling in Nepal. And India, for its part, claim the fault is Nepal's. Khom Raj Dahal, deputy director general of Nepal's department of water-induced disaster prevention, told The Kathmandu Post that India must be held squarely responsible for the devastation because it "did not carry out repair and maintenance work on the Kosi barrage and the embankment along the river, thereby violating the 1954 Nepal-India Kosi agreement". The Indian embassy in Nepal issued a statement saying that an Indian technical team had been ready and waiting to help, but was prevented from reaching the site on time by Nepal.

Water wars (or squabbles) are common in South Asia and India is usually portrayed as the villain of the piece. India and Pakistan have been squabbling over New Delhi's decision to build an additional reservoir on the Baglihar dam, which, Pakistan says, violates the 1960 Indus Waters Treaty. India and Bangladesh haven't stopped quarrelling over sharing the Ganga waters, despite their 1996 accord, because the Bangladesh National Party-led governments that succeeded the government that signed the agreement did not share the Sheikh Hasina-led Awami League's enthusiasm for India.

Despite several water-sharing agreements (such as the 1954 Kosi treaty and the 1996 Mahakali treaty), bad blood between India and Nepal prevented both sides from looking at water as a common resource which can be used for agriculture as well as electricity generation on both sides of the border. Nepal's mountain rivers could produce as much as 82,000MW annually as they flow down to the Indian plains. And India desperately needs power to fuel its rapidly expanding economy.

Even as the Kosi scorned man-made boundaries, destroying three million homes in Nepal and 2.5 million in India, (resulting in 42 deaths), New Delhi and Kathmandu got embroiled in a seemingly petty argument: Why was Nepal's Maoist Prime Minister Pushpa Kamal Dahal, or Prachanda, undertaking his first visit as head of state to China instead of India, as every other Nepalese prime minister has done? India allowed Maoist leaders such as Prachanda, finance minister Baburam Bhattarai and information minister Krishna Bahadur Mahara to live in disguise in India when they were being hunted by former king Gyanendra in 2006.

And New Delhi gives Nepalese nationals a vast number of privileges, including the right to "national treatment", for jobs in government and the army. The feeling here is that the Maoists are simply not sympathetic to India's security concerns. As far as water is concerned, India constantly cites the Bhutan example and wonders why Nepal can't be more like the hill kingdom which has allowed India to build several dams over rivers, produces electricity and sells surplus power to India.

As a result, Bhutan's per capita income is only second to Sri Lanka in the South Asian region. But the Bhutan comparison is bad diplomacy because it infuriates Kathmandu each time India makes it — Indian officials make it all the time. The Maoists, meanwhile, point out that India continued to support the Nepali Congress in the elections — as well as in the race for prime ministership — despite the party's mass unpopularity. So, when Prachanda flew to Sunsari district on the border to inspect the damage, he called the 1954 Kosi treaty a "historic blunder".

Agreement between the GoI and The GoN on The Kosi Project

Signed at Kathmandu, 25 April 1954; in force upon signature

This agreement made this twenty fifth day of April, 1954, between the Government of the Kingdom of Nepal (hereinafter referred to as the "Government") and the Government of India (hereinafter referred to as the 'Union').

1. SUBJECT MATTER. - Whereas the Union is desirous of constructing a barrage, head-works and other appurtenant work about 3 miles upstream of Hanuman Nagar town on the Kosi River with afflux and flood banks, and canals and protective works, on land lying within the territories of Nepal, for the purpose of flood control, irrigation, generation of hydroelectric power and prevention of erosion of Nepal areas on the right side of the river, upstream of the barrage (hereinafter referred to as the 'project');

And whereas the Government has agreed to the construction of the said barrage, head-works and other connected works by and at the cost of the Union, in consideration of the benefits hereinafter appearing:

Now The Parties Agree As Follows:

(i) The barrage will be located about 8 miles upstream of Hanuman Nagar town.

(ii) Details of the Project. - The general layout of the barrage, the areas within afflux bank, flood embankments and the lines of communication are shown in the plan annexed to this agreement.

(iii) For the purpose of clauses 3 and 8 of the

agreement, the land under the ponded areas and boundaries as indicated by the plan specified in sub-clause (ii) above, shall be deemed to be submerged.

2. (i) PRELIMINARY INVESTIGATION AND SURVEYS.-The Government shall authorise and give necessary facilities to the canal and other officers of the Union or other persons acting under the general or special orders of such officers to enter upon such land as necessary with such men, animals vehicles, equipment, plant, machinery and instruments as necessary and undertake such surveys and investigations required in connection with the said Project before, during and after the construction, as may be found necessary from time to time by the Chief Engineer, Public Works Department (Kosi Project) in the Irrigation Branch of the Bihar Government. These surveys and investigations will comprise aerial and ground surveys, hydraulic, hydrometric, hydrological and geological surveys including construction of drillholes for surface and subsurface explorations; investigations for communication and for materials of construction; and all other surveys and investigations necessary for the proper design, construction and maintenance of the barrage and all its connected works mentioned under the Project.

(ii) The Government will also authorise and give necessary facilities for investigations of storage or detention dams on the Kosi or its tributaries, soil conservation measures such as Check Dams, afforestation, etc., required for a complete solution of the Kosi Problem in the future.

3. Authority For Execution Of Works And Occupation Of Land And Other Property. - (i) The Government will authorise the Union to proceed with the

execution of the said project as and when the Project or a part of the Project receives sanction of the said Union and notice has been given by the Union to the Government of its intention to commence work on the Project and shall permit access by the engineer and all other officers, servants and nominees of the Union with such men, animals, vehicles, plants, machinery, equipment and instruments as may be necessary for the direction and execution of the project to all such lands and places and shall permit the occupation, for such period as may be necessary of all such lands and places as may be required for the proper execution of the Project.

(ii) The land required for the purposes mentioned in Clause 3 (i) above shall be acquired by the Government and compensation therefore shall be paid by the Union in accordance with provisions of clause 8 hereof.

(iii) The Government will authorise officers of the Union to enter on land outside the limits or boundaries of the barrage and its connected works in case of any accident happening or being apprehended to any of the said works and to execute all works which may be necessary for the purpose of repairing or preventing such accident: compensation, in every case, shall be tendered by the Union to the proprietors or the occupiers of the said land for all damages done to the same through the Government in order that compensation may be awarded in accordance with clause 8 hereof.

(iv) The Government will permit the Union to quarry the construction materials required for the project from the various deposits as Chatra Dharan Bazar or other places in Nepal.

4. Use Of Water And Power. - Without prejudice to the right of Government to withdraw for irrigation or any other purpose in Nepal such supplies of water as may be required from time to time, the Union will have the right to regulate all the supplies in the Kosi River at the Barrage site and to generate power at the same site for the purposes of the Project.

(ii) The Government shall be entitled to use up to 50 per cent of the hydroelectric power generated at the barrage site Power House on payment of such tariff rates as may be fixed for the sale of power by the Union in consultation with Government.

5. Sovereignty And Jurisdiction.-The Union shall be the owner of all lands acquired by the Government under the provisions of clause 3 hereof which shall be transferred by them to the Union and of all water rights secured to it under clause 4(i). Provided that the sovereignty rights and territorial Jurisdiction of the Government in respect of such lands shall continue unimpaired by such transfer.

6. ROYALTIES. - (i) The Government will receive royalty in respect of power generated and utilized in the Indian Union at rates to be settled by agreement hereafter. Provided that no royalty will be paid on the power sold to Nepal.

(ii) The Government shall be entitled to receive payment of royalties from the Union in respect of stone, gravel and ballast obtained from the Nepal territory and used in the construction and future maintenance of the barrage and other connected works at rates to be settled by agreement hereafter.

(iii) The Union shall be at liberty to use and remove

clay, sand and soil without lot or hindrance from lands acquired by the Government and transferred to the Union.

(iv) Use of timber from Nepal forests, required for the construction, shall be permitted on payment of compensation. Provided no compensation will be payable to the Government for such quantities of timber as may be decided upon by the Government and the Union to be necessary for use on the spurs or other training works required for the prevention of caving and erosion of the right bank in Nepal.

Provided likewise that no compensation will be payable by the Union for any timber obtained from the forest lands acquired by the Government and transferred to the Union.

7. Customs Duties. - The Government shall charge no customs duty or duty of any kind, during construction and subsequent maintenance, on any articles or materials required for the purpose of the project and the work connected therewith or for the bona fide use of the Union.

8. Compensation For Land And Property. - (i) For assessing the compensation to be awarded by the Union to the Government in cash (a) lands required for the execution of the various works as mentioned in clause 3 (ii) and (b) submerged lands, will be divided into the following classes:

    1. Cultivated lands.
    2. Forest lands.
    3. Village lands and houses and other immovable property standing on them.
    4. Waste lands.

All lands recorded in the register of lands in the territory of Nepal as actually cultivated shall be deemed to be cultivated lands for the purposes of this clause.

(ii) The Union shall pay compensation (a) to the Government for the loss of land revenue as at the time of acquisition in respect of the area acquired and (b) to whomsoever it may be due for the Project and transferred to the Union.

The assessment of such compensation, and the manner of payment, shall be determined hereafter by mutual agreement between the Government and the Union.

(iii) All lands required for the purposes of the Project shall be jointly measured by the duly authorised officers of the Government and the Union respectively.

9. Communications. - (i) The Government agrees that the Union may construct and maintain roads, tramways, ropeways etc., required for the project in Nepal and shall provide land for these purposes on payment of compensation as provided in clause 8.

(ii) Subject to the territorial jurisdiction of the Government the ownership and the control of the metalled roads, tramways and railway shall vest in the Union. The roads will be essentially departmental roads of the Irrigation Department of the Union and any concession in regard to their use by commercial and non-commercial vehicles of Nepal shall not be deemed to confer any right of way.

(iii) The Government agrees to permit, on the same terms as for other users, the use of all roads, waterways and other avenues of transport and communications in Nepal for bonafide purposes of the construction and maintenance of the barrage and other connected works.

(iv) The bridge over Hanuman Nagar Barrage will be open to public traffic but the Union shall have the right to close the traffic over the bridge for repairs, etc.

(v) The Government agrees to permit installation of telegraph, telephone and telegraph in the project area to authorised servants of the Government for business in emergencies provided such use does not in any way interfere with the construction and operation of Projects.

10. Use Of River Craft.-All navigation rights in the Kosi River in Nepal will rest with the Government. The use of any watercraft like boat launches and timber rafts within two miles of the Barrage and headworks shall not be allowed except by special licence under special permits to be issued by the Executive Engineer, Barrage. Any unauthorized watercraft found within this limit Shall Be Liable To Prosecution.

11. Fishing Rights:-All the fishing rights in the Kosi river in Nepal except within two miles of the Barrage shall vest in the Government of Nepal. No fishing will be permitted within two miles of the Barrage and Headworks.

12. Use Of Nfpali Labour.-The Union shall give preference to Nepali labour, personnel and contractors to the extent available and in its opinion suitable for the construction of the Project but shall be at liberty to import labour of all classes to the extent necessary.

13. Administration Of The Project Areas. In Nepal.- The Union shall carry out inside the project areas in the territory of Nepal functions such as the establishment and administration of schools, hospitals, provision of water-supply and electricity, drainage, tramway lines and other civic amenities

14. The Government shall be responsible for the maintenance of law and order in the project areas within the territory of Nepal. The Government and

Union shall, from time to time consider and make suitable arrangements calculated to achieve the above object.

15. If so desired by the Union, the Government agrees to establish special court or courts in the project area to ensure expeditious disposal of cases arising within the project area. The Union shall bear the cost involved in the establishment of such courts, if the Government so desires.

16. Future Kosi Control Works. - If further investigations indicate the necessity of storage or detention dams and other soil conservation measures on the Kosi and its tributaries, the Government agree to grant their consent to them on conditions similar to those mentioned herein.

17. Arbitration. - If any question, differences or objections whatever shall arise in any way, connected with or arising out of this agreement or the meaning or operation of any part thereof or the rights, duties or liabilities of either party, except as to decisions of any such matter as thereinbefore otherwise provided for, every such matter shall be referred for arbitration to two persons - one to be appointed by the Government and the other by the Union-whose decision shall be final and binding, provided that in the event of disagreement between the two arbitrators, they shall refer the matter under dispute for decision to an umpire to be,' jointly appointed by the two arbitrators before entering on the reference.

Co-Ordination Committee For Kosi Project

Whereas it is considered desirable to establish a forum for discussion of problems of common interest and in order to expedite decisions for the early completion of the Kosi

Project, it is agreed between the Union of India and the Government of Nepal to set up a Co-ordination Committee. The Committee will consist of three representatives from each country to be nominated by the respective Governments.

It is further agreed that the Chairman of the Committee will be a Minister of the Government of Nepal and the Secretary will be the Administrator of the Kosi Project. The Committee will consider such matters of common interest concerning the project including land acquisition, rehabilitation of displaced population, maintenance of law and order, soil conservation measures and such other items as may be referred to the Committee for consideration by the Government of Nepal or the Union from time to time.

The Committee shall meet as and when necessary at Kathmandu or at the barrage site or such other place as may be necessary at the discretion of the Committee. Travelling allowance for the journeys undertaken by the Committee shall be met by the Union according to normal rates in the Union. All other expenditure on staff, etc., of the Committee will be met by the Union.

9

River-Linking Concept of India

Fresh water has nurtured and sustained many civilisations, ancient and modern, including China, Egypt, Mesopotamia and the focus here, the future hydrological aspirations of India. However in comparative terms water as an essential human and ecological need makes up barely a tenth, of a thousandth, of all the liquid water on Earth. Mostly when visualising rivers in the abstract, they are seen as the dark blue curved line on a map. But this is only a small, final, part of the fresh water dynamics in a landscape.

A river is the sum of, or the collection in a larger geographic area, of a basin or catchment as a "funnel like" harvest of rainfall or precipitation, captured and flowing as run off, either on the surface, over land or as groundwater through rock strata, by the force of gravity to a low point at sea level. Sustained quantities of fresh, potable water for India's population are problematic because of the diversity and immense interaction between culture and landscape. Modern India is a union of 35 states and territories that in the year 1900 had a population of 238 million, expanding to 1.03 billion in 2001.

India is now the second most populous country in the world. This population has 28% urban residents and 72% rural dwellers, in approximately 600,000 villages. The 3,287726 square kilometres of India's political borders is made up of 13 river basins, some shared with neighbouring states, in major geographic regions of the Himalayan

Mountains, the Indo-Gangetic Plain, the Great Indian Desert, the Deccan Plateau and the Coastal Mountain Belts, with climates, from tropical wet, semi arid and arid.

Metaphorically, river basins or catchments can also be viewed as harvesting the cultural and political flow of the population from highland to lowland and countryside to urban dwelling. This interaction of the population with the "landscape" is also a creation of the "human mind" where the scenery is built up from the "strata" of memory and history, incorporating the physical influence and exploitation of rivers flowing over and through the landscape where a population dwells.

Climate Change

Although an environmental imperative, climate change is also a current fashionable topic of political debate. This debate oftentimes hinders and confuses the prophecies, forecasts and predictions of climate change and the focus of India's response to this challenge needs clarification. Firstly, with an increase in global temperatures glacial melt in the Himalayan Mountains would effect the amount of water run-off into rivers.

This water runoff dictates the rapidity and volume of a river's water flow. Two geographical and cultural significant rivers, the Ganga and Yumuna are dependant on the summer melting of glaciers for a uniform perennial water supply. Complete melting of Himalayan glaciers would result in an initial catastrophic flooding of the plains and deltas followed by a water shortage as the water table lowers from the lack of snow melt replenishment. Secondly, a major characteristic of India's weather is orographic precipitation, where rainfall, especially from water bearing air masses crossing the Arabian Sea, are forced to rise over India's mountain ranges unloading Monsoon on the landscape.

A significant feature of orographic precipitation/rainfall is that it leaves the opposite side of the mountain range, water poor, or technically in a "rain shadow" creating an arid region.

This is the primary reason for the engineering of an inter-basin water transfer system discussed below, which involves moving water from abundant river basins to water poor river basins. Monsoon's and their continuation are not just important for economic growth but the livelihood of a population who over the centuries, through custom and practice, have become dependant on them for agricultural production.

As an indicator of the dependence of the Indian economy and peoples lives on Monsoon, the revenue targets for 2004-5 financial year were based on a projected growth of a Gross Domestic Product (GDP) of 6 to 6.5% which are now uncertain because of the late arrival of the Monsoon and the extra spending needed for drought relief and a slow down in economic growth. Monsoon failure in India due to climate change would be catastrophic.

One might argue that the climate change debate has no justification for a critique in India's economic growth because the country's per capita green house emissions contributing to climate change is 25 times less than the average of the United States and 15 times less than the European average. As the Indian Secretary for Ministry of Environment and Forests, Prodipto Ghosh has said,

India is certainly not responsible for the mess. We are in fact victims of it. So why expect us to tighten our belts?

Unfortunately half a billion of India's population could be affected by a loss in water supply and a forecasted sea level rise of 40 cm will create 50 million homeless people, not including, possible environmental refugees from Bangladesh, South Coast Pakistan and Eastern parts of coastal Burma. India's emergence as a giant is dependent on how the Indian Government plans and prepares for climate change. The plan to interlink the rivers of India and create a new "national water grid" comes at a time when water scarcity discourses assume a nervous tone that is at once local and global, triggering fears of drought, lowering ground water tables and the further contamination of surface waters.

This initiative to link many of India's domestic and transnational rivers follows from the official interest in pursuing big projects for big solutions, a continuation of the canal-dam/food-power paradigm that began in colonial irrigation schemes and continued through twentieth century development projects. Today, the river-linking plan responds directly to opportunities available through global financing to design large-scale projects that address large-scale problems. This massive project seeks to provide increased amounts of surface water to growing, consuming human populations spread across rural and urban areas.

The first Task Force on River Linking established in 2002 aimed to augment irrigation, fulfill the increasing domestic and industrial needs for water, generate about 34.000 MW of power through hydro-electricity and facilitate waterway transportation through 30 link projects. This proposal is part of an emerging water nationalism—sketched out via a national "water grid"—to unite the nation's water resources conceptually and geopolitically. Alongside these quantity-driven approaches, the Government of India has, since the 1980s, planned and executed river action plans to prevent intrusion of raw wastewater into rivers. The aim has been to divert wastewater for treatment before routing the treated water back to rivers.

The GoI moved through British, Dutch, Japanese and Australian donors to fund the first and second phases of the first river program, the Ganga Action Plan. From this sprung other river action plans (Yamuna, Gomati, to name a few) designed to collect municipal, state and central funds in order to build and operate wastewater diversion and treatment systems. During this period, the understanding was that Public River uses, and in particular Hindu ritual uses, required pollution prevention schemes to improve water quality, especially in religious bathing areas. The aim of the river pollution prevention schemes was to restore water quality to bathing standard (now called Class B status), safe for public access and especially for bathing.

The first river action plans were eventually consolidated under the National River Conservation Directorate (NRCD) in the Ministry of Environment and Forests, and this body continues to carry along the water quality model in its pollution prevention programs. In the first ten years, officials in the NRCD had enough funds to contract treatment and diversion facilities through state governments. Now after attempts to develop cost sharing with state governments, the central government's projects are starved for the substantial funding they need. In Varanasi, the radio team toured the wastewater disposal and treatment facilities created under the Ganga Action Plan.

After almost twenty years of the Plan, we found the facilities in a dilapidated state of existence. Most were not running 24 hours a day or even every day of the week, portions of plants were lying dormant and not used, and staff had not been paid for months. The British had completed their projects, the Dutch were asked by the Government of India to discontinue as a project donor, and the Japan Bank for International Cooperation was considering new investment to salvage the facilities. In my memory bank, the current state of affairs was far bleaker than at the time the first large treatment plants were being constructed under the Ganga Action Plan (1985-1996).

The situation appeared worse: populations had grown; consumption behavior had changed to include more use and disposal of water, plastics, paper, and toxic substances; industries, cities, and farms were emitting heavy metals, pesticides and other toxic chemicals into surface waters at an alarming rate; and projects with big investments lay dysfunctional or without key parts to run properly (including uninterrupted electricity). Unfortunately the radio team found this scenario repeated in most of the other border cities.

Meanwhile, the Ganga Action Plan was passed off as a success as other river pollution prevention plans were developed on paper. Since most projects have been and continue to be starved for funds only the minimal work at infrastructure building has been accomplished. Meanwhile intensive public uses of rivers and ritual practices continue. Citizens are not barred from religious bathing at a sacred site but the physical/chemical quality of the river water they use is affected by upstream diversions, urban and industrial effluents, run off and more.

These change the quality and experience of use, even if they do not go so far as to undermine religious devotion to rivers as goddesses or worship practices more broadly. While the sacred purity of the Ganga may override all this— an issue of devotion I don't dispute—public uses bring citizens into direct contact with untreated effluent and wastewater, contacts with potentially severe human health consequences. Water quality, watershed ecology and ecosystem services are all affected by the increase in intensive uses of river water and river beds as effluent channels. Peer reviewed scientific research has documented the rise in levels of fecal coliform, bacteria, pathogens, and metals in rivers and the deterioration of water quality—in terms of BOD and DO—for fishing and public uses.

Yet these "pollution" considerations appear almost outdated now, as citizens and officials shift the public water discussion more passionately to the possibilities of transferring surplus water from one basin to another. The emerging interest in transference—entailing distribution among agricultural, urban and industrial users—appears to be shadowing the problem of pollution and the importance of the cultural practice of bathing in a sacred river.

The water quality model is giving way to a water quantity (flow, water potential) model, as statements about the growing needs of power, agriculture, industries and cities eclipse the importance of religious rituals. In the process, national policies move from a focus on river basins to a vision of a national water grid that connects water supplies through a network of canals. This vision falls in line with the shift in the policies of the World Bank, International Monetary Fund and Asian Development Bank from water quality to water quantity and flow models. This shift in emphasis from water quality to quantity began most noticeably in 2002 when the government resurrected with euphoria an older river linking plan developed two decades earlier by the National Water Development Agency (NWDA).

After 2002, it morphed in just two years from a sleepy, fund starved plan into a symbol of resource nationalism. The former and then current central government, the National Democratic Alliance, used sketches of the river linking plan in its manifesto, election campaigns and general references to sacred and life-giving rivers as it stirred up the technological motivation to move "surplus" waters across the national landscape. However since 2002, proponents of river linking have rarely mentioned or promised benefits to religious practices and uses. The push began in March 2002 when the governing body for the NWDA met for its semi-annual meeting.

In that meeting, the chairman stressed that institutional mechanisms were required to speed up the process of getting the concerned states of the union to reach a consensus on sharing surplus water. The governing body created a committee headed by the chairman of the Central Water Commission (also the chairman of the technical advisory committee under the NWDA) to look into this and discuss preparing the detailed project reports (DPRs) for each proposed link. However, before this committee began its work, the president of India made reference to the river-linking scheme in his address on the eve of India's Independence Day, August 15, 2002. He said:

Let us now look at a long-term problem. It is paradoxical to see floods in one part of country while some other parts face drought. This drought-flood phenomenon is a recurring feature. The need of the hour is to have a water mission, which will enable availability of water to the fields, villages, towns and industries throughout the year, even while maintaining environmental purity. One major part of the water mission would be networking of our rivers. Technological and project management capabilities of our country can rise to the occasion and make this river networking a reality with long-term planning and proper investment.

The president's message inspired some and worried others. Among the inspired was Supreme Court lawyer Ranjit Kumar who used his legal knowledge to respond to the issue in the court. At the time, Kumar was amicus curaie in a river case titled, News Item Published in Hindustan Times titled "And Quiet Flows the Maili Yamuna" v. Central Pollution Control Board and others, one of several cases in the Supreme Court addressing river flow and pollution. In 2002, with little knowledge of the NWDA's earlier reports, Kumar introduced an intervention application in the Hindustan Times case (then heard by Justice Kirpal's bench) to plead for consideration of the river linking scheme hailed by the President.

In his petition, he made references to population growth, flooding, erosion, and drought. He cited current disputes between states over the sharing of river water and added that the networking of rivers would solve these. In his concluding prayers, Kumar asked the court to issue appropriate directions, in the first instance, to form a "High Powered Committee" to look into the suggestion of networking rivers and issue further directions in consonance with this objective. Upon hearing the intervention application, the Supreme Court converted it into a writ petition, giving it a separate case name and number.

A day before his retirement, Chief Justice B. N. Kirpal proposed a new time frame for the envisioned scheme relying, in only a cursory manner, on the comments and reports on the subject made by various governmental and non-governmental agencies. On that day, the court made a suggestion that was interpreted by case respondents as an order before a response to the plan could be registered by citizens and officials in the respective states. The court stated that, "We do expect that the programme when drawn up would try and ensure that the link projects are completed within a reasonable time of not more than ten years".

With this, the court sped up a process envisioned by a series of bureaus under the government and gave legitimacy to a dormant plan, without considering earlier critiques of it. In December 2002, the Government of India issued a resolution constituting the Task Force on Interlinking of Rivers. The prime minister appointed a political officer at the rank of Union Cabinet Minister to chair the committee. When environmental programs such as river-linking are pushed along by public interest litigation, the epistemic community (those experts involved in assessing and analyzing a common problem and providing policy advice and guidance) expands slightly through use of the law.

Then generally the community divides into bureaucratic insiders and policy-thinking outsiders, pitting governmental against non-governmental scientists and professionals. This reproduces the split personality of the law, developed out of the paternalistic and authoritarian legacy of the colonial regime on the one hand and emancipatory constitutional provisions on the other. In environment cases, citizens use public interest litigation to contest bureaucratic powers and policies that make little provision for public participation.

Were it not for their legal interventions, citizens' groups would have no role in setting statutory environmental standards, applications for consent to pollute would not be published, and there would be no real opening for a public inquiry into polluting activities. At the same time, legal orders may legitimize and provide permissions for large-scale development projects that engage in intensive resource uses and leave aside the claims of the worst affected citizens. In short, the bench may be just as eager to promote large development projects – river-linking, dams, thermal power plants, highway projects and others – as it may be to check and correct the powers of the executive and legislative branches and industry players through continuing mandamus powers.

Current Debates

Almost immediately after the plan hit the public, a heated debate developed through the media. Additionally, local and national seminars and workshops were organized to debate scientific, technical and political issues and problems. Ramaswamy Iyer, a former secretary of the Ministry of Water Resources and prominent independent commentator on water issues, published an article in the Economic and Political Weekly. He wrote, "An almost abandoned idea has been given fresh currency; a dubious idea has been given legitimacy; and a wild-goose chase has been not merely sanctioned but mandated". Groups began meeting to discuss and oppose the plan a month after the Supreme Court issued its order.

Several Delhi-based NGOs organized a seminar series that began in Delhi and then moved to many other states of the union. Critics pointed to possible problems with the plan: increased salinity, water-logging and further pollution of surface waters as rivers are channeled and dammed in reservoirs; loss of water to evaporation by channeling; the impracticality of coursing water across the country, in terms of power and the challenges of terrain; the anticipated and unanticipated ecological and human consequences; the inaccurate and non-existent data on which to substantiate the classification of rivers into surplus and deficit; and the classified status of all government reports and documents related to river linking. Non-governmental experts were also arguing against the ways governments, corporations and banks lead nations into specific resource use projects by limiting the scope of debate, circumscribing official science and classifying data.

Many had scientific and professional experience documenting the previous and ongoing human impacts from dams and diversion projects, pollution prevention projects and other projects to privatize water. They used scientific knowledge and a humanist ideology of international appeal but had no formal legitimacy, no centralized or umbrella organization or agency to combine their individual perspectives. Without a centralizing agency, their organizational presence began to form through the coordination of seminars and email discussion initiatives. As increasing numbers of people began to discuss the official plan, viable expert communities formed all around the outside of official agencies. These openings were matched by the bureaucratic closure of the Task Force.

The Task Force began its work as a small group of government servants and then initiated a period of selective public gestures through informal meetings with some non-governmental experts and conference participants. Thereon, the Task Force members studied and prepared to implement the river-linking plan as they rewrote it, creating a new bureaucratic space outside existing ministries and agencies and taking over the data collection and decision-making powers once held by the NWDA. By August 2003, the Task Force had appointed a series of institutions and organizations to carry out research on the geological, hydrological, engineering and human dimensions of the plan, choosing its scientific and professional agencies from those it had worked with in the past.

During this period of committee formation, the Task Force provided limited and sporadic information to the public on its deliberations and movements and only after settling its institutional linkages put up a website of plans and activities in October 2003. The Indian courts are aware of the need for scientific data to set standards for environmental regulation and to monitor industrial emissions and discharges. The courts lead the way in promoting the use of science when they order the creation of committees and agencies to collect data needed to adjudicate a problem.

When the Kerala conference participants considered the possibility of collecting data using their own resources to show water quality or flow conditions in the targeted rivers and the human and ecological effects of previous and projected dams and diversions, they knew resources were very limited and independent monitoring laboratories and consultancies were few and far between. Justices usually appoint NEERI, the National Environmental Engineering Research Institute and the Central Water Commission – both government agencies with labs to test water, soil and air samples – to scientifically monitor and investigate problems brought to the attention of the bench. However, non-governmental groups mistrust both as stand-alone authorities.

Many NGOs and non-governmental scientists and professionals argue for neutral, independent bodies to conduct research and verify the reports of government-sponsored agencies. These citizens also find that the lack of baseline or historical data on the previous human and ecological effects of industrial practices and large-scale development projects stymies their ability to build a case. For instance, data on river flow and physico-chemical pollution, collected over time by the Ministry of Water Resources, the Central Water Commission and the Central Pollution Control Board, are selectively published. Studies connected to more politicized projects such as river-linking are classified and completely off limits to citizens and those outside the highest reaches of the concerned ministries.

From these concerns, the seminar participants emerged with a specific request: to see and discuss the NWDA's pre-feasibility and feasibility studies of the links proposed in the respective states. The NWDA refused to make them public, invoking their classified status. The Task Force, though privy to them, withheld on the pretext that negotiations with state leaders and affiliated research institutions were underway and could not be disclosed. The conference participants suspected that the Task Force had found the NWDA's reports incomplete and insufficient and was trying to revise the feasibility studies using better scientists and a broader frame of inquiry. Entering the debate as an observer in July 2003, the request to see the NWDA's feasibility studies had become a kind of resistance idiom for those opposing the plan.

Their objection was this: How could a country debate a problem and find a solution when key ecological and water engineering studies were withheld from the public and from outside peer review? Was there no room to reassess the plan legitimized by a hasty court decision and debate it? As concerned scientists and professionals in fields such as hydrology, geology, geography, social science, engineering, policy analysis and others, they had scientific and policymaking abilities not legitimized, though recognized, by official agencies and were trying to contribute to key decision-making processes.

While the July workshop participants concluded that they would have to arrange data collection activities on their own and in co-operation with universities and specific independent scientists, the problems of funding this scientific research and getting new sources of data accepted by the court remained firmly on their minds. By late fall of 2003, proposals and critiques of the river-linking plan were circulating widely through email lists, coordinated web sites, national and international media and diplomatic correspondence. Along with this, the problem of limited access to official plans and studies and to decision-making processes was raised again and again by non-official scientists and professionals.

Occasionally, a demand for disclosure and information was made within Parliament as members discussed water resources and river linking. In response to the closed-sourcing of government data, scientists, NGOs and other ecology experts outside government began to engage in an open-sourcing of science, using the information and knowledge generated in the public domain to critique and assess government plans. All this raised a series of questions about the processes of debate essential to the production of verifiable knowledge and "best practices." It also raised questions about the democratic process more broadly and the fundamental rights of citizens guaranteed under the Constitution.

When the ad hoc Task Force was dissolved in early 2005, the river linking data and material were transferred to the NWDA, and some of it is now presented on their web site. Iyer notes pressing problem areas for India in terms of water: grim forecasts of water scarcity or a water crisis and the related problem of food insecurity; persistent problems of drought-prone areas, arid zones, and other water-short areas; recurring flood-related damages and losses; bitter and divisive inter-State river-water disputes, and the growing ineffectiveness of the constitutional conflict-resolution mechanism; unresolved issues relating to rivers with Pakistan, Nepal and Bangladesh; the emergence of acute water conflicts between users (agriculture/industry/ drinking water) and between areas (rural/urban); difficulties of meeting the UN Millennium Development Goals for the provision of safe drinking water and sanitation facilities; the ominous depletion of groundwater aquifers in many parts of the country; the shrinking of wetlands; the pollution and contamination of water sources; the enormous waste of water in every kind of use (agricultural, industrial, municipal, domestic); and the uncertainties arising from predictions of climate change.

In order to deal with these problems, the government is banking on increasing access to rivers in relatively untapped areas, but the access is at first predicated on the need for increased hydropower rather than on the needs of increasing water supply to agriculture, industry or municipalities. The National Policy on Hydropower Development highlights the potential of the northeastern states in particular. Numerous dam and link projects are underway and proposed for this region. They are taken up individually under specifically named projects and not considered part of the larger river linking scheme.

River Basin Governance

Since June 2003, the Task Force chairman had tried to promote consensus among the Indian states on river basin transfers, as he established links with research and consulting agencies and garnered support from the public through domestic and overseas visits. Since inter-state river basin sharing agreements in India were already problematic and hotly contested, it was well known among experts in all groups that these deals would require additional quid pro quo arrangements. The fancy part of the interlinking concept was based on transferring water from the Brahmaputra at a reach in Arunachal Pradesh downstream from the Yarlung Tsangpo, the main tributary in Tibet.

From Arunachal Pradesh, a portion of the flow of the Brahmaputra would then be diverted via the Manas, Sankosh and Tista rivers through Nepal to the Ganga in India. From there, the additional waters would be directed via long-distance canals to the smaller rivers in the peninsular south, re-enacting, in a sense, the mythical descent of Ganga's waters. Indirectly, the river-linking scheme renewed contests over Asia's last water resource frontier, the glaciers of the Tibetan plateau. Before consulting neighbors, the Government of India declared it would study and implement where feasible the domestic links sketched out by the NWDA. By the end of 2003, the Task Force chairperson had consulted all chief ministers of Indian states, the World Bank and other donor bank officials.

However, higher-level discussions with neighboring nations on planned and existing water-sharing agreements moved at a decidedly slower pace. Little of these conversations reached the public until opposition started to form in Bangladesh and fears grew over China's plans to divert the Yarlung Tsangpo for its own needs. In other words, the Task Force's work to gain consent from the states began with the assumption that India held the upstream advantage by securing water from the Brahmaputra in Arunachal Pradesh and diverting it to the Ganga and then to the peninsular south. On governance, Ramaswamy Iyer, writes that the most visible manifestation of water politics has been in inter-State river-water disputes.

The dispute over the sharing of Cauvery waters has assumed enormous importance in the politics of Tamil Nadu and Karnataka. Similarly, the disputes over Ravi-Beas waters have occupied Punjab and Haryana. Iyer explains that the River Boards Act of 1956 was rendered inoperative by politics and that the establishment of any kind of organization at the river-basin level has been extremely difficult. In the Krishna Tribunal's Award, 'Scheme B' that envisaged a Krishna River Authority was not made mandatory and never came into operation.

In the Cauvery case, attempts to establish a standing, professional-cum-bureaucratic Cauvery River Authority had to be abandoned; instead a political Authority was set up (essentially as a mediating body, without any planning or managerial functions). Also rehabilitation and resettlement in the command area of projected reservoirs and the settlement of rural/urban and agriculture/industry water conflicts are based on politics. Historically, transnational rivers have been governed through international treaties and interagency compacts; today, as water uses grow more complicated politically, culturally and ecologically, river basin organizations are becoming viable alternatives to treaty commissions. Interests in water allocation, navigation rights, hydropower, and flood control are now contextualized in emerging models of integrated river basin management that include attention to ecosystem functions and services.

However, river basin organizations continue to be challenged, as they have been in India, by nation-state and transnational politics. The Ganges-Brahmaputra-Meghna (GBM) basin that India's river linking scheme aims to tap more intensively is made up of the catchment areas of three major river systems that flow through India, Nepal, Bhutan, the Tibet region of China, and Bangladesh. This huge system is second only to the Amazon and home to a population of over 600 million growing at a rate of 2 percent a year.

The Brahmaputra sub-basin is gifted with water wealth, hydropower potential and high biodiversity, while the waters of the Ganga and the Meghna sub-basins are heavily utilized for agricultural and industrial production, urban settlements, hydropower and everyday sustenance through religious, household and small-scale industrial practices. The five countries in this basin have different political motives and interests in water uses. Nepal and Bhutan, the upper riparian countries, have significant hydropower potential and favorable ratios of per capita water availability. Bangladesh accounts for only 8 percent of the total basin territory yet the hydrological catchment areas represent 88 percent of that country.

The Indian River linking project envisages construction of various structures for diversion and storage of water. If built, these structures could potentially cause inundation, backwater effects for upstream countries (Nepal and Bhutan) and reduction of water flows for downstream countries (Bangladesh). Information in advance and consultation with both upstream and downstream riparian countries with regard to such structures is necessary to avoid regional tensions. However, as Yaqoob notes, the importance of transnational discussions across this large basin are not mentioned in riverlinking documents; only inter-state dialogue within India is discussed.

To date, there has been little official discussion between India and other riparian countries on the river-linking scheme, and on its economic and environmental feasibility. Bangladesh is located on the world's largest alluvial delta of three large rivers, the Ganges, Brahmaputra, and Meghna, and sits within a complex network of other rivers. Together these rivers contribute more than 90 per cent of the annual stream flow and about 80 per cent of the annual freshwater inflow into the country. The river link project would interlink all but one of the 52 rivers Bangladesh shares with India. India and Bangladesh have debated the management of trans-boundary Rivers for decades, with Bangladesh focusing on their shortage of water during the dry season (January-May).

In theory, the 1996 Ganges Treaty was to divide the share of the Ganga waters at the Farakka barrage but in the years between the commissioning of the barrage and the final treaty implementation India had already diverted a significant share to create a more viable port in Kolkata. This period of water diversion dried up the Padma basin and created problems for agriculture and soil quality. More importantly, it led Bangladeshis to a very negative view of water sharing with Indians.

The Indo-Bangladesh Joint River Commission set up to oversee sharing of the Ganga waters from Farakka Barrage rarely met in the last ten years since the Ganges Treaty was instituted, despite the mandate that it meet two times a year. In late 2004, an international conference was organized in Bangladesh so that scientists, officials and activists across Bangladesh, India and Nepal could discuss these apprehensions, exchange data, and critique the viability of the plans. This conference and other educational and civic exchanges are building dialogue on pressing issues in the basin.

Official discussions, however, have been blocked by Indian authorities. Although India and Nepal have a long history of cooperation in irrigation and hydropower projects, the government of Nepal has adopted a very cautious approach towards the interlinking proposal and has shown neither opposition nor support. At the scholarly level, concerns have been raised in Nepal that India should have invited it to join in feasibility studies of the project. Nepal's concerns center on the social and environmental costs of the huge storages that India plans to construct on the shared rivers.

The construction of storage projects in Nepal is critical not only to hydropower generation but to mitigating floods in the neighbouring states of India and to augmenting the Ganges flow at Farakka. India has unilaterally undertaken a number of construction works and built various canals out of Himalayan Rivers along its Nepal border for irrigation purposes. The basins of Kosi, Gandak, Karnali, and Mahakali all have extensive links to accommodate the lean-season flows in India. A landlocked Himalayan country, Bhutan is almost entirely mountainous, with flatland limited to the broader river valleys and along the foothills bordering the Indian subcontinent.

With the exception of one small river that flows north, all rivers flow south to India. Hydropower potential is the most important feature and the single biggest revenue source for Bhutan, estimated at over 30,000 MW, out of which, safe and exploitable water resources potential is estimated at 16,000 MW. Today, the power sector contributes about 45 per cent to the gross revenue generation in the country and accounts for about 11 per cent of GDP. For the exploitation of its massive hydropower resources, Bhutan is fully dependent upon India. Besides being the largest aid donor to Bhutan, India has also assisted in a number of development projects in the country ranging from electricity to irrigation and road development.

The two countries have signed a memorandum of understanding to prepare detailed project reports on two hydropower projects. India and Bhutan have a brief history of strong cooperation, particularly in the hydro-power sector. With this India may receive an assured supply of cheap and clean energy and Bhutan would receive a significant revenue stream. Two of Bhutan's rivers — Manas and Sankosh (tributaries of Brahmaputra) — are included in the Indian River link plans. This cooperation and Bhutan's economic dependence on India may limit Bhutanese criticism or disapproval of the Indian plan.

Additionally, the ILR does not appear to pose threats of inundation and population displacement to the upper riparian Bhutan because her mountainous location, ideal for run-of-the-river schemes, needs no big reservoirs. The upper reach of the Brahmaputra River is known as the Yarlong Tsangpo in China. It is the sixth longest river in China. Until recently, China has not entered the hydro politics of the region except through occasional claims to parts of Arunachal Pradesh, a state with borders disputed by China since the drawing of the McMahon line.

Arunachal Pradesh is a de facto state in the Indian Union but the ongoing dispute creates ideological tension in the press from time to time. This resurfaced most recently in February 2008 when China offered assistance to India in developing hydropower projects in the state. Needless to say, the Indian government did not respond. Among the public, however, there is a continuing fear that China plans to divert the Yarlong Tsangpo to drought-ridden northwestern China.

China has been trying to overcome water scarcity problems in the country by building large dams and water diversion schemes. In December 2002, China launched a south-to-north water diversion project which consists of three south-to-north canals, each running more than 1,000 kilometres across the eastern, middle and western parts of the country. The project is considered China's largest water transfer scheme that will link together four of its seven major rivers. The major tributary to the Brahmaputra, the Tsango could be dammed at one of its many narrow passages and significantly affect downstream flow.

To date, there has been some Sino-Indian cooperation in data sharing. Through its three hydrological stations, all located along the Yarlong Tsangpo, China has been providing India with hydrological forecasts to mitigate floods in the latter's northeastern territory. China and India have already resolved their long historical dispute over Sikkim. Both are involved in forging close ties in sectors ranging from military to trade. As Yaqoob notes, the Ganges-Brahmaputra basin is identified as a basin with "the potential for political stresses in the coming five to ten years."

The parameters taken to identify 'basins at risk' are rapid institutional and/or physical changes from major planned projects in hostile and/or institution-less basins that may outpace the transnational capacity to absorb that change. On a more hopeful note, it is increasingly clear in official Indian circles (though not advertised to the public) that river linking, as a grand scheme, will never be doable in all its parts. Instead the scheme continues to create a more important unintended result: it draws together many kinds of experts and concerned citizen groups into a debate on water uses and the assumptions, projections and actual instances of water use as data are put into the public domain.

Still, as this debate goes on, state governments continue to enter into quiet arrangements and memoranda of understanding, especially in the northeast, to deal out water among claimants and arrange for projects that will hypothetically create "new" water. After the state governments create MoUs, the NWDA hires scientists, engineers, contractors, the "construction lobby" and other entities of its choice to research and implement a project. So the potential remains for piecemeal operations in the shadow of the river linking dream. In order to maintain its strong riparian position in the region, India has preferred bilateral water sharing agreements to a multilateral cooperative arrangement in spite of the enormous potential that exists in the GBM basin for collective development. As Yaqoob (2005) notes, a regional cooperative framework is necessary to achieve equitable water resource development in the shared basin.

The most successful river basin organizations usually have strong support among governments, consistent and cooperative engagements, and high levels of authority through formal instruments such as legislation. The hope of independent scientists and policy thinkers is that ongoing dialogue especially among scientists, NGOs and citizens will catalyze more official cooperation between countries. Since political and economic diversity and disparate political and cultural heritages can make decision-making difficult, it is important to have neutral and independent players or advisory groups to offer impartial expert advice.

Good river basin management also requires mechanisms for transparency, public participation, and accountability to ensure that local concerns are incorporated into transboundary decision-making. India's riverlinking scheme is a strong reminder that concerns over quantity now trump the focus on water quality in project plans (or dreams) and that, more exactly, smaller projects act in their shadow—in the hydropower plans slated for the continent's only remaining water rich region. This region will continue to be the place to look for water wars and visions of grand transfers alike, as the stronger centralized nation of China looks to garner more of the resources it needs from the Tibetan plateau and beyond. Its unlikely, however, that India will link the Brahmaputra to the Ganga through a series of connectors in the northeast now or into the future. There the terrain has the upper hand.

Colonial Influence

For thousands of years small-scale irrigation has been practiced in India and in the 19Th century British colonialists started major engineering works for agriculture in the landscape. Between 1836 and 1854 they built three large projects, developing the Upper Ganga Canal in Uttar Pradesh, the Upper Bari Doah Canal in Punjab and the Godavari Deta System in Andhra Pradesh, all to improve the mercantile economy and agricultural production of the colony. However one of the most damaging legacies of British colonialism was to be the dispute over the Farraka Barrage on the Ganga River.

The barrage diverts water into the Bhagirathi River with the intent of improving facilities at the port of Calcutta by flushing silt from the connecting lower reaches of the Hooghly River. The two tragic consequences of this project were to deprive East Pakistan/Bangladesh of valuable dry season water flows and create one myth of Indian malicious intent toward Bangladesh. Perhaps the major factor in the Farraka Barrage dispute is the multiple reports written only to allay fears over the viability of Calcutta's port and the ignorance to comprehend the impacts on the geographic region.

Between 1853 and 1952 there were 11 reports into the Hooghly, Bhagirathi and Ganga River impacts on Calcutta's future as a harbour with the longest research, of 9 years, being conducted between 1896 and 1905. Two of these reports recommended relocating Calcutta's harbour facilities. One might argue that this indecision and poor leadership created a legacy of dispute, mistrust and resentment toward Calcutta's inhabitants but it is difficult to believe that it was specifically created to agitate the future Bangladeshi Government because these political and environmental river machinations were commenced before partition of India and East Pakistan/Bangladesh.

Unfortunately this realisation does not alleviate the hardship of the current population who endure an ongoing cycle of extreme flooding and drought exacerbated by water diversion to Calcutta. Moreover one might argue that blaming the previous colonial masters for river problems of the present will not help India "emerge as a giant" but may explain the difficulty of being free of two scientific locations. Firstly the long term ecological management and conservation of river basins versus the economics and competition of food production, manufacturing, trade and commerce.

Also contemporary Calcutta may have inherited an outlook of a Western European Metropolis from an enclave of euro-centric science that is intellectually divorced from the Bangladeshi landscape. Therefore hydrological science inherited from colonialists and applied in Calcutta may have failed to appreciate the need of the region over the needs of the city. Furthermore language use and perception, such as the word "landscape," a 16th century language import from the Dutch "lanschap," defines "landscape" as a unit of human occupation or a jurisdiction with the ideal of reclaiming land from the sea and liberating from nature, a creation site of human culture, which may contribute to a Euro-centric outlook.

Therefore the environmental history, in the example of the Farraka Barrage pertains to India inheriting the British colonial example of taking, exploiting and exhausting not only the landscape but also the traditional cultures through economic aggression rather than long-term ecological management. The wider implications of this attitude, perception or belief of the colonial inheritance of environmental exploitation is that "development" be it sustainable, economic or technological is not just associated with rivers but imperative for India as a "river landscape" because demand is outstripping the capacity for natural resources to fuel economic growth.

Sustainable use of natural resources between the domains of environment, cultural protection and economic development could be achieved through public participation, inter-agency cooperation, national and local government coordination. One might argue it will be the response and cooperation of India's government, business sector and population that will determine what kind of giant India will become. In 1948, just after Indian independence A. C. Egerton, in address to the Royal Society, articulates a balanced approach to finding a way for India becoming a "giant;"

Do not be to attracted by all the glamour of western technology, it is wonderful but we in some ways have industrialised too far and not made the world happier thereby. You have a chance of distilling the best out of the West and fitting it into the age old civilisation of the East. If you can improve husbandry and the state of villagers with out going for too great a concentration of industry you may in the end gain greater happiness. The key note should be to copy and westernise but to fit the best of the new into the best of the old civilisation.

However one might argue that Edgerton's speech is a softening of condemnation for the colonisation process to justify, legitimise and authorise European rule. At the beginning of the 21st century a lingering Euro-centric view of Indian engineering, hydrology and mathematics is argued by both British and Indian historians, that it was as at its best in ancient times and fell from grace during Mughal rule.

But in reality these were reflections of the development of European science and technology from the dark ages, while Indian science came from waves of continuous and vigorous Sanskrit, Arabic and Persian manuscripts that were just not applied to industrialisation. The British colonial era saw a major expansion in water storage, transfer and irrigation that as a legacy has continued and intensified since 1947. In the year 2000 India's population reached 1.03 billion people with a forecast of it increasing to 1.8 billion by 2050. At present the average annual run off of water is 1800 cubic metres per person but by 2050 it will fall to 1000 cubic metres per person, suggesting that India is water stressed.

Kates, argues that India's success at gaining national independence from the British and its aspiration of economic development to provide for the basic necessities to the poor has ignored or been blinded to the fact that the environment does not exist as a space separate from human actions, ambitions and needs. Moreover "development" has become an accusatory word used by former imperialists to dictate how poor nations should be governed to alleviate poverty. Emphatically the environment is where people live and development is what governments do to improve that abode and therefore the two become inseparable.

Inter-Basin Water Transfer

India's dams have mostly been built for the purpose of irrigation and some for hydro power generation with half of the large projects built between 1970 and 1989. Most urban supplies of dam water feed the cities of Bangalore, Chennai, Delhi, Hyderabad and Mumbai for industrial manufacture of steel, fertiliser and textiles. In India there are approximately 4291 dams higher than 10 metres and 2342 dams higher than 15 metres. An increasing population demanding more food and protection from drought, flooding and the consequences of climate change have made current dams inadequate for the needs of the population because of the imbalance of water availability across the country.

However the west flowing rivers of Brahmaputra, Ganga/Maharati and Godavari have large storage's of water that could be transferred to water deficit areas for the development of irrigation, hydro-power generation, domestic and industrial water use. The National River Linking Project is a plan to transfer water from the water rich northeast or Himalayan Rivers to the water poor, Peninsula Rivers in southwest of India. The Indian National Water Development Agency (INMDA) has been carrying out feasibility studies since 1982 with the concept included in the 1987 National Water Policy and reiterated in a 2002 policy statement.

Recently in response to public interest litigation the Indian Supreme Court has ordered the Indian Government to complete the project within ten years and be fully operational by 2016. The project will transfer 173 billion cubic metres of water from the Ganga, Brahmaputra and Teesa Rivers through a series of canals, weirs, reservoirs and pipelines to the states of Uttar Pradesh, Rajasthan Maharashtra, Gujarat, Orissa, Andhra Pradesh, Karnataka and Tamil Nadu at a cost of over $US 120 billion. However Environment Impact Statements (EIA) in India are not reliable because of the lack of data for the different climatic zones, landscapes, culture and traditions that produce India's diversity of lifestyles, terrains, flora and fauna.

No standard environmental information database exists because it is viewed as a complex, cumbersome and a time consuming exercise. EIA for development projects is presently seen as a project level instrument and does not address the programs at the policy and planning level. One might suggest that if EIA are not addressed at the policy level then the cultural, social and spiritual impacts will have consequences more immediate in antagonizing the population to when construction attacks there personal beliefs and landscape. Moreover India's natural world will be decimated because of a lack of knowledge about the state of the environment.

Mega-Hydrological projects are not unique for development, nation building or as a panacea for water supply issues and problems. One might suggest they are a perquisite for "Emerging Giants." Jawaharlal Nehru's proclamation of Hindi Chini Bhai Bhai has a hydrological simile can be visualised through China's Three Gorges Dam Project, the worlds biggest hydroelectric scheme on the Yangtze River in central China will build a dam wall 175 m high and 2.3 km long generating 18, 200 MW of electricity costing $US 30 billion.

This will reduce China's coal consumption by 40 million tonnes a year, the equivalent of 12 nuclear power stations. Flooding in the worst year on record, 1954 killed 30,000 people and the Three Gorges will mitigate most of this disaster event. However the reservoir is 630 km to 690 km long and just over a kilometre across and will inundate 13 cities, 140 towns and 1352 villages relocating 1.2 million people. Farmers will be forced to move to less fertile land losing productivity. Furthermore the sediment build up will be as far as the biggest river port in South West China, Chonqing.

Like the proponents of the Indian River Linking project, Three Gorges Dam is decreed to have benefits that outweigh the severity of the human cost. One might suggest that "Western" critics are hypocritical when they venerate the achievements of their heritage, such as, 1st century AD Roman engineering of Nimes in Provence, France. Where the inhabitants decided they needed more water for their city than the landscape had available. Citizens spent 100 million sesterces building a massive symbol of human ingenuity.

Near Uzes, north of Nimes, Roman engineers found a water source strong enough to irrigate the baths and fountains of their city and made plans to divert water 50 miles through mountains and across valleys in a system of aqueducts and underground pipes. When engineers came to the cavernous gorge of the Gad River they erected a 3 tiered aqueduct, 360 metres long, 48 metres high, capable of carrying 35,000 cubic metres of water a day, so the inhabitants of Nimes would not have to suffer the indignity of a shallow bath. The construction of the National River

Linking Project has serious consequences for the people of India when it inundates 8, 000 square kilometres of fertile land and displaces 3 million people.

Unlike the Chinese and Roman examples the Indian project has international dilemmas because the scale of the construction has unknown environmental and economic outcomes for neighbouring Bangladesh and Nepal. Moreover the construction of Mega-Dams in the Himalayan Mountains risks the triggering of earthquakes in a seismically active region. Also dams will reduce the flow of sediment loads of the Ganga and Bramhaputra River which carry an average of $1.7-2.4 \times 10^9$ tonnes per year to an Indian and Bangladeshi river delta with an area of 20, 000 km2. Dams would trap sediment upstream with impacts on fisheries, forestry, coastline stability and a social cost for people who depend on these areas for their livelihood.

Gender

From a feminist perspective, one might argue, that the building of large-scale projects such as the National River Linking Project does not adequately address the needs of women and family members who would benefit more from small scale targeted programs. In natural disasters such as flooding, women are more affected than men because they are restricted to the home with responsibilities of an extended family.

Social or cultural objections often mean that women have never learned to swim or engaged in physical play that would give them skills in climbing and running to escape the impacts of natural disasters. Indian clothing fashion, saris and long garments hamper the movement when carrying young children, babies or assisting the infirm. Women carry the responsibility of giving birth, caring for children, the sick and elderly. During disasters and construction projects when male members of the family are absent, the risk of a break down in law and order increases the risk of women as victims in exploitive behaviours. Loss of employment or a partner can result in sexual harassment and a reliance on prostitution for food or a livelihood and in developing regions one of the few opportunities to avert poverty.

The focus on women's issues pertaining to their life dependant on a river and water development may provide an alternative to building a massive dam project. A micro personal empowerment project would achieve similar outcomes for the population and allow people to work with the landscape instead of trying to change it for human consumption. Emergency preparation, disaster readiness, the teaching of boat/raft handling techniques, as well as swimming, rescue skills and first aid are methods that can enrich communities and benefit the country by increasing the skill base and adaptability of its citizens.

Moreover flood proofing, design; mobile health clinics and limited relocation add flexibility to natural disaster areas. It could be argued that innovation in cultural expectations and female empowerment would help people in water troubled areas to adapt to their conditions rather than attempting to change the landscape with mega engineering project. The choice India can make as an emerging giant is to either invest in mega-engineering projects or in the knowledge enterprise and resourcefulness of its citizens.

Spiritual Impacts

In spite of the diversity of landscape and culture in Indian traditions, one might argue there is an overriding belief and respect for religious values relating to wealth, beauty, longevity, health, food, love and children and the association of these values with rivers. Simon Schama argues that national and cultural identities would lose their captivation if they did not have the mysticism of the associated landscape and a traditional topography that is elaborately mapped as a "homeland." One might argue that rivers are such a dynamic part of a landscape that one can understand their mystical veneration. Religious leaders deal with ecological change by separating the domains of Hinduism and science.

Hinduism is not necessarily opposed to the differences between modernity and tradition but incorporate them into the argument. These two domains are so specialised that that they do not converge, which minimilises but does not eliminate ideological conflict. Rivers are created by the merging of a multitude of tiny streams and rivulets that are sometimes dry and with no immediate obvious source. But whether they are minor or major, most have a particular spot that is identified as a spiritual or magical source, which becomes a site of worship and pilgrimage. This cultural construction of the landscape is usually accepted as tradition and the "source spot" becomes the location of temples, tanks, steps and structures to facilitate pilgrim visits.

India has relatively abundant water but rivers and urban supplies have become highly polluted and most of the population does not have basic sanitation systems or access to clean water and consequently dysentery, cholera, typhoid and hepatitis become health care burdens rather than just issues. Water in nature does have the ability to clean itself and modern inputs of organic waste, rotting vegetables, excrement and even crude oil, can be biodegraded by bacteria, consumed and metabolised and passed along the biogeochemical cycle in the landscape. Most components of domestic sewage may persist for only days to weeks in the environment but self-cleansing has its limits.

It is difficult to comprehend how Indian society could fail to understand the burden of polluted water but people have acquired this mystical belief in water, on the one hand and solid waste on the other that overwhelms the landscape with pollution. In India, water is considered the universal cleanser, whose rivers and lakes are the most contaminated in the world yet are accorded a supernatural quality of purification. Religious practitioners make a distinction between purity and cleanliness when considering waste water having an impact on people and the environment.

For instance the "Mother Ganga" could become unclean but she could never be impure. Spiritually the river

Ganga is a Goddess who possesses the power to absorb and absolve human and worldly impurities and can stave off the degenerating contempt of Indian societies without defiling herself. Water pollution through spiritual acts of purity, fertility and worship by ablution is a counter argument to government criticism. Water health programs and accusatory officials are claimed by religious leaders and gurus that they are the ones who actually create the pollution they claim to control because of corruption and inefficiency.

Separate domains of action exist in the population where Indian Government departments administer resource development and management through the judiciary and political enforcement. Litigious rules and regulations with the consequent fines and penalties supposedly control navigation, fisheries, dams, water extraction and natural disaster response. However religious institutions, sectarian organizations, temple committees and trusts although not legally recognised are respected by the population as a moral truth.

Moreover religious practice uses ablutions, meditations and worship from sacred texts, folk and oral narratives that teach empower and obligate a person to enter a sacred place. But unlike the government officials, priests and holy men do not punish people for their transgressions but teach and direct them through spiritual practice and ritual. Conversely religious practice and precedent can inhibit and restrain development solutions.

For instance, Ahluwalia argues that a major decline in public saving of 1.7% of GDP in 1996-7 to -2.7% 2001-2002 is because the government borrowed money to finance fiscal deficits from expenses in food and fertiliser subsidies, which resulted in a budgetary burden of 1.4% in 2002-2003. Ironically in rural areas where fertiliser is in demand, human excrement is flushed away with gallons of water rather than composted for its nutrients. Indian's can spread animal dung in a garden or burn it for stove fires but their own excrement induces such revulsion when it can be composted into dark crumbly fertiliser within a year.

10

India-Bangladesh Battle for Water Sharing: An Impact of Tipaimukh Project

Himalayan Dams pose threat to Bangladesh

India, Pakistan, Nepal and Bhutan have planned a total of 552 hydropower projects in Himalayan region, of which some have already been built and some are under construction that may have far-reaching impacts on downstream Bangladesh, informed sources said. Himalayan region is the centre point from where scores of small and large Asian rivers originated and run through. The Indus, Ganges, Brahmaputra, and Irabati are some of those. Bangladesh shares water of 54 rivers with India and 3 with Myanmar. "If those upstream countries divert normal water flow through these dams, it will dry up many Bangladeshi rivers ruin irrigation system, kill lives in the water bodies. On the other hand, if they do not manage water properly it will inundate a big part of the country during rainy season," Joint River Commission (JRC) Member Mir Sajjad Hossen told The New Nation.

A study of the 'International Rivers', an US based non-governmental organisation that protects rivers and defends the rights of communities, revealed that India has already built 74 dams, Nepal 15, Pakistan 6 and Bhutan 5 in

Himalayan region in the recent years. It also found that 37 Indian, 7 Pakistani and 2 Nepalese dam are under construction in that area. The study also identified that India has planned to build 318 dams, Nepal 37, Pakistan 35 and Bhutan 16 more dams in this region to add over 1,50,000 Megawatts (MW) of additional electricity capacity in the next 20 years. Sajjad Hossen said that the proposed and under construction dams, Tipaimukh dam is one of those, will change downstream flows, affecting agriculture and fisheries and threatening livelihoods of many people in Bangladesh.

"These countries are supposed to share information with Bangladesh before taking any such step of building new dams, but they are not doing so. We have asked them for information. What we can do if they do not obey the river interlinking rules," said Hossen expressing helplessness against upstream powerful countries. The author of the 'Mountains of Concrete: Dam Building in the Himalayas' Shripad Dharmadhikary wrote: "If all the planned capacity expansion materialises, the Himalayan region could possibly have the highest concentration of dams in the world. This dam building activity will fundamentally transform the landscape, ecology and economy of the region and will have far-reaching impacts all the way down to the river deltas."

Bhutan is planning a capacity expansion of about 10,000 MW in the next 10 years. Among the projects being planned for the near future are the 1,095 MW Puntansangchu-I and the 600 MW Mangdechhu projects. Nepal is planning to install hydropower capacity of 22,000 MW in the coming years. For its own needs, Nepal plans to add 1,750 MW by the year 2020-2021, mostly through small and medium projects. Rest, mainly from the bigger projects, is planned for selling power to India. Pakistan has plans to add 10,000 MW through five projects by the year 2016. Another 14 projects totalling about 21,000 MW are under study for construction by 2025. The government is pushing for the immediate implementation of the massive 4,500 MW Diamer-Bhasha project.

India declared its intentions with the launching of the "50,000 MW Initiative" on May 24, 2003. This initiative fast tracked hydropower development by taking up time-bound preparation of the Preliminary Feasibility Reports (PFRs) of 162 new hydroelectric schemes totalling around 50,000 MW. India has plans to build this capacity by 2017 and then, in the 10 years following, to add another 67,000 MW of hydropower. Construction is ongoing for many of the projects including the 2,000 MW Lower Subansiri project, the 400 MW Koteshwar project and the 1,000 MW Karcham Wangtoo, to name a few.

Many of these projects are already under construction. Due to various obstacles of dams, barrages and hydropower projects in Himalayan region, the source of water of rivers, Bangladesh get lesser water in rivers flowing throughout the country. The lean water flow in the rivers has already cast negative impact on ecology, aquatic life, and irrigation. According to the Ganges treaty, signed in 1996, Bangladesh and India will equally share water if water flow is up to 70,000 cusec or less in the Farakka barrage point. Bangladesh will get 35,000 cusec of water and India will get the rest if water at Farakka point is between 70,000 and 75,000 cusec.

If water at Frakka point reaches more than 75,000 cusec, India will get 40,000 cusec and Bangladesh will get the rest. But India never followed these terms and conditions of the accord and released meagre quantity of water for Bangladesh, it was alleged. The JRC statistics shows that Bangladesh did not get its proper share of water since signing of the treaty. In 1999 Bangladesh got 1,033 cusec of water at Teesta barrage point against its normal requirements of 10,000 cusec of water. After JRC meeting in 2000 the water flow rose to 4,530 cusec, in January 2001 it reduced to 1406 cusec, in January 2002 to 1,000 cusec, in January 2003 to 1,100 cusec, in November 2006 to 950 cusec, in January 2007 to 525 cusec and in January 2008 to 1,500 cusec.

Due to less quantum of water supply through Teesta barrage thousands of acres of land in the country's northern districts lack irrigation posing threat to Boro rice cultivation. Around 15 small rivers are also drying up and about to die due to the same reason. The Teesta River itself becomes a thin canal for less volume of water supply from the upper riparian Indian part. The rivers include: Kortoa, Dudhkomol, Jingira, Dhorla, Bangali, Ghaghot, Atrai, Akhira, Manas, Katakhali, Ichamoti, Punorvoba, Burighora and Dhauk also drying due to less water supply. WDB officials said sustainability of these rivers is impossible unless India supplies adequate water through the barrage.

Habitat and Ecosystems

Over 73% of the Brahmaputra River watershed's originial forest is gone. The remaining forests are disappearing at 10% per year. Currently only 4% of the land is in protected areas. The area supports 4 endemic bird habitats and one RAMSAR-listed wetland.126 fish species also call the Brahmaputra basin home (WRI). The ecoregion covering the Brahmaputra River in northeast India harbors India's largest elephant population, the world's largest population of the greater one-horned rhinoceros, tigers (Panthera tigris), and wild water buffalo (Bubalus arnee) (WII 1997). The ecoregion overlaps with a high-priority (Level I) ecosystem that extends north to include the subtropical and temperate forests of the Himalayan midhills.

The known mammal fauna consists of 122 species, including 2 near-endemic species. Of these, the pygmy hog and the hispid hare are confined to the grassland habitats. At present, twelve protected areas cover about 2,500 km of intact habitat, or 5 percent of the ecoregion. Of these, Manas, Dibru-Saikowa, Kaziranga, and Mehao are the larger and more important reserves. Mehao extends over two other ecoregions and is only partially within this ecoregion. Kaziranga has the world's largest population of the greater one-horned rhinoceros, estimated at 1,100 individuals.

Because of the large number of wide-ranging large vertebrates in this ecoregion, additional protection is urgently needed. Specifically, habitat connectivity should be provided within the Buxa-Manas complex and the Barail-Intanki-Kaziranga complex to allow elephants to disperse and migrate. The ecoregion represents the swath of semi-evergreen forests along the upper Brahmaputra River plains.Assam Valley semi-evergreen forest, Assam alluvial plains semi-evergreen forest, eastern submontane semi-evergreen forest, sub-Himalayan light alluvial semi-evergreen forest, eastern alluvial secondary semi-evergreen forest, sub-Himalayan secondary wet mixed forest, and Cachar semi-evergreen forest. But most of the ecoregion's original semi-evergreen forests have been converted to grasslands by centuries of fire and other human influences.

Only small patches of forests now remain. Tipaimukh Dam is not an isolated project; it is part of a comprehensive Indian plan of using rivers that flow from India into Bangladesh, and, hence, needs to be viewed in the general context of sharing of international rivers by these two countries. In general, India has been using its upper riparian position and its economic and financial strength to take unilateral steps with regard to the flow of these international rivers. Most of these unilateral steps have been of diversionary character, diverting the water flow to destinations inside India and thus reducing the flow of water into the rivers of Bangladesh.

Glaring examples of such diversionary interventions are the Farakka Barrage on the Ganges and the Gozaldoba Barrage on the Teesta. India has undertaken numerous other diversionary and flow-controlling structures on most of the 54 rivers shared by Bangladesh and India. These diversionary projects of India go against the international norms regarding sharing of international rivers. In particular, they violate Bangladesh's right to prior and customary use of river water. The entire economy and life in Bangladesh have evolved on the basis of rivers. Any major change in the flow of these rivers is, therefore, seriously disruptive for Bangladesh.

Furthermore, river intervention structures affect the flow of sediments, which are vital for deltaic Bangladesh, which is facing submergence by rising sea level caused by global warming:

(a) First, Bangladesh does not yet have the necessary facts to assess the changes in Barak flow to be caused by Tipaimukh.

(b) Second, dams can also be a source of destabilisation, not only in the extreme situation of dam-break, but also in the often recurring situation when the excess water needs to be released to protect the dam from overflow. Such unplanned releases lead to unexpected floods. For example, the unusual 2008 floods in Bihar were caused by unexpected release of water by the dams that India has constructed on the Ganges tributaries near Nepal.

(c) Third, for Bangladesh to benefit from stabilisation of the Barak flow, it has to have a say in the release of water at Tipaimukh. This would suggest that Tipaimukh should be under joint control of India and Bangladesh. As of now, Tipaimukh will be entirely under Indian control, and the water release decisions will be made by India alone, putting Bangladesh at the mercy of the Indian officials operating Tipaimukh. Such a helpless situation is not in Bangladesh's interests.

(d) Fourth, river flow contains not only water but also sediments, which are very important for deltaic Bangladesh. One damaging impact of Tipaimukh will be reduced sediment volume in the Barak flow.

(e) Fifth, Bangladesh has to assess the costs and benefits for her economy of the seasonal changes in the Barak flow caused by Tipaimukh. For example, boro, which is cultivated in the haor areas that become dry in winter, is the main crop for many in the Surma-Kushiara basin. If Tipaimukh increases winter flow, cultivation of boro in these areas may not be possible. Without detailed studies it is difficult to say whether the net economic impact of the cross-season stabilisation of the Barak flow will be positive for Bangladesh.

(f) Sixth, there is also the issue of ecology to consider. The flora and fauna of the Surma-Kushiara-Meghna basin have developed on the basis of a certain seasonal pattern of the river flow. Detailed studies are necessary to gauge the environmental and ecological impact of Tipaimukh.

Worldwide experience shows that large-scale interventions in rivers do not prove to be that beneficial in the long run. The hydropower generated often proves to be meagre and costly. The irrigation carried out on the basis of diverted water often proves wasteful and leads to salinity and deterioration of the soil quality, so that diversionary projects end up harming not only the basin from which water is withdrawn but also the area to which water is transported (at a great cost). The reservoir submerges large areas of land, destroying the ecology and displacing thousands of (often most vulnerable) indigenous people, causing permanent problems of alienation and insurgency.

The reservoir also becomes a source of methane, undercutting the emission reducing potentiality of the hydropower generated. The reservoir and the upstream flow often become a cesspool of pollution. Dams obstruct sediment flow and the free movement fish stock. While many of the damages prove to the permanent, dams themselves become obsolete due to sedimentation, filling up of the reservoir, etc. In view of these negative consequences many are now skeptical about dams, barrages and other large-scale river intervention projects. It is an open question whether Tipaimukh dam will be beneficial in the long run and in net terms even for India.

Many in India are opposed to the Tipaimukh dam. They include, indigenous people, state governments of Manipur and Mizoram, environmentalists, river activists, human right advocates, and even economists and social scientists. By providing various monetary benefits and offering free electricity, etc., the North East Electricity Production Company (NEEPCO), the current Tipaimukh implementing agency, has been able to pacify the state governments. However, in India, opposition to Tipaimukh continues. India should not undertake water diversionary project (such as at Fulertal or at other points) on the Barak River under any circumstances. India should refrain from water diversionary projects on other rivers shared with Bangladesh. Bangladesh, India, and the other countries of the sub-continent should abandon the current commercial approach to rivers and to adopt the ecological approach.

Delhi going ahead to build Tipaimukh Dam

Amidst mounting protests both at home and in lower-riparian Bangladesh, India is going ahead with the plan to construct its largest and most controversial 1500 mw hydro-electric dam project on the river Barak at Tipaimukh on the common borders of three northeastern states of Assam, Manipur and Mizoram. Officials and experts in Dhaka fear the unilateral Indian move to construct the massive dam and regulate water flow of the Barak, which feeds both the Surma and Kushiara rivers in Sylhet, will have lasting adverse effects on livelihoods, ecology and environment in a vast region of Bangladesh. Moreover, people living in the vicinity of the hydro-electric project in Manipur, costing over 5,000 crore Indian rupee, fear submersion of vast areas on the Indian side too.

One of the largest river systems in Bangladesh — the Meghna with its distributaries — is fully dependent on the waters rolling down from the Surma and Kushiara. A massive construction on the Barak River will adversely affect the water flows of the Meghna and its distributaries. Against this backdrop, tension is growing over reports that the Indian prime minister laid the foundation stone of the project recently. Meanwhile, people in greater Sylhet under the banner of Shahjalal Samaj Kalyan Parishad plan to hold a rally at Court Point in the divisional city today, protesting the Tipaimukh project. In India too, protests have been going on for years in the northeastern region as many people living in the Barak catchment areas fear permanent flooding of their areas due to the impact of the dam.

According to reports from across the border, the Naga Women Union of Manipur protested Manipur State Government's signing of agreement with the North-Eastern Electrical Power Corporation (NEEPCO) for constructing the project. It feared that due to the dam-induced submersion, 15,000 people would be rendered landless and homeless. The Naga People's Movement for Human Rights (NPMHR) also condemned the government decision of constructing the 162.8 metre-high dam. Tawhidul Anwar, a senior member of Indo-Bangla Joint Rivers Commission (JRC), told The Daily Star yesterday, "We have no confirmed reports about Manmohan Singh (Indian premier) laying the foundation stone during his recent visit to northeastern India. But we have come to know for sure India has started updating the Tipaimukh DPR".

Dhaka formally protest against New Delhi's plan for construction of a dam which may adversely affect Bangladesh's ecology, after a new government takes over in India, a senior Bangladeshi minister said Saturday. Indian plans for construction of a multi-purpose dam on the Tipaimukh River might cause an ecological catastrophe for its downstream neighbour Bangladesh, Finance Minister AMA Muhith told reporters after a meeting in Dhaka. He charged that the proposed dam could lead to desertification in the north-eastern region of Sylhet, while also drying up the Surma, Kushiara and Meghna rivers downstream. "We cannot allow this disaster to take place," the minister said, calling on Bangladeshis to campaign against the Indian project, which has also drawn protests inside India itself.

Bangladesh will send a delegation to visit the project areas after the new Indian government assumed office to see their plan and understand the possible impact. "We'll solve the problem through bilateral discussion," he said. In April, Indian Foreign Secretary Shiv Sankar Menon in a surprise visit to Dhaka had requested Bangladesh to send a delegation at the project site to assess the impact of the project in the downstream. Bangladesh has long asked India to refrain from building the dam, to be located at the confluence of the Barak and Tuivai rivers. India began soliciting international bids for the dam in early 2006. The Barak River feeds Bangladesh's Surma and Kushiyara rivers in the north-east, eventually flowing into Meghna, one of the three main rivers in Bangladesh. India plans to complete the project by 2012.

Two senior cabinet ministers, who hail from the region (Sylhet), spoke about their plan to resist the construction of the dam at the Annual General Meeting of Jalalabad Association at Bangladesh Shishu Academy auditorium. "The dam will desert the greater Sylhet region," Finance Minister AMA Muhith told the meeting. He said, the Tipaimukh dam will dry up the rivers Surma, Kushiara and Meghna as well as the haors. "It's the responsibility of every citizen to resist the dam," he said, adding that a plus point is that the Indian people in the surrounding areas of the project like Karimganj and Monipur are also against the project. Muhith said by implementing the project, India will withdraw waters from international river Barak for irrigation purpose, which will desert the land in Bangladesh's northeastern region. "We cannot allow this disaster to take place."

Even as Delhi is all set to begin work on the Tipaimukh hydroelectric project, a multipurpose high dam inclusive, upstream of a major river system of Bangladesh, Dhaka seems oblivious to all relevant developments. The Rs 5,163-crore Tipaimukh plan, which has been on the drawing board for nearly 40 years, is set to be built on the river Barak, which bifurcates into two streams as it enters Bangladesh as the rivers Surma and Kushiara. The Meghna originates at the confluence of the Surma and the Kushiara. Goutam Chakraborty, the state minister for water resources, told New Age Sunday evening that the government did not know anything about the foundation stone laying of the Tipaimukh project.

"Earlier we had protested against implementing the Tipaimukh project through the joint rivers commission of the two countries," he said. "We have requested India to provide detailed information about the project. But they remain taciturn," Goutam said. Secretary to the water resources ministry, Omar Faruque Khan, said, "The government will look into the latest development regarding the Tipaimukh project." The Tipaimukh plant, which was delayed after the Manipur State Assembly had raised objections, has led to protests in India and its downstream neighbour Bangladesh as the project will cause economic, ecological and human catastrophes in both countries.

The residents of the Indian states concerned who are likely to be displaced and affected on account of the project have been staging protests and making representations to their respective state and the union governments, saying that thousands of people will suffer as the construction of the dam will submerge 73 villages, many sacred sites and cultivable land and violate their inalienable human rights. The people of the localities where the dam is proposed to be built have sought constitutional protection, particularly with a view to safeguarding the tribal people, their land, belief, culture and history.

Expressing grave concern over the possible consequences of the dam, the protestors said in a recent memorandum submitted to the central government of India, "Once the dam is built, the land, covering an area of 275.5

sq km, will be submerged permanently." Meanwhile, experts in Bangladesh have expressed their apprehension about the project that is sure to block the flow of the country's major riverine network in the north-east and have further disastrous consequences downstream. They claim that it could hit the country fatally, or have consequences of no less magnitude than the Farakka Barrage across the Ganges to the north-west of Bangladesh.

Tipaimukh to become another Farakka

Dr. Soibam Ibotombi of Dept. of Earth Sciences, Manipur University says that the dam will be a geo-tectonic blunder of international dimensions: The site selected for Tipaimukh project is one of the most active in the entire world, recording at least two major earthquakes of 8+ in the Reichter Scale during the past 50 years. The proposed Tipaimukh HEP is envisaged for construction in one of the most geologically unstable area as the proposed Tipaimukh dam axis falls on a 'fault line' potentially active and possible epicenter for major earthquakes.

While Hydroelectric projects are typically considered greener than other power generation options in short term, it has significant long-term impact to the environment like changes in the ecosystem, destroying nearby settlements and changing habitat conditions of people, fish and wildlife. Especially in the densely populated countries like India and Bangladesh, where rivers are lifelines, projects like Tipaimukh will create adverse effect to a huge number of population and their habitats. No wonder right from the start this project faced protests from potentially affected people in India, and the recommendations of the WCD (World Commission on Dams)".

The people of Manipur have been fighting legally to stop the project but have so far been unsuccessful. The Indian government is going ahead with the plan. The Sinlung Indigenous People Human Rights Organisation (SIPHRO) of India said that "the process for choosing it (the project premises) ignored both the indigenous people and the recommendations of the WCD (World Commission on Dams)". People of Zakiganj formed a human chain at Amolshid in the upazila protesting Indian move to construct a dam on the river Borak at Tipaimukh in the Indian state of Manipur. Acid Santrash Nirmul Committee, Sylhet, staged the protest against the controversial dam project, 100-km upstream of eastern border of Sylhet district. The river Borak bifurcated into two flows and entered Bangladesh as Surma and Kushiyara through Zakiganj border.

Zakiganj Pourasava (municipality) Mayor Iqbal Ahmed and Sylhet City Corporation Councillor Koyes Lodi also joined the human chain programme.

The Indian government initiated the project about a decade ago, but could not go ahead in the face of widespread agitation from its own people at times. Even some 25 peoples' forums like that of Tipaimukh Dam Resistance Committee have been formed there to protest the move. With reference to some experts' opinion, the discussion meeting was told that implementation of the dam project mainly aimed at producing electricity would cause a disastrous situation in the Meghna basin, especially the greater Sylhet and Mymensingh region, during the dry season due to withdrawal of water in the upper stream. Also, they said, there are apprehensions of recurrent flooding during the monsoon due to possible release of water. It will be another Farakka, the speakers said, urging the people to resist the move.

Ignoring its promise, India in the last four years has refrained from sharing technical information with Bangladesh about building the Tipaimukh Dam in the bordering Manipur state, triggering public uncertainty and outcry over its possible negative impact on the neighbouring country. While India has not started construction of Tipaimukh dam on the Barak River near Manipur-Mizoram border, it had floated international tender in 2005 and opened the bid in 2006 during the era of former BNP-Jamaat alliance rule. In 2005, India promised to share with Bangladesh the project design, which is pending till date.

Besides, the country also did not share any study report on the dam's impact on downstream regions. Experts told The Daily Star the construction of Tipaimukh dam would impose a great environmental threat to Bangladesh as four major rivers in the Meghna basin — the Meghna, Kalini, Surma and Kushiyara — lie downstream the Barak, locally known as 'Ahu'. Amid such concerns, the prime minister has recently said an all-party parliamentary committee will visit India to know about the issue. The schedule of this visit has not yet been set. Indian response to Bangladesh's worries has so far been remained confined within officially informing the government that they have not started any construction yet.

At a Joint River Commission (JRC) meeting in September 2005 held in Dhaka India formally assured Bangladesh that they would not divert any water for their irrigation project, he said. Hiding any information by the upper riparian countries about the use of common rivers is considered as violation of the international water management convention. The expert warn of an increase in salinity in the Meghna-Surma basin, unusual floods in hoar region, reduce in water flow in the Surma, Kushiyara and Meghna rivers in certain period, damage to the country's ecosystem and agriculture patterns in Sylhet region, among other impacts of the dam.

A chain of severe impacts is very likely as Bangladesh gets 7-8 percent of its river waters through the Barak. Negative impacts of any large dam are very widely known around the globe. A detailed study by the World Dam Commission published in 2000 says adverse impacts of any large dams are irreversible for the lower riparian region. The study after reviewing 1,000 dams from 79 countries concludes in its report: "The environmental impacts of dams are more negative than positive ones and in many cases dams have led to irreversible loss of species and ecosystems."

Indian High Commissioner to Dhaka Pinak Ranjan Chakrabarti at a meeting with Communications Minister Syed Abul Hossain recently said though his country will have sole control over water flow at the proposed dam site, it would not make any barrage. He also said Bangladesh would not be 'affected' by the dam. However, experts fear once the dam is set up, it may reduce the natural monsoon flood patterns in the Sylhet region, adversely affecting cultivation and livelihoods on a vast scale.

"It will increase the risk of floods at the end of monsoon and hamper the agriculture patterns during winter," said Ainun Nishat, eminent river expert of the country. Rainfall patterns are changing due to climate change and a lot of rainfall takes place at the end of monsoon, said Ainun Nishat. If it rains at the end of monsoon, it will open the spillway gates of the dam and unusual floods will occur here, he added. They would preserve the water during monsoon after building the dam and release it in winter, which will increase the water flow downstream. "The land downstream the Barak in Sylhet region is wetland, where people grow crops during winter when it gets dry. If they release water during winter the wetland will be inundated and it will be a great impact on our agriculture," Nishat warned.

An increase in water level in the winter will cause a major impact on the ecosystem if the wetland gets inundated, he added. He however said without checking every piece of information it is not possible to measure the total impact of Tipaimukh dam. The experts fear India may hold up water flow during dry season and divert water at the proposed Phulertal Barrage 100 kilometres downstream Tipaimukh and 100 km upstream Amalshid in Sylhet. The Phulertal barrage would have a direct bearing on the Surma, Kushiyara and Meghna rivers due to diversion of water for irrigation purposes in northeastern India. On hydropower component and rock fill dam, India claims no damage would occur to Bangladesh, but Bangladesh fears upstream water flow regulation. Director General of Water Resources Planning

Organisation (WARPO) Jalaluddin Md Abdul Hye said, "We don't have enough information to talk about the issue."

Information surfaced in different websites says several Indian organisations and civil society bodies are protesting the dam considering its negative impacts. The websites also say the Expert Appraisal Committee (EAC) of India has found the design of the dam contains many errors, omissions, gaps, lacks in scientific rigour and falls far short of compliance of normative standards set by the scientific and academic community in India and the world. The Action Committee against Tipaimukh Dam (ACTIP), a platform protesting the dam, along with some other local committees from Manipur and Mizoram submitted a memorandum on March 14, 2007 to the president and prime minister of India in protest against the project.

They mentioned in their memorandum that once the project is implemented, an area of 286.20 square kilometres land will go under water forever. Eight villages situated in the Barak valley will be completely inundated leaving over 40,000 people landless and more than 90 villages, mostly in Tamenglong district, adversely affected. Besides, about 27,242 hectares of cultivable land will be lost. The Barak waterfalls and Zeilad Lake, which are connected with the history of the Zeliangrong people, an indigenous community in India, will go forever underwater. All folklores and legends will have no monuments' proof and it will become a makeup story for the next generation.

In the memorandum they said the mega-dam proposed in Tipaimukh will smother this river, change its age-old knowable and reliable nature, and drown them all in sorrow forever. The project is not for the common people, they said, appealing to the government to let the Ahu run free.

International Convention and Ganges Water Sharing Treaty

According to the International Convention on Joint River Water, without the consent of the downstream river nation no single country alone can control the multi-nation rivers. But India does not care for these international laws despite being a signatory of this convention. If India constructs the dam without the consent of Bangladesh, it will also violate the article 9 of Bangladesh-India Ganges Water Sharing Treaty, 1996. Asked about a possible solution, Ainun Nishat said the solution has to be political. He added in the Ganges Water Sharing Treaty both the countries agreed to manage all the joint rivers on bilateral basis. "So under the Gages Water Sharing Treaty, both the country can resolve by sharing information and a joint team can study the adverse impacts on both the countries," Nishat added.

India handed over a number of primary project proposals to Bangladesh in 1979 and 1983. Later they conducted detailed studies about the project and completed the final design and environment impact assessment but did not share those with Bangladesh. According to the primary project proposals, the height of the Tipaimukh damn was fixed at 161.8 metres and length 390 metres to contain at lest 15.9 million cubic metres of water.

Pollution in the Ganges Brahmaputra Delta Plain

Indian 'Green Lady' and former environment minister Maneka Gandhi was worried that in early 21st century the Indian provinces may be involved in battles due to irrational water sharing. National Water Development Agency (NWDA) of India to carry out 560,000,000,000,00 Indian rupee (50 Rupees= 1 US Dollar) a project to link 37 rivers through similar number of canals and 32 dams. Indian Prime Minister's personal initiative helped prioritise this project, while the President directed a 'Task Force' in August 2002 to complete the project within 10 years.

India is apparently stressing on the Hormon Doctrine, which originated in the United States in 1895, but has never gained universal acceptance. It is conveniently forgetting various provisions of the Montevideo Declaration of

American States (1933), the views of the 1977 UN Water Conference held in Mar del Plata, the decision of the Lake Lanoux Arbitral Tribunal in the dispute between Spain and France and those of legal experts from the International Law Commission. The Indian plan envisages transfer of water of the Ganges and its tributaries to Maharashtra, Rajasthan and Gujarat.

Similarly, it also plans to divert the waters of the Brahmaputra and its tributaries to the Ganges and from there to the Godavori, Krishna, Pennar and Cauvery basins through Subrnarekha in West Bengal and Mahanadi of Orissa. Again the Brahmaputra and the Teesta would be connected to take waters from the former to the latter and from the latter to the Farakka Barrage. For this purpose they need some 30 connecting canals which (if joined) together would be around 10,000 km in length. Besides nine big and 24 small dams—four of them in collaboration with Bhutan and Nepal—would also be built as required in the master plan.

India also plans to produce 34 million KW (kilowatt) waterpower under the same project. The policymakers, moreover, in India believe this river-link project is worth the huge expenditure as they take the multi-faceted benefits from this project into consideration. Another thing that added motion to the Indian government's initiatives in materialising the project is a verdict of the Indian Supreme Court. The court verdict, which came after a public interest case was filed with it, ordered the government to realise the project by December 31, 2016.

Indian President APJ Abdul Kalam has spoken in favour of this project recently while the BJP govt. has been calling it "Indian's dream project" and promising to materialise it for quite some time now. Notable water expert, Tauhidul Anwar Khan, Member of the Joint River Commission has also very correctly pointed out that India's unilateral move to inter-link the trans-boundary Rivers contravenes existing Articles of the 1996 Treaty between Bangladesh and India with regard to the sharing of the Ganges Waters at Farakka. According to him, such a scheme would be contrary to the body and spirit of Articles 2(2) and 9 of this Treaty and would affect providing of due share of common river's water to a co-riparian.

Consequences for Bangladesh

Such steps would have disastrous impact on the economy of Bangladesh, its ecology, the livelihood of its people, its eco-system. It will also in the long run lead to internal displacement of millions of its citizens. Specialists have also pointed out that implementation of such a project would most certainly lead to more severe flooding in the monsoon and worse droughts in the lean season. Such vagaries would also contribute to increased salinity across the country and sharp fall in sweet water levels. These factors would juxtapose to eventually destroy the largest mangrove forest in the world, the Sunderbans.

According to a Washington Times report on September 20, the Indian plan would cause severe flooding during the monsoon rains and worse drought during the dry season in Bangladesh. Centre for Development and Environment Policy at the Indian Institute of Management in Kolkata as saying that once the Indian plan is implemented, the world could lose the richest fisheries in south Asia. Bandhopadhyaya points out that salinity would also make inroads into the region, affecting thousands of hectares of arable land [and] affecting the lives of millions of people living on agriculture in Bangladesh.

Mangrove forests too, he says, will be disastrously affected as they depend on the steady rise and fall of tides for their roots to breathe. Arresting the natural flow of rivers could be a death knell for the world's largest remaining coastal forest a World Heritage site shared by the delta regions of Bangladesh and India. The wisdom of linking up rivers is not beyond question because more than 70 percent of Indian River water is polluted by linking them and then allowing them to enter into Bangladesh will poison all our water bodies, human beings and wildlife.

The International Law Association (ILA)'s Helsinki rules-1967 and the International Law Commission (ILC)'s second report on the Law of Non-navigational Uses of International Water Courses-1986, both prohibit co-riparian states from altering the flow of an international water course, so as to cause either substantial or appreciable harm to another.

Both adopt the equitable balance approach with regards to sharing the waters of an international drainage basin. Similarly, the Salzburg Resolution of the Institute of International Laws in 1961 stated that the right of a sovereign state to use the waters of a shared river is limited by the right of utilisation of other states interested in the same water course. In it's general commentary the ILA states that "Any use of water by a basin state, whether upper or lower, that denies an equitable sharing of uses by a co-basin state/states, conflicts with the community of interests of all basin states, in obtaining the maximum benefit from the common resource.

Certainly, a diversion of water that denies a co-basin state an equitable share is in violation of International Law". While Farakka barrage alone has adversely affected our 40,000,000 (four crore) people of Bangladesh, crippled our agriculture, fisheries, navigation, hydro-morphology, industry, forestry, poultry and other relevant sectors; the Mohanada and the Teesta barrages that were not left uncommissioned by India. By and large Farakka, Mohananda and Teesta barrages together have resulted severe ecological and climatic degradation in Bangladesh resulting in the desertification of the north and north-western parts of the country, destroying the Sunderban forest, the largest mangrove forest of the world, including its flora and fauna, posing serious threat to Mongla Port, and intensifying flood, flash flood, cyclone and draught.

Bangladesh response to Indian River-linking Proposal

The Congress-led Indian government has decided to implement a controversial river-linking project for unilateral withdrawal of water from trans-boundary Rivers despite widespread concern over and protest against the mega-project within India and in Bangladesh. The government will take up the issue for a comprehensive review any time this month, the Indian Supreme Court was reportedly told Monday. Indian solicitor general told the court that the government had decided to continue with the project, the New Delhi-based Times News Network reported Tuesday.

The solicitor general told the court that the issue would be placed before the cabinet in September for a 'comprehensive review'. The Indian government sought six weeks time to get back to the court. The case is posted for further hearing eight weeks from now, the Times News Network added. Dhaka, meanwhile, remains in the dark as the no detail communications have been made by New Delhi since the government of Prime Minister Manmohan Singh assumed office in May this year. The government is, however, aware of the Indian move, Water Resources Secretary Dr M Omar Faruque Khan told New Age Tuesday. "All of us in the lower riparian country should stand together against such a project irrespective of political views as the project may bring about ecological disaster."

Dhaka has already expressed grave concern over the project and called upon New Delhi not to implement it as it is meant for withdrawal of water from the rivers Brahmaputra, the Ganges and Barak, main sources of surface water in Bangladesh, ignoring the interests of other riparian countries. The move in the Indian court came within days of Congress MP Jairam Ramesh's statement that inter-linking of rivers could lead to severe ecological and rehabilitation problems. "The first requirement for managing floods on a long-term basis in East and North East is a viable, durable water-sharing agreement in the Ganga, Brahmputra and Barak basin involving the states of eastern India, Nepal, Bhutan and Bangladesh," he said while participating in a recent discussion in Rajya Sabha, the upper house of the Indian Parliament.

"As the river-linking project makes headway, more inter-state and inter-country dissensions are likely to surface," Dr Sudhirendar Sharma, who heads the Delhi-based Ecological Foundation and specialises in water issues, told New Age during his recent visit to Dhaka. The Indian initiative would be another 'death trap for Bangladesh, even more deadly than Farakka. According to the initial plan, 37 rivers will be inter-linked to transfer water to regions facing scarcity through 30 links across 9,600 kilometres, connecting 32 dams.

Water from the Brahmaputra will flow into the Ganges, which will be connected to the Mahanadi and the Godavari. The Godavari will be linked to the Krishna, then the Pennar and the Cauvery. The Narmada will flow into the Tapi and the Yamuna into the Sabarmati. This huge inter-basin transfer is to be completed by 2016 with an estimated cost of $112 billion.

The concept of "surplus" or "unused" water

The most important question that needs to be addressed is whether or not there is any "surplus" or "unused" water in Brahmaputra River. The concept of "surplus" or "unused" water is an ironic one. The water that flows in Ganges-Brahmaputra-Meghna (G-B-M) basin is the reason why there exists the deltaic country called Bangladesh to start with. The sediments laid down by these rivers built the delta over millions of years that we call Bangladesh today. Needless to say that there is a very complex ecosystem, including the Sunderbans, that is supported by the freshwater flow in these rivers. Any diversion of water also means proportional diversion of sediments.

Any lack of sediment flux to the delta and coastal plains will cause accelerated drowning the coastal region in the face of rising sea-level. In essence, it is already happening due to the impact of Farakka Barrage and will certainly accelerate if other barrages (e.g. the proposed Ganges Barrage, and Mowa Barrage). The people of Bangladesh,

India, and Nepal living in the Ganges-Brahmaputra-Meghna basin share common history, heritage, and friendship that go back to the time immemorial.

India as the largest country in the basin has the responsibility to protect the interests of her own people, as well as the interests of all her neighbors. The Govt. of India should take initiatives to develop an integrated water resources development plan based on the principles of equity and respect of her neighbors, which in turn will strengthen the regional stability, security, peace, and prosperity.

China's Move to divert Tibetian Rivers

Chinese leaders are drawing up plans to use nuclear explosions, in breach of the international test-ban treaty, to blast a tunnel through the Himalayas for the world's biggest hydroelectric plant. The proposed power station is forecast to produce more than twice as much electricity as the controversial Three Gorges Dam being built on the Yangtze River. The project, which also involves diverting Tibetan water to arid regions, is due to begin as soon as construction of the Three Gorges Dam is completed in 2009. China will have to overcome fierce opposition from neighbouring countries who fear that the scheme could endanger the lives and livelihoods of millions of their people.

Critics say that those living downstream would be at the mercy of Chinese dam officials who would be able to flood them or withhold their water supply. China's state-run media reported that the project would form part of a national strategy to divert water from rivers in the south and west to drought-stricken northern areas. The reports said that a 38 million kilowatt power station at Muotuo on the Yarlung Zangbo River in Tibet would harness the force of a 9,840ft drop in terrain over only a few miles.

The capacity of the station would make it the world's largest power generation facility, much bigger than the 18 million kilowatt plant at the Three Gorges. The cost of drilling the tunnel through Mount Namcha Barwa has not yet been announced, but appears likely to surpass £10 billion. At the bottom of the tunnel, the water will flow into a new reservoir and then be diverted along more than 500 miles of the Tibetan plateau to the vast, arid areas of Xinjiang region and Gansu province. Beijing wants to use large quantities of the plentiful waters of the south-west to top up the Yellow River basin and assuage mounting discontent over water shortages in 600 cities in northern China.

Yang Yong, a geologist who has explored the river, said the dam could become an embarrassing white elephant amid growing signs that the volume of water flowing in the Yarlung Zangpo could shrink. He said: "Environmental conditions in the upper reaches of the river continue to deteriorate, with glaciers receding and tributaries and lakes going dry." Tibetan activists have warned that the plans are likely to devastate the lower reaches of the Yarlung Zangbo, which flows south where it becomes the Brahmaputra. This river irrigates the northern plains of Assam state in India before flowing through Bangladesh and emptying into the Bay of Bengal.

River linking - A Millennium Folly

Considered to be the "mother of all projects", interlinking of rivers is projected as the one and the only solution to all water problems - droughts and floods. Never before has any proposal won the unstinted support of the apex court, the first citizen and the chief executive of the country, all at the same time. The book is a collection of articles by experts who dissect and analyze the proposed project from various angles. Amongst other issues, the book brings into the focus the question of the rights of the riparian countries.

Authors assert that riparian rights are not being taken cognizance of and that a unilateral decision by India without a fully consulted prior consent of the concerned countries can injure the already fragile political atmosphere in South Asia. The idea of interlinking of the rivers of India is described by - from the President down to local leaders in the less water endowed areas - as the perfect win-win solution for addressing the twin problems of water scarcity in the western and southern parts of the country and the problem of floods in the eastern and northeastern parts.

The claims and statements of politicians, do not, however, substitute comprehensive scientific assessment, so that one can know whether by the proposed interlinking, the right quality and quantity of water would be stored and delivered at the right time in the right places...and all this would be achieved in the most cost-effective manner. For this, what is needed is sound professional assessment of the technical proposals based on the latest interdisciplinary systems knowledge. Unfortunately, as far as the proposal for interlinking is concerned, there is little information available to the open world of science, beyond some lines drawn on the map of the country.

Unless the scientific basis and technical details of the proposal are made available for open professional assessment, the justifications that are being propped up for the project will remain mere exercises in the act of guessing on the part of the people, and professing on the part of the water resource officials. Such silence about the technical details of the proposals also has other implications. For example, in contrast with the official prescription for interlinking of rivers, there are strong opinions that India's water crisis is caused by the mismanagement of water resources and the solutions do not lie in supply side augmentation. Iyer (2000), a former Secretary of Water Resources of the country corroborates this fact, with the view that:

Large scale supply side augmentation has been prescribed by the engineers as the only way for the satisfaction of water requirements of the developing countries. As a result, political leaders at all levels have sold the idea of solving the water problem by harnessing the huge monsoon run-off. The reductionist view of engineering is unable to recognise the ecological significance of the unhindered flows in the river as critical to drainage, transportation of sediments, recharge of groundwater, maintenance of the delta and highly productive estuarine ecosystems and related biodiversity. Hence, it finds little difficulty in locating 'surplus' river basins! India's plan of inter-linking trans-boundary rivers to create a new "national water grid" seeks to provide increased amount of surface water from trans-boundary rivers to other parts in India. The plan traces its idea back to India's Water Resources Minister K.L. Rao's proposed National Water Grid of 1972 and Captain Dastoor's Garland Canals of 1977.

India has always conceived inter-linking rivers to transfer water from so-called "surplus" areas to so-called "deficit" areas within its territory. During the negotiations in 1977 on the Ganges Water Agreement, I distinctly remember that a senior member of India's delegation disclosed informally to me that if the India's canal link proposal (Jogighopa to Farakka) through Bangladesh, linking Brahmaputra with the Ganges, was not accepted, India eventually would transfer water from Brahmaputra to the Ganges through its territory above Bangladesh. If India proposes to inter-link its peninsular rivers (Mahanadi-Godavari-Krishna-Pennar-Cauvery), without affecting its neighbours, Bangladesh has nothing to say as the rivers involved are within the territorial jurisdiction of India.

When India attempts to inter-link Himalayan Rivers (Ganges-Brahmaputra-Meghna) without explicit agreement of Bangladesh, it raises serious concerns from the point of view of two international law principles: (a) state responsibility, and (b) law of international rivers. Besides the above principles of law, the plan comes within the ambit of Article 9 of the 1996 Ganges Water Treaty wherein both Bangladesh and India agreed "to conclude water sharing Treaties/Agreements with regard to other common rivers."

Political Agenda

At a conference on "Regional Cooperation on Transboundary rivers: Impact of the Indian River-Linking

Project" held in Dhaka from December 17-19, 2004, many Indian speakers, mostly experts on water resources management, have expressed strong reservations on the inter-linking plan of rivers on serious technical and environmental grounds. Among them is an India eco-activist, Ms. Medha Patekar who leads the National Alliance of People's Movement, a network of over 150 mass-based movements. During an interview with The Daily Star, she revealed the real motives behind the inter-linking river plan. She said: "Water has become an electoral issue in India and river linking project is a political agenda.

The government of India looks at the project as a sort of gift to the voters." Furthermore, it has been reported that the people of Bihar, Orissa, Assam, West Bengal, and Karnataka are opposed to the project. On December 19, India's High Commissioner to Bangladesh, Veena Sikri, at the conclusion session of the conference reportedly defended the linking plan. She argued that firstly it is a plan only, not yet a "project," and secondly India's share of water per capita is much less than that of Bangladesh (she has been quoted placing India at 2,200 cubic metres per capita versus Bangladesh's 19,600).

It seems implicit from the statement of the High Commissioner that the plan or concept of inter-liking rivers is a step in the right direction to mitigate flood and drought situation in India. It is obvious that being the official representative of the government of India, she has to defend government's policy and plan.

Big Power Dynamics

At a conference on "Regional Cooperation on Transboundary rivers: Impact of the Indian River-Linking Project" held in Dhaka from December 17-19, 2004, many Indian speakers, mostly experts on water resources management, have expressed strong reservations on the inter-linking plan of rivers on serious technical and environmental grounds. Among them is an India eco-activist,

Ms. Medha Patekar who leads the National Alliance of People's Movement, a network of over 150 mass-based movements. During an interview with The Daily Star, she revealed the real motives behind the inter-linking river plan. She said: "Water has become an electoral issue in India and river linking project is a political agenda.

The government of India looks at the project as a sort of gift to the voters." Furthermore, it has been reported that the people of Bihar, Orissa, Assam, West Bengal, and Karnataka are opposed to the project. On December 19, India's High Commissioner to Bangladesh, Veena Sikri, at the conclusion session of the conference reportedly defended the linking plan. She argued that firstly it is a plan only, not yet a "project," and secondly India's share of water per capita is much less than that of Bangladesh (she has been quoted placing India at 2,200 cubic metres per capita versus Bangladesh's 19,600).

It seems implicit from the statement of the High Commissioner that the plan or concept of inter-liking rivers is a step in the right direction to mitigate flood and drought situation in India. It is obvious that being the official representative of the government of India, she has to defend government's policy and plan. Bangladesh does not wish to make the water issue an international one unless it is pushed back to the wall. In 1976, Bangladesh had to raise the issue of the sharing of the Ganges water at the UN General Assembly.

Despite strong opposition from India, the General Assembly found the issue as one that might endanger peace and stability in the region. India realised that there was no way to get out of the issue and agreed to a Consensus Statement of the President of the General Assembly, rather than a UN General Assembly resolution. The statement of November 26, 1976, urged India to commence negotiations immediately in Dhaka with Bangladesh, that eventually resulted in the conclusion of the 1977 Ganges Water Agreement. Internalisation of the water issue does not seem to be a ready option for Bangladesh, given the current state of bilateral relations with India. India has only to abide by the provisions of the 1996 Ganges Water Treaty and rules of international law on uses of international/trans-boundary Rivers.

This is not a big ask from India because India has to respond to the lawful right of Bangladesh on uses of waters of common rivers through cooperative basis. The construction of Farakka Barrage and its operation in 1975 demonstrates that if India wants to undertake interventions (such as dam, barrage, or other river construction work) on the natural flow of trans-boundary rivers, it will do so despite Bangladesh's opposition. India is an upper riverine country and is placed in an advantageous position vis a vis lower riverine Bangladesh. Bangladesh has to realise this hard fact.

Self-reliance

Bangladesh has to rely on its own plan of water management and utilisation. No outside country will do this for Bangladesh. Self-help is the first call of the game. It seems that due to reasons known only to the authorities, Bangladesh has not adequately focused on water utilisation projects in the country and did not reportedly fund sufficiently in water sector. A budget break-up per year for water sector may disclose this fact. The Ganges Barrage project within Bangladesh was conceived in the 70s. Short canals from the Ganges Barrage would have led water into the moribund rivers of the delta, using them to distribute water for salinity control in the Sunderbans, consumption for domestic and industrial use, and irrigation.

When Teesta Barrage was built in Bangladesh, it was constructed by Bangladeshi personnel and the government deliberately excluded foreign experts. The idea was that the personnel, thus trained and skilled during the construction of the Teesta Barrage, would be utilised to construct the Ganges Barrage in the country. However nothing seems to have advanced so far on the Ganges Barrage project. The Ministry of Water Resources of the government of Bangladesh has at various times commissioned pre-feasibility studies for barrages and associated canals at locations on both the Ganges and Brahmaputra rivers.

Experts say that the studies have recommended works on water utilisation of rivers. If the water works would be in place, it would have led to increased amount of water into the North Central, North West, and South West areas of Bangladesh. Experts say that the government of Bangladesh also undertook studies that came to be known as the New Line, a proposal to build barrages on the Brahmaputra and the Ganges within Bangladesh and link them with a canal further south.

This would have allowed both Bangladesh and India to access all the waters of the Ganges and Brahmaputra. The proposal did not proceed. Another proposal, the Farakka-Paksi-Mawa Complex (FPMC), was suggested by a foreign expert, J.S.A. Brichieri-Colombi, of University of London. The proposal was designed to allow both Bangladesh and India to abstract their legitimate share of water from the main rivers, while avoiding some of the problems rose with other proposals. The designer thought it a "win-win" solution for both countries. The proposal, according to the designer, would have benefited Bangladesh as follows:

1. Irrigation supply to areas short of groundwater in North West and South West of Bangladesh;
2. Salinity control in South West and South Central areas in Bangladesh; Salinity control in South West and South Central areas in Bangladesh;
3. Bridges over Padma (Ganges);
4. Freshwater to Sundarbans in Bangladesh;
5. Water supply to Dhaka;
6. Improved navigation on main rivers in and around Dhaka;

7. Erosion control in vicinity for barrages; and

8. Drainage pumping in wet season.

India, on the other hand, would have access to 50 percent share of the Brahmaputra for use and freshwater to Sunderbans in West Bengal. The FPMC did not proceed. The days of adequate supply of water have gone. Fresh water availability is a matter of concern because of the growth of population. According to UN estimate, by 2050, Bangladesh's population is expected to grow to 200 million. Unless Bangladesh seriously undertakes water utilisation plans, it will be left high and dry. Bangladesh is endowed with an adequate number of water resources experts in the country and their assistance needs to be sought at an urgent level.

There is no room for complacency or sentimentality. Many Bangladeshi experts have suggested creating a national body for Integrated Water Resource Management and Development to advise the government on strategies to address, among others, the optimal utilisation of land and water in the country. Meanwhile, steps for water conservation and avoidance of waste are to be undertaken pending the suggested water intervention projects. Recycling and reuse of water is the way to go for the future.

Farming technology on drought-prone areas has to be introduced. Awareness of appropriate choice of crops among farmers is to be disseminated and optimum use of available water is to be made. Although accusing India of diverting water unilaterally from common rivers makes sense, it may not by itself resolve Bangladesh's problems. It seems that Bangladesh needs to be self-critical of its own actions during the last 33 years on water utilisation from its rivers. As a sovereign country, Bangladesh has to stand on its own legs and consider relevant water projects for mitigating floods and droughts in the country.

The bottom line is unless Bangladesh does for itself, no country will come to our aid for a situation in which Bangladesh has appeared to have overlooked its national interests. We live in a world of hard reality. Self-interest rules the day. According to the British Prime Minister Lord Palmerston, there are no permanent friends or enemies. What is permanent is self-interest and that has to be pursued vigorously.

Bibliography

1. Abraham, K., *Ethiopia from Bullets to the Ballot Box: The Bumpy Road to Democracy and the Political Economy of Transition* (Lawrenceville, NJ: The Read Sea Press, Inc., 1994).
2. Abu Zeid, M. A., 'The River Nile and Its Contribution to the Mediterranean Environment', Paper presented at the Stockholm Water Symposium, 10-14 August 1992, Stockholm, Sweden.
3. Adhana, H., 'The Roots of Organised Internal Armed Conflicts in Ethiopia, 1960-1991', in Trevdt, T. (ed.), *Conflict in the Horn of Africa: Human and Ecological Consequence of Warfare* (Uppsala: EPOS, 1993).
4. Badenoch, N., *Transboundary Environmental Governance* (Washington DC: World Resources Institute, 2002).
5. Banerjee, B. N., *Can the Ganga be Cleaned?* (Delhi: B.R. Publishing Corporation, 1989).
6. Basson, M. S., van Niekerk, P. H. and van Rooyen, J. A., *Overview of Water Resources Availability and Utilization in South Africa* (Pretoria: Department of Water Affairs and Forestry, 1997).
7. Beach, H. L., Hamner, J., Hewitt, J. J., Kaufman, E., Kurki, A., Oppenheimer, J. A. and Wolf, A. T., *Transboundary Freshwater Dispute Resolution: Theory, Practice, and Annotated References* (Tokyo: UNU Press, 2000).
8. Beaumont, P., *Environmental Management and Development in Drylands* (London: Routledge, 1989).

9. Burchi, S., 'National Regulations for Groundwater: Options, Issues and Best Practices', in Salman, S. M. A. (ed.), *Ground Water: Legal and Policy Perspectives* (Washington DC: World Bank Technical Paper No. 456, 1999).

10. Caponera, D. A., 'International Water Resources Law in the Indus Basin', Paper presented at the Regional Symposium on *Water Resources Policy in Agro-Socio-Economic Development*4-8 August 1985, Dhaka, Bangladesh.

11. Caponera, D. A., 'Ownership and Transfer of Water and Land in Islam', in Faruqui, N. I., Biswas, A. K. and Bino, M. J. (eds), *Water Management in Islam* (Tokyo: UNU Press, 2001).

12. CGWB, *Background Note: Colloquium on Strategy for Ground Water Development* (New Delhi: Central Ground Water Board, 1996).

13. East Pakistan Water and Power Development Authority. (1964) Master Plan.

14. Government of Bangladesh. (1976) White Paper on the Ganges Water Dispute.

15. Government of Bangladesh. (1983) Bangladesh Irrigation Water Rate Ordinance no.31.

16. Government of Bangladesh. (1985) Groundwater Management Ordinance no. 27.

17. Government of Bangladesh. (1986) National Water Plan.

18. Government of Bangladesh, Ministry of Water Resources. (1992) Irrigation Water Rate Rules.

19. Homiman, B.G., *Amritsar and Our Duty to India*, T. Fisher Unwin, 1920

20. Hough, Richard, *Mountbatten: Hero of our Time*, Weidenfeld and Nicolson, 1980

— *Edwina, Countess Mountbatten of Burma*, Weidenfeld and Nicolson, 1983

21. Indian National Congress, *Report of the Commissioners Appointed by the Punjab Sub-Committee*, New Delhi, Deep Publications, 1920

22. Ismay, General the Lord, *Memoirs*, Heinemann, 1960

23. Ispahani, M.A.H., *Quaid-i-Azam Jinnah As I Knew Him*, Karachi, Forward Publications, 1966

24. Jalal, Ayesha, *The Sole Spokesman: Jinnah, the Muslim League and the Demand for Pakistan*, Lahore, Sang-e-Meel Publications, 1992

25. Jinnah, Quaid-i-Azam Muhammad Ali, *Speeches as Governor-General*, Karachi, Pakistan Publications, 1963 —*Speeches*, Lahore, Sang-e-Meel Publications, 1989

26. Jones, Thomas, *Whitehall Diary*, Oxford University Press, 1969

27. Kabir, Humayun, *Muslim Politics 1906-47 and Other Essays*, Calcutta, Firma K.L. Mukhopadhyay, 1969

28. Kaye, John William, *A History of the Sepoy War in India, 1857-58*, W.H. Allen, 1880

29. Lambton, Anthony, *The Mountbattens: The Battenbergs and Young Mountbatten*, Constable, 1989

30. Lapping, Brian, *End of Empire*, Granada, 1985

31. Lewin, Ronald, *The Chief*, Hutchinson, 1980

32. Munawwar, Muhammad, *Dimensions of Pakistan Movement*, Rawalpindi, Pap-Board Printers, 1989

33. Muni, S.D. and Arnuradha, *Regional Co-operation in South Asia*, New Delhi, National Publishers, 1984

34. Naidu, Sarojini (ed.), *Mohammad Ali Jinnah: His Speeches and Writings, 1912-1917*, Madras, Ganesh, 1918

35. Nanda, B.R., *Mahatma Gandhi*, Delhi, Oxford University Press, 1958

36. O'Dwyer, Sir Michael, *India as I Knew It 1885-1925*, Constable, 1925

37. Patel, I.J., *Sardar Vallabhbhai Patel*, Publications Division, Ministry of Information and Broadcasting, Government of India, 1985

38. Philips, C.H. (ed.), *The Evolution of India and Pakistan, 1858 to 1947: Select Documents*, Oxford University Press, 1962

39. Philips, C.H. and Wainwright, M.D. (eds.), *The Partition of India: Policies and Perspectives*, George Allen & Unwin,

1970

40. Pirzada, S.S. (ed.), *Foundations of Pakistan: All-India Muslim League Documents*, Karachi, National Publishing House, 1969 — *Quaid-i-Azam Jinnah's Correspondence*, Karachi, East and West Publishing Company, 1977

41. Ross, Alan, *The Emissary: G.D. Birla, Gandhi and Independence*, Collins Harvill, 1986

42. Royle, Trevor, *The Last Days of the Raj*, Michael Joseph, 1989

43. Sadullah, Mian Muhammad *et al*, (eds.), *The Partition of the Punjab*, 4 Vols., Lahore, National Documentation Centre, 1983

44. St. Aubyn, Giles, *Queen Victoria: a Portrait*, Sinclair-Stevenson, 1991

45. Sarkar, Sumit, *Modern India 1885-1947*, Macmillan, 1989

46. Saiyid, M.H., *Mohammad Ali Jinnah*, Lahore, S.M. Ashraf, 1945

47. Tinker, Hugh, *The Foundations of Local Self-Government in India, Pakistan, and Burma*, Athlone Press, 1954

48. Tuker, Francis, *While Memory Serves*, Cassell, 1956

49. Tully, Mark & Masani, Zareer, *From Raj to Rajiv: 40 Years of Indian Independence*, BBC Books, 1988

50. Wrench, Sir John Evelyn, *The Immortal Years, 1937-1944*, Hutchinson, 1945

51. Zaidi Z.H. (ed.) *M.A. Jinnah — Ispahani Correspondence, 1936-1948*, Karachi, Forward Publishing Trust, 1976

52. Zetland, Lord, *Essayez: the Memoirs of Lawrence, 2nd Marquess of Zetland*, John Murray, 1956

Index

Protect the marine environment by preventing and c 16

Prove to be an enduring economic burden on the int 19

Provide protection to fishermen, including assisti 16

Q

Qualitative descriptions 65

Quantitative findings in context 86

Quota 24

R

Raising canal water charges 57

Rather slow 24

Recognition that cooperation is essential to allev 145

Regional South Asian Strategies 137

Responsibility for providing Water 50

Restrictions on the depth of borewells 55

Right to Water 49

Rights over Groundwater 47

Rights over Surface Water 46

River Basin Governance 262

River Linking Project 91

River Linking Project Issue 93

Roman Empire 2

S

Seabed Committee 8

Seabed Mining 8

Selecting Alternatives 180

Selecting alternatives 178

Serious Environmental Non-compliance 113

Serious lapse 120

Shall take measures 28

Shallow Tubewell 166

Sharing, pumping and pricing 175

Signed at Kathmandu 234

Simulation 169

Some Case Study 62

Southern African Development Community 74

Sovereignty And Jurisdiction 238

Sri Lanka in 1974 and 1976 16

Stage one — data collection 77

Stage three — contextual evaluation 82

Stage two — data analysis 78

Submit an annual report to the two governments 130

Supplemental irrigation 57

Supply of Water 52

Supreme Court Decision 119

T

Take measures for the safety of life and property 16

Tapi Irrigation Development Corporation Act, 1997 46

Technology Transfer 27

Territorial sea 1, 9, 11, 14, 33

Thailand and Indonesia, on the trijunction point, 17

The geopolitics of the Farakka-Paksi-Mawa Barrage 170

The Maldives in 1976 16

The Sea 10

Tipaimukh Dam 97

Tipaimukh Hydrological Dam 95

www.ingramcontent.com/pod-product-compliance
Lightning Source LLC
Chambersburg PA
CBHW070809300326
41914CB00078B/1911/J